On Artillery

On Artillery

Bruce I. Gudmundsson

PRAEGER

Westport, Connecticut
London

Library of Congress Cataloging-in-Publication Data

Gudmundsson, Bruce I.
    On artillery / Bruce I. Gudmundsson.
      p.   cm.
    Includes bibliographical references and index.
    ISBN 0–275–94047–0 (alk. paper).—ISBN 0–275–94673–8 (pbk. :
alk. paper)
      1. Artillery, Field and mountain. I. Title.
UF400.G83   1993
358.1′2—dc20   93–17105

British Library Cataloguing in Publication Data is available.

Library of Congress Catalog Card Number: 93–17105
ISBN: 0–275–94047–0 (HB)
     0–275–94673–8 (PB)

First published in 1993

Praeger Publishers, 88 Post Road West, Westport, CT 06881
An imprint of Greenwood Publishing Group, Inc.

Printed in the United States of America

The paper used in this book complies with the
Permanent Paper Standard issued by the National
Information Standards Organization (Z39.48–1984).

P

Contents

Preface

Since the 1940s, the English-speaking world has seen very few books published on the subject of field artillery. Of these, the overwhelming majority come from the prolific pen of Ian Hogg. Of late, however, this unfortunate situation has been mitigated by some first-class scholarship. J. B. A. Bailey has surveyed the largely periodical English-language literature to produce a magisterial volume entitled *Field Artillery and Firepower*. Shelford Bidwell and Dominick Graham have explained the history of twentieth-century British artillery in their *Firepower*, while Christopher Bellamy, in *Red God of War*, has done the same for the Soviets. Boyd L. Dastrup has written *The Field Artillery: History and Sourcebook*, a short reference volume that is the very first to cover the development of field artillery from the Middle Ages to the present in terms of technology, organization, tactics, and doctrine, along with biographical profiles of the leading figures in this development, and bibliographical essays about the most important writings on the subject. U.S. Army field artillery, which has been neglected since Frank E. Comparato published *Age of the Great Guns* in 1965, is soon to be the subject of a book written by the staff of the U.S. Army Military History Institute.

Because these excellent works are generally available, I have chosen to pay less attention to the British, Russian, and American experiences and more to what will be new to most English-speaking readers, the field artillery of the French and German armies of this century. This approach not only uncovers hitherto inaccessible material but also serves as a reasonable substitute for a broader treatment of the subject. For while the

French and German experiences do not encompass the entirety of the recent history of field artillery, the contrast between the two provides a good way of examining the major issues that affected many other armies during the period in question.

Strictly speaking, this book is a work on field artillery in conventional war. It therefore pays little attention to the use of artillery in "special cases," such as airborne, airmobile, amphibious, guerrilla, urban, or mountain warfare.[1] Neither does it give much information on such topics as the employment of antiaircraft artillery, coastal artillery, or siege artillery. Indeed, when these areas are mentioned at all, the reader can be sure that it is because of their influence, at a given time and place, on the employment or development of field artillery.

Credit for getting this book started belongs to William S. Lind, of the Center for Cultural Conservatism, and Dan Eades, of Praeger Publishers. The former made me realize that there was a need for a serious book on artillery tactics. The latter, working with little more than a few notes scribbled on a paper placemat, convinced me that there was an audience. Mary J. Porter of the Breckenridge Memorial Library greatly facilitated my research by locating and procuring books that I could not otherwise have obtained in the time allotted to this project. Colonel Robert Hamaïd of the French military archives at Vincennes also went out of his way to help me obtain important materials during my short stay in France.

Important financial support (and not inconsiderable moral encouragement) came from the Marine Corps Command and Staff College Foundation, which, among other things, paid for my archival research in France. In particular, I would like to thank my fellow Marines, Colonel Charles J. Goode, Jr., and Colonel R. W. Crain, as well as Brenda K. Drennan and Nancy L. Koontz. I would also like to thank the family of General Gerald R. Thomas, USMC, whose generosity provided the funds spent by the Staff College Foundation on behalf of this book.

Major John J. Sayen, Jr., USMCR, in addition to providing access to his extensive library, applied his considerable knowledge of weapons and organization to the task of checking the technical details of this book. He also kindly allowed me to use material that originally appeared in *Tactical Notebook*, the information service of the Institute for Tactical Education. Additional help with sources came from Dennis Showalter of Colorado College.

Finally, I would like to thank Lee-Ann, Kathleen, and Brian for their love, patience, and support during the four years of evenings and weekends that it took to write this book. Needless to say, all errors of fact and interpretation are my own.

NOTE

1. Those interested in the question of artillery in guerrilla warfare and airmobile operations will gain much from reading Robert H. Scales, Jr., *Firepower in Limited War* (Washington, DC: National Defense University Press, 1990).

On
Artillery

1

The Shadow of Sedan

The artillery of Europe entered the twentieth century under the shadow of the Franco-Prussian War of 1870–1871. For the tacticians, the battles of that conflict were rich in lessons for the employment of modern cannons. For the armorers, the fact that the victors had been a full generation ahead in field gun technology spurred an arms race that was to last for half a century. While this arms race certainly brought profit to the merchants of death, it made life difficult for the tacticians. For before they had completely digested the tactical implications of the artillery technology used in the Franco-Prussian War, that technology changed radically. And, although some clues to the impact of the new field guns were provided in wars fought on the periphery of the civilized world, no consensus on their proper use was reached before the outbreak of World War I.

From the vantage point of the late twentieth century, the salient characteristic of the artillery battles of the Franco-Prussian War was technological asymmetry. The German breech-loading guns were vastly superior—in terms of range, accuracy, and, perhaps most important, reliability of fuses—to their mostly muzzle-loading French counterparts. The crew of a standard German field gun, a four-pounder of 80mm caliber, could throw an explosive shell 3,800 meters and be reasonably sure that it would explode at the end of its journey. Their French counterparts, armed with their 86.5mm four-pounder, could send a projectile 3,150 meters. However, only at ranges of 1,400 to 1,600 meters and 2,650 to 2,950 meters did the fuse of the explosive shell work. At other ranges, it was simply an inert projectile, an overpriced but underweight piece of hollow solid shot.[1]

One result of this critical weakness on the part of the French artillery was the impunity with which the German artillery could assemble large numbers of guns close to one another. At Sedan, five German corps employed groups of ninety guns or more as grand batteries massed in one line under one commander. At one point in that battle, 540 guns, 80 percent of the German guns present for duty on the battlefield, formed a single grand battery.[2]

When it came to infantry weapons, the relative positions of the French and the Germans were reversed. The French *Chassepôt* rifle, with its reliable mechanism, flat trajectory, and longer range, was vastly superior to the Dreyse "needle gun" with which most of the German infantrymen were equipped. The immediate and predictable result was that, except under exceptional conditions, the German infantry was unable to move forward against the fire of the French infantry. This was particularly true when the French infantry was reinforced by a few field guns firing shrapnel at short ranges.[3]

The German solution to this problem was to divide into two phases. The first was the artillery duel, wherein the German artillery made good use of the ability to bombard the French guns at ranges at which the latter were ineffective. The second was the close-in fight, during which the Germans dissolved their "grand batteries" and pushed their guns forward into positions from which they could, fighting as single batteries, sections, and even individual guns, provide immediate support to the attacking infantry. In most cases, this close-in fighting was costly for the artillery.[4] It was particularly costly, however, when the Germans had failed to knock out or drive off the enemy artillery before moving forward.[5]

To the military historians and doctrine writers of the era immediately following the Franco-Prussian War, the technical asymmetry upon which the German approach of 1870 had been based was either forgotten or relegated to footnotes. Instead, that generation of European soldiers who enjoyed the long peace that stretched from 1871 to 1914, eager to learn the lessons of a war that had turned Europe upside down in the course of a few weeks, derived from their study of the Franco-Prussian War two articles of faith. The first was the need to mass field guns, that is, to put as many batteries as possible in a single location under the direct control of a single commander. This would allow division, corps, and even army commanders to use massed fire as a means of decisively influencing the action on the battlefield. The second was the need to silence the enemy's guns before the battle proper, the battle between the main bodies of the opposing armies, could begin.[6]

The chief apostle of the two-phase artillery battle was the premier German artillerist of the Franco-Prussian War, Prince Krafft zu Höhenlohe-Ingelfingen. Writing in the 1880s, he argued that while improved field guns might increase the ranges at which the two phases would be fought, the essential pattern of battle would remain the same as in 1870.

> The artillery fight will be carried on in the same manner as formerly, except that the ranges will be longer. It will commence [at a range of 5,000 yards or more] with a "cannonade," by which I mean a more or less ineffective fire, which must be opened in order to draw the attention and the fire of the enemy's artillery upon our batteries, and thus to prevent it from annoying the advance of the infantry. . . . Then the officer commanding the troops will decide where he proposes to make his real attack. When he has made up his mind on this point, the artillery will advance up to the edge of the zone of shrapnel fire (about 3,500 yards), and will endeavor to obtain the advantage in the combat with common shell. The moment of time at which this advantage becomes palpable will be the earliest at which the officer commanding the troops will be in a position to determine when he will commence his attack. This also will be the moment at which the artillery can first resolve to engage in the decisive artillery duel; for this purpose it will advance by successive fractions, without ceasing its fire and making use of any cover which the ground may afford. If, as a result of this duel the defender's artillery is silenced, then the moment will have arrived for the officer commanding the troops to let loose his infantry . . . the infantry will thus first reach the enemy half an hour after the end of the artillery duel. It will carry out its advance of from 1,500 to 2,000 yards under cover of the shrapnel fire of its artillery, which should be used to shatter the enemy's infantry.[7]

There were, of course, differences in the way each army applied the lessons of the Franco-Prussian War. Most artillerymen, for example, respected the killing power of modern rifles, and therefore opposed any scheme that would put gun crews in the sights of infantrymen. The Germans, on the other hand, were less concerned about losing gunners than they were about letting their infantry face enemy rifle fire alone.[8] "It is to be established as a principle," intoned the German regulations, "that our own infantry never have to do without the support of the artillery. Therefore, the artillery must not, in decisive moments, avoid even the heaviest infantry fire."[9]

These differences notwithstanding, the principles of massed grand batteries and the artillery duel soon became the twin pillars of European artillery doctrine. In Germany, they were enshrined both in the regulations for the field artillery (beginning with the edition of 1876) and the books of such respected experts as Hoffbauer, von Schell, and Baron Thürheim. In France, they found their way into the first Field Service Instructions published after the war. And in Austria, they became the foundation for the official artillery manual published in 1878. Indeed, of the four great Continental powers of the time, only Russia failed to adopt the German approach to artillery tactics.[10]

Tangible proof of this conversion could be found not only in the official and private literature of each nation but also in the reorganization of artillery units. The battery of six or eight guns—long considered the largest permanent tactical unit—tended more and more to be permanently grouped with other batteries into a larger tactical organization. Called "groups" (*groupes*) in France, "divisions" (*Abteilungen*) in Germany, and (*Divisionen*) in Austria, these collections of two, three, or four batteries soon lost the ad hoc character indicated by their names and took on all the trappings of permanent battalions.[11]

In Germany, where the practice of grouping batteries into permanent battalions had first taken hold, the artillerymen went two steps further. Battalions were paired to form regiments. Regiments, in turn, were paired to form brigades, each of which formed the artillery of an army corps. From the point of view of the German field artillery as an institution, the formation of artillery regiments and brigades provided high-level jobs for field artillery officers. From the point of view of tactics, it provided the corps commander not merely with a single artilleryman who would be responsible for the massing of his guns but also with two major subunits that could, if needed, be attached to divisions.[12]

While the writers of tables of organization and books on tactics digested the lessons of the Franco-Prussian War, scientists, engineers, and inventors kept changing the weaponry available to gunners. Improvements in metallurgy meant that guns of a given weight could fire larger shells. The replacement of black powder with smokeless powder both improved range and made firing batteries easier to conceal from the enemy's field glasses. Fixed ammunition—putting the propellant in a metal cyclinder and attaching the projectile to that cylinder before loading—combined with improved breech mechanisms to increase rates of fire by a factor of three or four.

The result of all of these changes was a class of weapons that might best be described as "quick-loaders." Seventy or more kilograms lighter than the weapons they replaced, quick-loaders were drawn by the same six-horse teams and were thus significantly more mobile than the previous generation of field guns. Their calibers were smaller (about 75mm against the previous norm of 87mm) but their ranges were greater (5,000 to 8,000 meters, as opposed to a previous average of about 4,000). Displacing weapons that fired about two rounds per minute, these new field guns fired six or seven.[13]

The projectile of choice for the quick-loaders was shrapnel, a type of round that had been invented at the beginning of the nineteenth century but made reliable only toward the end. Composed of a relatively thin container filled with eight to ten grams of metal shot and a small bursting charge, the shrapnel shell was designed to burst a few meters from the enemy infantry and, acting like a giant shotgun, shower them with small projectiles. The fuse of choice for shrapnel shells was a simple burning time fuse, cut according to the distance at which the gunner wished to have the shell explode.[14]

That the almost universal use of quick-loaders (or, at the very least, older weapons modified to approximate the virtues of quick-loaders) did not undermine the doctrinal consensus that followed the Franco-Prussian War is a tribute less to the inertia of the military mind than to the way the soldiers of the time understood the implications of the new technology. In particular, the increased use of shrapnel made enemy artillery more dangerous to friendly infantry at ranges (over 2,000 meters) at which the infantry could not effectively reply. This made imperative the silencing of the enemy guns before the infantry could be sent forward.

At the same time, the fact that most field guns could fire common shell 1,500 to 3,000 meters further than they could throw shrapnel (5,000–5,500 versus 6,500–8,000) meant that there was a zone in which artillery could maneuver outside the range of the enemy's most powerful killer of men and horses and yet, if massed and willing to spend a large number of common shells, still have a decisive effect on emplaced batteries.[15]

Another contributor to the retention of tactics designed for a previous generation of weapons was a by-product of the use of smokeless powder. In the days of black powder, the cloud that soon enveloped a gun position was a real hindrance to effective fire. The more smoke there was, the harder it was for the battery officers to see the target, estimate range, correct the fall of shot, and evaluate damage. Putting a number of batteries together exacerbated this problem. Once black powder was replaced by smokeless powder, however, batteries massed with other batteries could see as well as batteries operating alone. Thus, even though the technical basis for the lessons of the Franco-Prussian War had changed, the teachings derived from those lessons were truer in 1900 than they had been in 1875 or 1890.[16]

Such lessons, however, could not stand forever in the face of changing technology. As the armies of Europe were investing millions in their new quick-loaders, the weapons designers were fast at work on the next generation of field gun.[17] For weapons small enough to be used as field artillery, the practical limits of chemistry, metallurgy, shell design, and even the ergonomics of loading had been reached with the quick-firer. The one area where there was still room for improvement was in the reduction of recoil.

From its inception in the late Middle Ages until the beginning of the twentieth century, the limit on the rate of fire of field artillery was not so much the method of putting the projectile in the weapon but Newton's Third Law of Motion. Every time a field piece was fired, the "equal and opposite reaction" to the propelling explosion caused it to jump back a few inches. This meant that if any degree of accuracy was required, the gun had to be manhandled forward and reaimed before it could be fired again. This, in most cases, took far more time than the simple process of loading the weapon.

In the 1880s artillery makers began producing guns with sophisticated mechanisms for absorbing the recoil of the gun so that while the barrel might move, the carriage would stay still. These early recoil-absorbing guns, however, were either too big or too small to be used as field artillery. Guns in fixed emplacements (like naval or fortress guns) could be provided with large (and heavy) recoil-absorbing mechanisms. Small-caliber guns could have their recoil absorbed by a combination of springs, spades, and the simple expedient of having the gunner sit on the carriage during firing. Unfortunately for the field artillery, the smallest weapon of the fortress category was far too heavy to be pulled by horses. Likewise, one of the largest weapons of the small-caliber category—the Nordenfelt 8-pounder—threw a shell weighing less than four kilograms out to distances of no more than 3,500 meters.[18]

Solving the problem of recoil in field guns, however, was only a matter of time. As was the case with the automobile and the heavier-than-air flying machine, inventors and engineers in a number of countries were simultaneously investigating the problem. In Germany, the upstart firm of Heinrich Ehrhardt had offered quick-firing guns to the army as early as 1896.[19] In Russia the Putilov factory was working on quick-firing guns of an entirely different design. The first country out of the gate, however, was France. In 1897, one year after German batteries started to receive their model 1896 quick-loading 77mm gun, the French Army adopted a 75mm quick-firing field gun designed by a team of French ordnance officers.

The German 77mm gun could fire eight 6.85-kilogram shells in a minute, whereas its French counterpart could spit out between twenty and thirty slightly heavier (7.2 kilogram) projectiles. Thanks largely to a "long recoil" mechanism, the carriage of the French model 1897 field gun remained perfectly still during the entire cycle of loading and firing.[20] And despite the violent force with which the barrel recoiled with every shot, the piece as a whole was so stable that the gunner had only to make minor adjustments to the sights to fire the next round.[21]

Between 1897 and 1901, the Germans (and the rest of Europe) were unaware of their inferiority in the area of field guns. Good security kept spies away from both blueprints and performance data. An elaborate disinformation plan that included the fabrication of actual guns that used "short recoil" mechanisms similar to those then being developed in Germany kept the German authorities believing that they were on the right track. It was not until the first time the French 75mm gun was used in combat—in China, during the pursuit of a band of retreating Boxers—that Germany learned how well armed their once and future enemy actually was.[22]

After a number of incidents in which the fire of one of two French 75mm guns succeeded in driving off large numbers of normally fearless Boxers, the new weapon was put to the test in a deliberate assault against a fortified Chinese village defended by 2,000 men. The French forces consisted of two and a half companies of Zouaves and a pair of "75s." Beginning their advance at 1,500 meters, the two guns advanced by bounds—one firing while the other one moved forward. At 600 meters the French crews stopped moving forward and concentrated their efforts on maintaining the liveliest possible fire while the Zouaves rushed forward with fixed bayonets. Almost completely suppressed by the fire of two field pieces, the Chinese were unable to resist. The French took the village at the cost of one wounded man.[23]

In the five years that followed the unveiling of "Mademoiselle Soixante-Quinze" (Miss Seventy-five), as the French 75mm gun soon became known, the armies of the world rushed to obtain quick-firing guns of their own. Between 1901 and 1905, Russia, Denmark, Sweden, Norway, Portugal, Switzerland, the Netherlands, and the United States all adopted 75, 76.2, or 77mm field pieces capable of similar feats. Great Britain departed from this general trend only insofar as caliber was concerned. Its 83.8mm weapon (designated the "18-pounder") was, nonetheless, a true quick-firing piece able to deliver over twenty rounds a minute.[24]

In the less-developed world—the Balkans, Latin America, and Asia— governments spent fortunes to acquire quick-firing guns before their neighbors could, and the merchants of death grew fantastically rich in the race to provide antagonists with the revolutionary weapon. Thus, by 1905, the German Army not only was equipped with a field gun less capabale than that of every northern European army, but its artillery regiments were full of weapons that were inferior to those that German firms of Krupp and Ehrhardt were selling overseas.[25]

Once recognized, this state of affairs was quickly remedied by extensive modifications to the model 96 field gun. Most of the new features—the mechanisms for absorbing recoil in particular—were taken from the Ehrhardt export guns.[26] The result was the *Feldkanone 96 neuer Art* (new version), a weapon that could fire twenty aimed shells a minute. Better late than never, Germany was finally a member of the quick-firing club, and her incomparable military intelligentsia soon led the way in the work of divining the effect that these new weapons would have on the battlefield.

Almost all writers on tactics—whether official or unofficial—soon agreed that quick-firing guns should be equipped with steel shields. Since the dawn of gunnery, gun crews had been well advised to stay clear of the gun, its carriage, and its wheels at the moment of firing. Gunners who ignored this advice did it only once, for the force with which field pieces recoiled was considerable. Needless to say, fitting an armored shield on such a weapon made no sense. It would merely encourage gunners to risk being run over by recoiling gun carriages. Once field pieces stopped moving backward every time they were fired, however, protecting gunners from shrapnel and rifle fire made a great deal of sense.[27]

The efficacy of such shields was demonstrated both on the test range and in battle. In 1909, Danish artillerymen fired 270 shrapnel shells against a battery of quick-firing guns set up 2,000 meters away. Although the shields were frequently hit, only five shell fragments or unexploded shells managed to penetrate the shields. In the same year, during street fighting in Constantinople, a battery of quick-firing guns was sent into action against rebel infantry at a range of 500 to 600 meters. Although the enemy rifle fire was heavy, the only casualty among the gunners was an NCO who was shot through the head while trying to peer around his gun shield.[28]

Danish experiments and internal unrest in the Ottoman Empire notwithstanding, the great laboratories for testing the new field guns—both quick-firing and quick-loading—were the battlefields of the Second Anglo-Boer War (1899–1902), the Russo-Japanese War (1904–1905), and the Balkan Wars (1912–1913.) That the experience of these wars failed to lead to a consensus about the best way to employ the new weapons was partially due to the biases of those who reported on the war and those who received the reports. Much credit, however, must also be laid at the feet of the tendency of the lessons drawn from one conflict to contradict those of the previous one.

From the point of view of artillery, the salient characteristic of the battles of the Second Boer War was asymmetry. In every case, the British were able to bring far more artillery to the battlefield than their Boer adversaries. At Colenso (December 15, 1899) the British had forty-four guns; the Boers had five. At Pieters Hill (February 23–27, 1900) the British opposed seventy pieces to ten Boer pieces. And at Paardeberg (February 19–27, 1900), the ratio was ninety-one to six in favor of the British.[29]

This overwhelming advantage notwithstanding, the battles of the Boer War were far from the "turkey shoots" that the artillery ratios would suggest. Part of the problem was one of equipment. The Boer artillery was bought from various French, German, and British merchants of death after 1896.[30] The field guns were thus of the quick-loading variety—not yet as stable in firing as the French model 1897 75mm gun but, thanks largely to their fixed ammunition, far quicker to load than the British 15-pounders.[31]

There were, as a result of this disparity, incidents in which a handful of Boer quick-loaders was able to get the better of a much larger number of the older British guns. On February 5, 1900, at Brakfontaine, a hill north of Spion Koop, three Boer 75mm guns kept thirty-six British field guns and an infantry brigade under fire for the better part of the day, during which time the British guns were unable, because of the range, to reply in kind. Although the British only took thirty-four casualties in the incident— the British maneuver was a feint rather than an attack—the apparent strength of the Boer artillery was enough to deprive the British commander of his will to continue. The next day he called off his offensive, complaining to his superiors that the Boer positions were too strong to assault and that his artillery was "outclassed" by the Boer guns.[32]

A far larger part of the problem was a consistent failure on the part of the British to present the Boer artillery with any sort of dilemma. The British generally insisted on fighting a separate counterbattery battle before beginning the infantry attack. If the Boers chose, as they most often did, to keep their guns both silent and well hidden during this bombardment, they risked very little damage as the British shells fell over the countryside. The fact that the Boer guns were rarely assembled as complete batteries combined with the inability of British shrapnel shells to function at long ranges to further reduce the danger from British bombardment.[33]

The British failure to make their infantry and artillery work together made life easier for the Boer infantry. If the British bombarded at long ranges with their heavier guns, the Boers lay on the ground near their dugouts. They knew that, with the exception of the rare shell that happened to land inside a Boer shelter before exploding, there was little danger from British high-explosive shells. (The blast of the lyddite filling was so weak that during one bombardment a few brave Boers were seen boiling coffee on the ground outside their dugouts.)[34] If the British got close enough to fire shrapnel from their field guns, the Boers crouched in their shelters, no longer making coffee but still relatively safe from the fast-flying cones of shrapnel balls a few inches above them.

If the British had made their artillery and infantry attacks simultaneous, the Boers would have been in a different position. Their gun crews would have faced the difficult choice of firing on the foot soldiers, thus exposing themselves to the fire of the British artillery, or remaining silent, and thus increasing their chances of being overrun. Their infantry would also have faced a Hobson's choice. If they stood up in their trenches to fire, they would take casualties from shrapnel. If they remained deep in their trenches, they would allow the British infantry to cross their field of fire unmolested.

The battle of Colenso (December 15, 1899) was typical in this respect.[35] The fighting strength of the Boers—five 75mm field guns, one 120mm howitzer, and no more than 4,300 rifles—was spread among the hills overlooking the point where the railroad crossed the Tugela River. The British, numbering close to 18,000—four brigades of infantry, five batteries of field artillery (thirty 15-pounder field guns), fourteen long-range naval guns mounted on improvised carriages, and some mounted troops—moved toward the Tugela along the railroad line. The British aim was to force a passage. The Boer aim was to stop them.

The action commenced with the long-range shelling of the Boer positions by six of the naval guns. Firing lyddite shells at 4,000 meters, these guns had little trouble hitting the hills where the Boers were hiding. From the point of view of the British officers observing the scene through their field glasses, the bombardment was devastatingly effective. It was so effective, in fact, that no Boer could be seen on the hills where they had been observed the day before.

Fearing that the Boers might have evacuated their positions, and mindful of his mission to cover the advance of the infantry, the commander of the British field artillery moved forward alone with two field gun batteries. These were stopped 1,000 meters in front of the Boer trenches by rifle bullets and shrapnel shells that poured in from three of the four points of the compass. The long-range bombardment, it turned out, had done little to disturb the Boers. It was not even sufficient to irritate them into breaking their fire discipline.

The British gun crews fought bravely for an hour, coolly working their guns despite the steady rain of small projectiles that struck one of their number every minute and a half. Although the Boers did not speak of it, it is reasonable to believe that the British got their range and were able to arrange for some of their shrapnel shells to burst over the Boer position. Such counterfire would explain the relatively low casualties of the gunners standing unprotected in an open field.

When the field guns ran out of ammunition, the crews retreated to the shelter of nearby depressions. A few minutes later, some British infantry arrived on the scene. The Boers were able to concentrate their fire on this new threat, while the crews of the abandoned guns (and, to a large extent, the British leadership as a whole) were less concerned with defeating the Boers than with avoiding the disgrace of letting artillery pieces fall into the hands of the enemy.

In the meantime, the bombardment of the naval guns continued. High-explosive shells fired behind the Boer positions were effective in denying the latter the benefit of interior lines. Although the rapid shifting of tactical reserves was not part of the Boer repertoire, the fact that the most likely routes for doing this were interrupted by bursting shells would have made such a move costly for a formed body of men. This embryonic interdiction fire was, however, a two-edged sword preventing the British from attempting any sort of attack into the Boer rear area.

If, of course, the officers commanding the naval guns had been able to distinguish friend from foe, this would not have been a problem. At 4,000 meters, however, it was hard to determine who was wearing Imperial khaki and who was clothed in the homemade corduroy of the Boers. Thus, when British infantry were able to drive a party of Boers from their trenches, the naval guns were not able to exploit the opportunity presented by an enemy unit moving slowly in the open. From their vantage point, the long-range artillerists could see that somebody was moving in their field of fire. Because they could not tell the nationality of this target, they declined to fire.

Their victory notwithstanding, the Boers missed opportunities at Colenso. Just as the British batteries had gone into action with little sense of the need to cooperate either with each other or with the infantry, so the Boer pieces produced purely local effects. The dispersal of the guns that denied the British artillery a single target upon which to concentrate its efforts also deprived the Boers of the decisive effects that could have been obtained by the simultaneous fire of their five field guns and one howitzer on a single, exposed target. The problem was not one of range— the battlefield at Colenso was about 5,000 meters wide and the Boer weapons could easily reach to 6,000 to 7,000 meters—but of doctrine and command arrangements.

The Boers were fighting a defensive war for the preservation of their independent way of life. The defensive attitude that they took led them to be generally satisfied with holding the British at arm's length and prevented the development of the idea that they should press advantages to the point of annihilating large British units. The habits of thought developed in the course of small-scale, close-range battles against poorly armed Zulu and Matabele did not require the Boers to think of a battle as having any reality apart from the men in their sights. Once those men were gone, the battle was over.

As a result, the Boer guns were rarely used as a means of influencing the battle as a whole. Rather, they were employed as larger versions of the main Boer weapon—the magazine rifle. Despite the fact that the Boer gunners were formed in batteries with a separate chain of command, each gun, once distributed, came under the effective command of the elected leader of the Boer riflemen occupying the immediate area. The only gun that remained at the disposition of the overall Boer commander at Colenso was the one next to his command post, which he used to signal his command to open fire.[36]

Despite the defects of their armed forces and partially because of the inability of the Boers fully to exploit those defects, the British won the Boer War. Perhaps because the war had not been the walkover that everyone had expected, or perhaps because the war coincided with a flowering of British military professionalism, the British Army soon embarked on a thorough reexamination of its way of doing business. For the infantry, this meant a dramatic increase in the emphasis placed on rifle marksmanship and field craft. For the artillery, there was a complete rearmament and a total revision of regulations.

By 1914, the British field artillery was among the most modern in the world. The mainstay of its equipment was the 18-pounder, the largest quick-firing field gun to be adopted by a major army before World War I. This deviation from the norm—the shell fired by this weapon was two pounds (just under one kilogram) heavier than the projectile fired by the next biggest field gun, the French 75mm—can be explained by the desire of Boer War veterans for a weapon capable of having an impact on entrenched riflemen.

The published doctrine of the British artillery, likewise, owed much to lessons gleaned from fighting the Boers. Regulations dealing with defense flattered the Boers with almost complete imitation. If the enemy had a superiority of artillery, they advised, guns were to be dispersed along the infantry firing line as batteries (of six guns) or sections (of two guns). These guns should be placed so as to take advantage of opportunities for taking the attackers in the flank, to enfilade their advancing skirmish lines, or to place the attackers in a cross fire.

If, however, the British were the ones with the superior artillery, their field guns were to be massed. In the attack, these massed guns should concentrate their fire on that section of the enemy line where the infantry planned to attack. This fire should remain on that line until the infantry got so close that there was danger of their being hit by friendly fire. At that point, the fire should be shifted to the rear of the enemy position, to prevent reinforcement of the line.

The enemy artillery was no longer the primary target of attacking guns. There was to be no artillery duel preceding the infantry attack. If, however, the enemy artillery posed a danger to the infantry attack, it was to be fired on. And if the enemy artillery fired on the British artillery, the latter was not to try to hide; rather, it was to keep firing, so as to keep the pressure off its attacking infantry.[37]

No other nation went so far in applying the almost universal truism that artillery was a supporting arm, justified only by its role as an auxiliary to the infantry. Whether or not memories of whole battalions pinned by rifle fire were dancing in the heads of the officers who embraced this doctrine, it was clearly based on a South African assumption. The major danger to attacking infantry was the enemy infantry. As a consequence, the chief duty of the artillery was to help the infantry gain fire superiority over its opposite numbers.

NOTES

1. Friedrichfranz Feeser, *Artillerie im Feldkriege. Kriegsgeschichtliche Beispiele* (Berlin: E. S. Mittler und Sohn, 1930), p. 98; W. Heydenreich, *Das moderne Feldgeschütz* (Leipzig, G. I. Göschen'sche Verlagshandlung, 1906), p. 69; C. Romain, "Les Responsabilités de l'artillerie française en 1870," *Revue d'artillerie*, Jan. 1913, pp. 241–42.

2. Prince Krafft zu Hohenlohe-Ingelfingen, *Letters on Artillery* (Quantico, VA: U.S. Marine Corps, 1988), pp. 49–52. (Hereafter cited as Krafft, *Letters on Artillery*.)

3. The French *obus à balles* was provided with a time fuse that was effective at ranges less than 1,400 meters. Romain, "Les Responsabilités de l'artillerie française," pp. 243–44.

4. Casualties (killed and seriously wounded) among German artillerymen in the Franco–Prussian War were slightly greater than those among cavalrymen (6.5 percent of strength versus 6.3 percent) and not as different from those of the infantry (17.6 percent) as would be the case in twentieth-century wars. The figures are from Klingenhöffer, "Über das Begleiten des Infanterieangriffs durch die anderen Waffen, insbesondere die Artillerie," *Jahrbücher für die deutsche Armee und Marine*, July 1914, p. 117.

5. For examples, see Romain, "Les Responsabilités de l'artillerie française," pp. 255–60.

6. Prussia, Kriegsministerium, *Exerzir-Reglement für die Feldartillerie* (Berlin: E. S. Mittler und Sohn, 1892), pp. 138, 151; Krafft, *Letters on Artillery*, pp. 275–76.

7. Krafft, *Letters on Artillery*, p. 318.

8. See, for examples, Krafft, *Letters on Artillery*; Wilhelm Balck, *Tactics*, trans. Walter Krueger (Fort Leavenworth, KS: U.S. Cavalry Association, 1914), vol. 2, pp. 355–56; and the comments made by British officers on the British munitions manufacturer Nordenfelt's talk before the Royal United Service Institution on Jan. 13, 1888—recorded in Thorsten Nordenfelt, "Quick Firing Guns in the Field," *Journal of the Royal United Service Institution* 32, no. 143 (1888): 1–24.

9. Prussia, Kriegsministerium, *Exerzir-Reglement für die Feldartillerie*, p. 138. For those interested in delving further into this subject, the noted historian of the German army, Dennis Showalter, recommends Michael Howard, *The Franco-Prussian War* (London: Macmillan, 1961); and C. von Hoffbauer's *Die deutsche Artillerie in den Schlachten und Treffen des deutsch-französischen Krieges 1870–71*, 3 vols. (Berlin: n.p., 1873–1878).

10. "Taktik der Feldartillerie. 1874–98," in *Das Militärwesen in seiner Entwickelung während der 25 Jahre, 1874–1898*, ed. Pelet-Narbonne (supplement to *Von Löbell's Jahresberichte über das Heer- und Kriegswesen 1898*), pp. 636–37, 646.

11. As was often the case with their army at this time, the British were notoriously backward in this regard. They did not form permanent brigade divisions until after the Boer War. Robert S. Scales, Jr., "Artillery in Small Wars: The Evolution of British Artillery Doctrine, 1860–1914" (Ph.D. dissertation, Duke University, 1976), pp. 69–74, 267–68.

12. For a detailed treatment of the employment of such units, see Adolph von Schell, *The Tactics of Field Artillery*, trans. A. E. Turner (London: Harrison and Sons, 1889).

13. The figures are derived from the table appended to part II of Heydenreich's *Das moderne Feldgeschütz*. Appendix A to Heydenreich's book contains particulars on the major types of artillery pieces in use in this century.

14. Named for the British artillery officer Henry Shrapnel, the late-eighteenth-century inventor of a family of spherical shells for muzzle-loading smooth bores, the shrapnel shells fired by the rifled cannon of the turn of the century bore little resemblance to their namesakes of the Napoleonic Wars.

15. The limitation here was the fuse. Common shells used impact fuses, the action of which was independent of range. Burning time fuses, however, were only long enough to last the time it took for the shell to fly 5,000 to 5,500 meters. Again, the figures are from vol. 2 of Heydenreich's *Das moderne Feldgeschütz*.

16. "Taktik der Feldartillerie. 1874–98," p. 648.

17. In these larger weapons, the excess recoil was absorbed by pistons and/or springs.

18. Nordenfelt, "Quick-Firing Guns in the Field," pp. 2–3.

19. Schirmer, "Die Technik im Dienst der schweren Artillerie vor und im Weltkriege," Franz Nicholas Kaiser, ed. *Das Ehrenbuch der deutschen schweren Artillerie*, vol. 2 (Berlin: Verlag Tradition Wilhelm Kolk, 1934), pp. 446, 470.

20. Konrad Haussner, the German inventer of this technique, first proposed it while a Krupp employee. Krupp officials declined to act, and Haussner moved on to the Ehrhardt works, where he obtained both French and German patents. Ibid.; and Michel de Lombarès, "Le '75,'" *Revue historique des armées*, 1975, pp. 96–102.

21. The French 75mm gun was not perfectly stable in all conditions. On slick ground, it could move back as much as six feet with each shot. See, for an example of this phenomenon, Paul Lintier, *My Seventy Five* (London: Peter Davis, 1929), p. 197.

22. Lombarès, "Le '75,'" pp. 96–110; J. Schott, "Material der Artillerie," *Von Löbell's Jahresberichte über das Heer- und Kriegswesen* 27 (1900): 370–71.

23. Lombarès, "Le '75'," pp. 109–10. This incident was reported to German readers by U. von T., "Taktik der Feldartillerie," *Von Löbell's Jahresberichte über das Heer- und Kriegswesen* 29 (1902): 302.

24. These figures are derived from the table in appendix A. For a more comprehensive overview of the artillery parks of the major powers on the eve of World War I, see the regular feature "Recent Development of Field Artillery Material on the Continent" in *Journal of the Royal Artillery* at that time.

25. For colorful descriptions of this arms race, see William Manchester, *The Arms of Krupp, 1587–1968* (Boston: Little, Brown, 1968), ch. 9; and Guiles Davenport, *Zaharoff* (Boston: Lothrop, Lee, and Shepard, 1934). The details of Italy's failure to acquire quick-firing guns in this period are provided in von Graevenitz, "Ein italienische Angriff auf das italienische Feldartillerie-Material," *Militär-Wochenblatt* no. 157/158 (1905): 3644–3648. For details on the Ehrhardt gun, see L. R. Kenyon, "Recent Development of Field Artillery Material on the Continent," *Journal of the Royal Artillery* 29, no. 1 and 2, 60–73.

26. The big winner in this episode was Krupp. In the space of ten years, it had been able to sell the German field artillery two full sets of field guns. The big loser was the German Army. After paying a total of 340 million marks (140 for the first set of guns and 200 for the second), it was still armed with a weapon inferior in range and rapidity of fire to the decade-old French 75mm. Manchester, *The Arms of Krupp*, p. 249; John Batchelor and Ian Hogg, *Artillery* (New York: Charles Scribner's Sons, 1972), p. 15.

27. Those who went on record as opposing shields seem not to have understood the almost complete stability of the true quick-firing guns. See, for example, U. T., "Taktik der Feldartillerie," p. 340.

28. From an article in the *Artilleristische Monatshefte* of May 1909, quoted in Wilhelm Balck, *Tactics*, vol. 2, p. 219.

29. Ibid., p. 296. At Paardeberg, the British artillery was not able to cooperate closely enough with the infantry to throw the Boers out of their position. Rather, the British won because of unsanitary practices on the part of the Boers. After their attacks failed, the British besieged the Boers in their camp. Constant shelling killed a large number of horses and oxen in the Boer camp. The Boers dumped the carcasses in the Modder River, their only water supply. The disease that soon followed, combined with the sufferings of the women and children in the camp, broke the Boer will to resist. For a detailed and touching description of the siege that followed the battle, see Byron Farwell, *The Great Anglo-Boer War* (New York: W. W. Norton, 1990), pp. 205–16.

30. At the beginning of the war the Boers had nineteen quick-loading 75mm field guns from Creusot, Krupp, and Vickers-Maxim. In addition, they had four six-inch (150mm) guns from Creusot, four 4.7-inch (120mm) howitzers from Krupp, and thirty 1.45-inch (37mm) "Pom-Poms." Prussia, General Staff, Historical Section, *The War in South Africa*, trans. W.H.H. Waters (London: John Murray, 1907), p. 30.

31. These weapons could fire between eight and twelve aimed rounds per minute. E. S. May, *Field Artillery with Other Arms* (London: Samson, Low, Marston, 1898), pp. 327–39.

32. John P. Wisser, *The Second Boer War, 1899–1900* (Kansas City, MO: Hudson-Kimberly, 1901), p. 217; and Farwell, *The Great Anglo-Boer War*, pp. 190–91.

33. U. T., "Taktik der Feldartillerie," pp. 343–44. The fuses of the shrapnel shell for the standard British field gun of the war (the 15-pounder breech-loader) could be set for distances up to 3,360 yards. Prussia, General Staff, Historical Section, *The War in South Africa*, p. 30.

34. At this time the British high-explosive shells were filled with lyddite. Ibid., pp. 227–28.

35. The following narrative is derived from ibid., pp. 50–78. I also consulted Farwell's *The Great Anglo-Boer War*, an accurate and very readable account that contains much of the tactical detail missing in the histories written by military officers in the decade after the war.

36. For a glimpse into the mentality of a Boer commandant, see Charles Parsons, "Narrative of a Boer," *Journal of the Royal Artillery* 29, no. 1 and 2 (1903): 6–16.

37. Balck, *Tactics*, vol. 2, pp. 465–66.

2

The Quick-Firing Revolution

Even as the British were codifying the lessons of the Boer War, the events of the Russo-Japanese War (1904–1905) were proving that their applicability was less than universal. Moreover, despite the fact that the war was fought in Asia, the scale of its battles and the character of the armies were much closer to those usually associated with a general European war. Whereas the engagements in South Africa generally involved less than a full division on each side, the Japanese and Russians maintained in the theater of operations forces many times larger than the combined civil populations of the two Boer Republics. And whereas the military leaders of both sides of the Boer War fell easily into the category of amateurs, the Japanese and Russian armies were officered, down to the platoon or gun section level, almost entirely with professionals.

The disparity between the artillery parks in Korea and Manchuria, though noteworthy, was considerably less than the difference between the British and Boer arsenals. The principal Japanese field gun was the Arisaka, a 75mm quick-loader optimized for lightness and maneuverability. With the ability of its carriage to absorb much of the recoil and two strong men to manhandle it back into battery after each shot, the Arisaka could fire six to seven shots a minute. Its Russian counterpart was the model 1900 Putilov, a 76.2mm quick-firer that, because of imperfections in the recoil system, could fire either quickly or accurately, but not both. Although considerably heavier than the Arisaka, the Putilov could pump out over twenty rounds in sixty seconds.[1]

The Putilov also had a considerable advantage in range. It could fire high-explosive shell out to 6,400 meters and shrapnel out to 5,600 meters. The Arisaka, on the other hand, could reach only to 5,500 meters with shell and 4,500 with shrapnel. The Putilov had a further advantage in its heavier shell—at seven kilograms it weighed two full kilograms more than the Japanese shell. These differences were somewhat mitigated by the Russians' failure to provide their field gun batteries with high-explosive shells. Nonetheless, most contemporary observers (including the Japanese, who made immediate and extensive use of any Putilovs that they captured) considered the Russian field gun a far superior weapon.[2]

Once again, however, possession of a superior weapon was no guarantee of victory. Even superior numbers of superior weapons could not compensate for poor tactics. For though the Russians had far more artillery in the theater of war than the Japanese and, in most of the encounters, more pieces on the battlefield, the Japanese were invariably able to concentrate overwhelming artillery fire at the critical time and place.[3]

The Japanese ability to concentrate the fire of their artillery was greatly facilitated by the fact that they were generally on the offensive. They could pick the time and place of the combat and distribute their guns accordingly. Their exploitation of these opportunities, however, must be credited to their doctrine. Drawing on the ancient tradition of Bushido and the teachings of their more recent German mentors, the Japanese soldiers of 1904–1905 placed great value on achieving decision in battle. It was not enough to drive away the enemy; he had to be annihilated.

To that end, the Japanese frequently massed the fire of many batteries. The six batteries (thirty-six guns) of each division were routinely grouped together so that they could bring the combined weight of their fire on a single target. Where the Japanese hoped to make a breakthrough, they brought up even more guns from their general reserve (which consisted of two brigades of eighteen batteries each) to make even larger grand batteries. Like the massed guns of an infantry division's artillery, these larger assemblages of guns were often used to attack targets as small as single Russian batteries.[4]

The Japanese willingness to mass their artillery had its roots in formal doctrine. Like the other first-class armies of the day, that of Japan had taken to heart the generally accepted lessons of the Franco-Prussian War. What made such massed fire possible, however, was the peculiar organizational culture that rendered the Japanese of the time such formidable enemies. More specifically, massed artillery fire in this era depended on a certain kind of disciplined initiative—individual decisiveness in pursuit of a common goal—that was characteristic of the Japanese officer of the turn of the century.

Without radios or even field telephones, the higher artillery commanders who organized the massing of batteries could not issue detailed orders. At best, they could pick a general area that offered suitable firing positions and convey a general idea of what was to be done. All other orders had to come from the subordinate battalion or battery commanders. The task of these junior officers, then, was to first understand the intent of the higher artillery commanders and then actively cooperate with each other, with a minimum of actual communication, to fulfill that intent.

This virtue of silent cooperation was most apparent when the Japanese concentrated the fire of a number of batteries without massing the batteries themselves. In some cases, these concentrations were garden variety concentrations—a number of batteries firing at a single target. At other times, two or more batteries firing from different positions would put a Russian position in a cross fire. With shrapnel shells, the effect of such a cross fire, which greatly reduced the value of many forms of cover, was often devastating.[5]

The Russian artillery, on the other hand, generally fought as single batteries. They did this for a number of reasons. First, their batteries were both larger (eight guns versus six) and capable of firing more shells (sixty or so per minute versus thirty per minute) than their Japanese counterparts.[6] Second, they lacked the "German" doctrine of massed fire, preferring to keep a reserve of limbered guns as insurance against unforeseen circumstances rather than choosing a single point at which to "go for broke."[7] Most important, the Russians were less able to mass because they lacked the Japanese knack for silent cooperation.

Technology, in the form of a field telephone set and a mile of cable for each Russian battery, provided a partial solution. Field telephones allowed Russian brigade commanders to micromanage the fire of their three to six batteries.[8] By the end of the campaign, moreover, the Russians were forming grand batteries of their own, which might number from thirty to sixty guns.[9] The Russians rarely succeeded, however, in concentrating as much artillery fire at the right time and place as the Japanese, for they never had all of their guns in action at the same time.

As a result of all of these factors, the Japanese generally enjoyed artillery superiority throughout the campaign. While Russian guns were almost always able to inflict losses upon the Japanese, and often helped to repel particular assaults, the Russian artillery did not prevent either the Japanese artillery or the Japanese infantry from doing its job. This is not to say that the Japanese artillery was generally successful in silencing the Russian batteries. On the contrary, the bulk of Russian batteries put out of commission by the Japanese forces were overrun by infantry rather than shot to pieces in the style of the Franco–Prussian War.

The reason for this was the increased tendency to place batteries in completely masked positions, and so to give up the convenience of direct fire for the protection offered by indirect fire. Russian guns in the open, even if protected by field fortifications, had been easily dispatched by the concentrated fire of thirty or more Japanese guns.[10] It did not take the Russians long, however, to cure themselves of the habit of putting guns on the crests of hills and in other exposed places. As a result, the Japanese found themselves in the impossible position of trying to find batteries in the shadows of hills—shadows that might cover millions of square meters of ground.

The Japanese solution to this problem was to violate the strict interpretation of the lessons of the Franco–Prussian War and attack anyway. As long as the Russian guns were busy trying to silence the Japanese guns (which were commanded by officers who knew that they could never completely silence the Russian guns), they would not be able to molest the Japanese infantry. In other words, the chief service rendered by the Japanese artillery was drawing the fire of the Russian artillery.[11]

Although this does not seem to have happened in Manchuria, the logical Russian response to such a situation would have been the abandonment of the artillery duel in favor of the concentration of all available artillery fire against the Japanese infantry. The Russians, after all, were defending from prepared positions against infantry advancing in the open. Therefore, they had far less to fear from the liberation of Japanese guns from the artillery duel than the Japanese had to fear from the sudden availability of Russian field pieces.

Given the variety of insights that could be drawn from recent conflicts, each nation's military leadership was free to judge the impact of the quick-firing gun according to its own lights. In addition to being influenced by local interpretation of the news coming from the battlefields of Manchuria, these views were the product of the particular situation in which each army found itself. While the peculiarities of geography and strategic position played their role in forming these opinions, the greatest influence on how an army received quick-firing artillery was internal—the result of the interplay between new ideas and preexisting doctrine. This can clearly be seen in the example of the two greatest artillery powers at the beginning of the twentieth century, the German Empire and the French Republic.

Prior to the introduction of quick-firing weapons, the French and German artillery doctrines were remarkably similar. This was no accident. Following their defeat in the Franco-Prussian War, the French adopted many concepts and practices from their once and future enemy. At the most prosaic level, the French adopted German techniques such as adjustment of fire by bracketing. On a higher plane, the French adopted the German practice of massing batteries for the artillery duel and then releasing them so that they might move forward to support the infantry combat. If there was a difference between the French and German doctrines of the quick-loading era, it was that the French were somewhat more reluctant than the Germans to expose their gunners to infantry fire.[12]

The first French reaction to the appearance of their 75mm quick-firer was to exchange this standoffish attitude for a more aggressive stance. Attempting to push to the limit the twin advantages of a high rate of fire and armored gun shields, a group of French artillery theorists envisioned a battlefield where four-gun batteries moved forward rapidly in search of positions from which they could fire at medium (1,000 meters) ranges in direct support of infantry battalions, regiments, and brigades. The task of these batteries would be to smother targets—whether groups of enemy riflemen or exposed enemy batteries—with "whirlwinds" (*rafales*) of three or more 75mm shells fired as fast as they could be shoved into the breech. The moral effect of these whirlwinds, these Frenchmen believed, would deprive an enemy of the ability to resist the charge of the French infantry that followed in their wake.[13]

The fact that quick-firing guns did not jump with every shot did much more than make them better direct-fire weapons. It also simplified the tiny adjustments in windage and elevation necessary for effective indirect fire. This was realized from the beginning of the quick-firing era—French experiments with 75mm field guns firing from defilade took place as early as 1897.[14] It was not, however, until the decade just before the outbreak of World War I that the consensus among French artillerymen, no doubt influenced by reports coming from the battlefields of the Russo-Japanese War, shifted again. While a certain fondness for employing artillery in small parcels—battalions of twelve field guns or batteries of four—was retained, the emphasis on getting close to the enemy was replaced by an increased interest in firing from defilade or, at the very least, masked positions.[15] The French field artillery regulations promulgated in 1910 went so far as to refer to the use of direct fire as an "exceptional case." At the same time, the exclusive dependence upon *rafales* was replaced by a more measured policy of matching the rate of fire to the task at hand.[16]

The differences between German and French artillery doctrine were reflected in the way each army organized its basic field artillery units. French batteries had four guns each; German batteries had six. French batteries were easy to hide but relatively fragile. One gun out of commission would seriously impair the firepower of the unit. German batteries required 50 percent more space and were thus harder to provide with suitable defilade positions. Because of their larger size, however, they were significantly more robust.[17]

The doctrines of each country were also related to the way artillery officers were trained. Whereas a French battery commander tended to be a graduate of the École Polytechnique, a school that might best be described as a combination of the Massachusetts Institute of Technology and West Point, his German counterpart was a product of either a cadet school or a gymnasium. Thus, while the German artillery officer was certainly no mathematical illiterate, the French gunner was usually more comfortable in the world of numbers. The German artillery officer, on the other hand, was a tactician before he was a technician.

The heart of the difference between the artillery doctrines of France and Germany lay in the way that French and German officers viewed their troops. Confident in (and perhaps even somewhat fearful of) the enthusiasm and initiative of their soldiers, French military professionals saw their role as providing structure and discipline to compensate for the inherent chaos of the battlefield.[18] German officers, on the other hand, were more comfortable with such chaos. In fact, one could go so far as to say that some found it liberating, even pleasant.[19] Their great fear was that their subordinates would decline to play an active role in battle.[20]

This fundamental disagreement was most clearly reflected in the different philosophies of command and control. Despite all the rhetoric about the natural initiative of the French soldier, the French approach to artillery command and control provided very little latitude to artillery commanders. The French theory was that since artillery units existed to support infantry units, they had to be directly controlled by infantry commanders. The German philosophy, on the other hand, gave a great deal of freedom to the leaders of artillery units. The relationship of German artillery units to infantry units was one not of subordination but of cooperation.

The French artillery regulations of 1910 provided for two means of controlling artillery fire. The first was "high-level connection" (*liaison par le haut*), the placing of an artillery battery, battalion, or regiment under the operational control of an infantry company, battalion, regiment, or brigade for the duration of a particular mission. The second was "low-level connection" (*liaison par le bas*), the orders given by that infantry commander to his subordinate artillery commander. This latter relationship was both informational, with the infantry and artillery commanders discussing what each arm could and could not do in a particular situation, and legal, with the infantry commander being the formal superior of the artillery commander.[21]

The French of the prewar period further fragmented their artillery by assigning particular units to particular tasks. Thus, specific batteries were designated as infantry batteries (*batteries d'infanterie*) and given the task of subordinating their choice of targerts to the wishes of the infantry. Others, the counterbatteries (*contres-batteries*), had no other assignment but to fire on enemy artillery. This division of labor occurred even when the batteries of a regiment were, in accordance with the French preference, located close to each other and under the direct control of a single commander.[22]

The Germans had no such arrangements. In keeping with an "artistic" approach to tactics dating back to the Prussian reformers who fought against Napoleon in the German wars of liberation (1813–1815), they saw great danger in restricting, a priori, the freedom of leaders to organize and employ their forces. Thus, German artillerymen saw danger not only in the fact that the French artillery was divided between missions but also in the inflexibility of the arrangements once they were made.[23]

In further contrast to the French, who massed their batteries but divided the fire of those masses, German artillerymen were increasingly more willing to separate their batteries as long as they could concentrate the fire of as many of those batteries as possible on single targets. At long distance—before the infantry fight began—these targets were usually the enemy artillery. At closer ranges, the target would tend to be enemy infantry blocking the advance of the German infantry. The choice of targets depended less on range than on the conduct of the battle as a whole.

The key idea at work here was the *Schwerpunkt*, the decisive point in space and time upon which a commander focused his efforts in order to produce a decisive result.[24] As a battle developed, the division commander would designate his *Schwerpunkt*. It then became the duty of the senior artilleryman in the division—the artillery brigade commander—to concentrate his artillery fire in such a way as to support the division commander's bid for victory. In other words, the artillery *Schwerpunkt* was to be aligned with the *Schwerpunkt* of the infantry division.[25] "If it is established where the decisive attack is directed," wrote a retired German general in 1910, "the artillery must place an overpowering fire there."[26]

For these reasons, the chief German means of providing for cooperation between the two combatant arms was what the author of the French artillery regulations of 1910 called "connection by sight" (*liaison par la vue*). The commander of the massed artillery of a division would look over the battlefield, determine what was going on, and decide what his batteries should do to influence those events. Likewise, the commanders of artillery regiments, battalions, batteries, and even single sections or guns pushed forward into the firing line were charged with understanding the larger tactical situation and doing what was necessary.

The one point upon which both the Germans and the French of the decade before 1914 were in essential agreement was the indecisiveness of the artillery duel. As early as 1890, some French and German authorities were arguing that a duel between two artillery forces of equivalent size and composition located in defilade would only rarely result in the destruction of one and the triumph of the other. By 1905, the idea that field guns, even after an enormous expenditure of ammunition, would not be able to knock out an appreciable number of opposing field guns, had become widespread in both France and Germany. By 1910 it was firmly enshrined in the professional literature.[27]

The corollary to this thesis was that while physical destruction of batteries in defilade was nearly impossible, it was still both necessary and possible for field artillery units of an attacking force to do their utmost to interfere with the work of the defenders' field artillery. This consisted of keeping the enemy batteries as a whole under a sustained hail of shrapnel that would make it much more difficult for the enemy gunners to complete the myriad tasks—bringing up ammunition, moving the guns, giving orders, observing the enemy—necessary to effective firing. If officers, horses, or drivers were killed or wounded by this fire, so much the better. The main object of such fire, however, was to minimize the power of the enemy artillery until the infantry fight could be settled.[28]

The terms applied to such fire varied. The French artillery regulations of 1910 used the noun *neutralization* to describe the effect. Colonel Paloque, the author of a substantial work on artillery tactics published two years later, was even less confident in the power of counterbattery fire. He preferred to use the verbs *gêner* and *empêcher*—literally, "to bother" and "to obstruct." The Germans, far less specific than the French as to the effect desired, used verbs such as *bekämpfen* (combat) and *niederkämpfen* (overpower).[29]

For most French authorities on the subject, interference with enemy fire was best achieved by the continuous fire of a number of batteries devoted exclusively to counterbattery fire (the aforementioned *contres-batteries*). On the other hand, the Germans tended to resist any such fixed division of labor. They therefore saw the neutralization of the enemy artillery as a task carried out simultaneously with other tasks, the number of batteries devoted to counterbattery fire increasing or decreasing as the situation required.[30]

Just as there was a relationship between doctrine and battery organization, so the French and German philosophies of command and control were reflected in the organization of higher-level artillery units. On the eve of World War I, the French had two types of field artillery regiments. Regiments of four battalions (48 guns) were assigned to active corps. Regiments of three battalions (36 guns) were assigned to active divisions. The battalions that made up these regiments were identical in equipment and training. Each consisted of three batteries of four 75mm field guns. The chief difference between the regiments was function. The smaller regiments marched with the divisions and answered directly to the division commander. The larger regiment, combined on occasion with a battery or two of heavy field howitzers from the field army's reserve, served as the corps commander's reservoir of artillery.[31]

The Germans also made a distinction between corps and divisional artillery. In 1914, the artillery brigade of each active division was divided into three battalions of 77mm light field guns and one of 105mm light field howitzers. The corps artillery battalion was composed of four batteries of 150mm heavy field howitzers.[32] Rather than try to control this powerful battalion himself, the corps commander invariably assigned it to one of his divisions, where it came under the direct orders of the commander of that division's artillery brigade.[33]

The Germans, thus, had but one echelon of command (the division) concerned with the employment of field artillery. At the very least, this facilitated the formation of an artillery *Schwerpunkt* by the division. The French, on the other hand, divided responsibility for field artillery between corps and division commanders, each of whom had a "proprietary" artillery regiment. The virtue of this system was that it ensured that the commanding generals at both echelons would have the means of intervening in a battle.

On paper, at least, this arrangement was not supposed to detract from the ability of a French corps commander to mass most or even all of his artillery. Though this seems to have been more a vestige of the late nineteenth century, when the army corps was the echelon primarily concerned with the employment of field artillery, each French army corps had an artillery brigade commander. Despite the trend in the regulations that decreased his power relative to that of division commanders, he was still the titular head of all field artillery in the corps. He was thus the logical choice to command any grouping of artillery larger than a regiment.[34]

In one sense, the French and German field artillery organizations presented a contrast between the old and the new, with the Germans playing the role of the conservatives whose doctrine had evolved slowly from that derived from the Franco–Prussian War and the French serving as the force that pushed the implications of a new technology to their limits. In another sense, the roles were reversed. The Germans were willing to experiment with howitzers and mobile heavy artillery while the French stuck close to a single innovation that, once made, seemed to preclude further innovations.

These differences, however, did not exist in a vacuum. In both cases they were part and parcel of larger views of war that were as different from each other as Clausewitz was from Jomini, and fear of panic was from fear of inertia. How these different approaches to field artillery fared against each other, thus, would depend largely on how the two larger doctrines interacted on the field of battle.

NOTES

1. de Négrier, *Lessons of the Russo-Japanese War*, trans. E. Louis Spears (London: Hugh Rees, 1906), p. 43; U.S. War Department, *Reports of Military Observers Attached to the Armies in Manchuria During the Russo-Japanese War* (Washington, D.C.: U.S. Government Printing Office, 1906–1907), pt. 5, reports of Edward J. McClernand and William V. Judson (hereafter referred to as McClernand and Judson, *Reports*), pp. 118–19; pt. 1, reports of W. S. Schuyler, J. F. Morrison, Carl Reichmann, and Peyton C. March (hereafter referred to as Schuyler et al., *Reports*), pp. 266–67.

2. U.S. War Department, *Reports of Military Observers Attached to the Armies in Manchuria During the Russo-Japanese War*, pt. 3, report of Joseph E. Kuhn (hereafter referred to as Kuhn, *Report*), pp. 30–31; Schuyler et al., *Reports*, pp. 266–67.

3. The relative strengths are summarized in de Négrier. *Lessons of the Russo-Japanese War*, p. 44.

4. Schuyler et al., *Reports*, pp. 196–97, and 266–67.

5. Ibid., p. 269.

6. These figures are derived by multiplying the maximum rate of fire for each gun by the number of guns in a battery. The figures for a Russian battery are confirmed by an Austrian translation of a Russian report of field firing exercises in 1901. "Concurrenzschießen der russichen Feldartillerie," *Streffleurs österreichische militärische Zeitschrift*, 1902, p. 265.

7. R. G. Cherry, "Russo-Japanese War, the Employment of Field Artillery from June to October, 1904," *Journal of the Royal Artillery* 39, no. 4 (July 1912): 154.

8. Schuyler et al., *Reports*, p. 267.

9. de Négrier, *Lessons of the Russo-Japanese War*, p. 51; Schuyler et al., *Reports*, p. 240.

10. Cherry, "Russo-Japanese War," p. 154; Schuyler et al., *Reports*, pp. 266–67; and de Négrier, *Lessons of the Russo-Japanese War*, p. 44.

11. Cherry, "Russo-Japanese War," p. 157.

12. The French term for a bracket (*fourchette*) seems to be a translation of the German word for the same thing (*Gabel*). Both words have the everyday meaning "fork." For a description of what it was like for a French artilleryman to be subject to bracketing during the Franco-Prussian War, see Alexandre Percin, *Souvenirs militaires, 1870–1914* (Paris: Editions de l'Armée Nouvelle, 1930), pp. 81–87. A detailed treatment of this episode in English can be found in "Range Estimation," *Tactical Notebook*, January 1992.

13. One should be careful not to overstate the influence of the French cult of the offensive in the decade before World War I. While many *phrases lapidaires* can be found in the literature of the time to prove that French military science had degenerated into a species of pep rally, there is a great deal of evidence that the slogans were balanced by other considerations. See, among others, Paddy Griffith, *Forward into Battle* (Chichester, U.K.: Anthony Bird, 1981); "Plan 17," *Tactical Notebook*, July–Nov. 1992; "French Drab Uniforms, 1903–1913," *Tactical Notebook*, July 1992.

14. It is to these experiments that modern artillerymen owe two familiar aspects of their trade: the use of mils as a means of measuring angles and the use of the fingers of the outstretched hands as an analogue for the distance between a target and a reference point. Percin, *Souvenirs militaires*, p. 208. Introduced by the Swiss in 1864, the mil had the advantage of having a simple and easily computed relationship with all means of measuring distance. Regardless of whether the distance was calculated in meters or feet, a mil was always 1/1000 of that distance. Thus, a mil was always one foot at 1,000 feet or ten meters at 10,000 meters. "Current Field Artillery Notes," *Field Artillery Journal* 10, no. 1 (Jan.–Feb. 1920).

15. This development can be seen in the number of articles in the *Revue d'artillerie* dealing with the problems of indirect fire and/or advocating its use.

16. France, Ministère de la Guerre, *Règlement provisoire de manoeuvre de l'artillerie de campagne, (Titre V, L'Artillerie dans le combat)*, (Paris: Imprimerie Nationale, 1911), pp. 8–11. (This manual is hereafter referred to as *Règlement provisoire*.)

17. Wilhelm Balck, *Tactics*, trans. Walter Krueger (Fort Leavenworth, KS: U.S. Cavalry Assn., 1914), vol. 2, p. 248.

18. Jean Defrasne, "La Peur et la panique devant la pensée militaire française," *Revue historique des armées* (1978): no. 1, pp. 84–109.

19. These feelings do not find complete expression until after World War I. See, for the classic example, Ernst Jünger's two wartime diaries, *The Storm of Steel: From the Diary of a German Stormtroop Officer on the Western Front* (London: Chatto and Windus, 1929), and *Copse 125: A Chronicle of the Trench Warfare of 1918* (London: Chatto and Windus, 1930).

20. Wilhelm Balck, whose writings are so often cited in this book, was perhaps the most prolific of the German proponents of open order tactics. The leading advocates of mass tactics were Fritz Hoenig and Jakob Meckel. For more on the debate between mass tactics and "Boer tactics," see Bruce Gudmundsson, *Stormtroop Tactics: Innovation in the German Army, 1914–1918* (New York: Praeger, 1989), ch. 2, or his "A Lesson from the Boers," *Military History Quarterly*, Summer 1989, p. 38. For a political explanation of mass tactics see Bernd F. Schulte, *Die deutsche Armee, 1900–1914. Zwischen Beharren und Verändern* (Düsseldorf: Droste Verlag, 1977).

21. *Règlement provisoire*, pp. 18–23. These ideas, inserted into the French regulations by General Alexandre Percin when he was inspector general of the French artillery (1906–1911), are thoroughly explained in his *Le Combat* (Paris: Librarie Félix Alcan, 1914), pp. 165–213.

22. Anonymous, "Taktische Strömunguen und Bewaffnungsfragen in der französischen Artillerie," *Vierteljahreshefte für Truppenführung und Heereskunde* 10, no. 3 (1913): 573–75; and U. von T., "Taktik der Artillerie des Feldheeres," *Von Löbell's Jahresberichte über das Heer- und Kriegswesen* 39 (1912): 299. Not all French artillerymen liked these designations. Colonel Paloque advised that the artillery be divided into two parts. The first was to cooperate directly with the infantry; the second was to remain under the control of the division commander. The first was to attack any enemy unit that interfered with the work of the infantry; The second was to attack targets of concern to the division as a whole. Paloque, *L'Artillerie dans la Bataille* (Paris: Octave Doin et Fils, 1912), pp. 254–55.

23. "Thus it must be established: whosoever practices tactics must be entirely free in the manner of employing his troops. The man for whom the method of employing his troops is preselected does not practice troop leading in the sense of an art, but rather its technique. And if in tactics the form is taken for the essence, then it is no longer art, but a handicraft." Gertsch, *Vom russich–japanischen Krieg*, quoted in Wilhelm Balck, "Gedanken eines Regimentskommandeurs über den Winterdienst der Infanterie," *Jahrbücher für die deutsche Armee und Marine*, Jan. 1912, p. 156.

24. For more on this concept, see Bruce Gudmundsson, "Fieldstripping the Schwerpunkt," *Marine Corps Gazette* (Dec. 1989); and "Focus of Efforts," *Tactical Notebook*, Oct.–Nov. 1991.

25. For an early expression of this idea, see "18.," "Die Neuordnung der deutschen Feldartillerie," *Jahrbücher für die deutsche Armee und Marine*, Feb. 1914, pp. 174–77.

26. Graf von Haslingen, "Ausbildung für den Krieg: Zusammenwirken von Artillerie und Infanterie," *Jahrbücher für die deutsche Armee und Marine*, Jan. 1910, p. 9.

27. Balck, *Tactics*, vol. 2, pp. 354–55, 418–19; U. von T, "Taktik der Artillerie des Feldheeres," pp. 297–98; Paloque, *L'Artillerie dans la bataille*, pp. 271–73, 354; *Règlement provisoire*, pp. 8–11.

28. Paloque, *L'Artillerie dans la bataille*, pp. 353–59, 378–79.

29. *Règlement provisoire*, p. 13; Paloque, *L'Artillerie dans la bataille*, pp. 375–78. The German terms appear throughout the literature of the period. The reference at hand was Wilhelm Balck, *Entwickelung der Taktik im Weltkriege* (Berlin: Eisenschmidt, 1922), p. 332.

30. "Judicious distribution of duties between various artillery units in action is one of the most important tasks of the higher artillery commanders." Balck, *Tactics*, vol. 2, p. 423.

31. Paloque, *L'Artillerie dans la bataille*, p. 244, 284–86.

32. Each battery of field artillery had six pieces. Each heavy field howitzer battery had four 150mm pieces. Balck, *Tactics*, vol. 2, pp. 253–55. For more on the role of howitzers, see Ch. 3 of this work.

33. The idea of making the division the focus of artillery employment antedated the widespread provision of 150mm heavy field howitzers. See "18.," "Die Neuordnung der deutschen Feldartillerie."

34. Anonymous, "Die Organization und Taktik der französischen Feldartillerie," *Vierteljahreshefte für Truppenführung und Heereskunde* 8, no. 2 (1911): 345–54.

3

Howitzers

During the first three months of World War I, everywhere that German met Frenchman on the field of battle, the story was the same. The French field guns were able to fire further, faster, and more accurately than their German opposite numbers. On occasion, this led to stunning local success.[1] For most practical purposes, however, that did not matter. While the German gunners had the tactical sense to put their shells where they would have the most impact on the larger battle, the French gunners were rarely in a position to cooperate effectively with their infantry.[2]

In addition to the advantages offered by their superior tactical doctrine and training, the Germans possessed a significant technical advantage in their large inventory of howitzers. In the mobile warfare of 1914, the heavier German howitzers were often able to outrange the *soixante-quinze*, striking at batteries that were completely unable to reply in kind. Even when they were within the firing fan of French field guns, German howitzers were often able to make themselves immune from French fire by taking up defilade positions. For while the flat-trajectory 75mm gun could fire from certain kinds of defilade positions, its ability to deliver plunging fire was severely constrained.[3]

When, in the fall of 1914, mobile warfare gave way to trench warfare, the benefits accruing to the side that possessed the larger howitzer park increased considerably. The more obvious advantage was the howitzer's better ratio of weight of shell fired to weight of piece firing. Less obvious, but equally significant, was the markedly greater degree of accuracy offered by howitzers firing at long ranges against the type of targets likely to predominate in trench warfare.

A carriage that can mount a given field gun can generally mount a howitzer of a significantly larger caliber firing a significantly larger shell. In 1916, for example, the U.S. Army 3-inch (76.2mm) field gun weighed the same as the American 3.8-inch (96mm) howitzer. The field gun shell weighed fifteen pounds, while the howitzer shell weighed thirty pounds. There was a similar relationship between the U.S. 4.7-inch gun and the U.S. 6-inch howitzer. The gun fired a 60-pound shell, while the howitzer, mounted on a carriage of similar size, fired a 120-pound shell.[4]

The greater size (and therefore volume) of their shells allowed howitzers to deliver a larger amount of explosive with each round fired. This meant not only that direct hits did more damage but also that near misses stood a greater chance of doing harm to the occupants of a trench and to the structural integrity of the trench itself. This greater "weight of metal" (the expression should be "weight of explosive") more than compensated for the somewhat slower rate of fire of World War I era field howitzers.

The accuracy advantage of howitzers is well illustrated by an article published in the *Field Artillery Journal* in 1916. Using empirical data from the range firing of U.S. 3-inch (76.2mm) field guns and 4.7-inch (120mm) howitzers, the author, Major E. D. Scott of the U.S. Army, calculated that less than half as many howitzer shells as field gun shells were needed to score the same number of direct hits on a given section of trench. The advantage of the howitzer over the field gun was particularly marked at ranges between 2,000 and 3,000 meters, where an average of two and a half field gun shells was needed to achieve the same probability of a hit as one howitzer shell.[5]

Table 3.1
Number of Rounds Needed to Score One Hit on a Standard Trench—1916

Range (yards)	Number of Rounds 4.7-inch Howitzer	Number of Rounds 3-inch Field Gun
1000	6	14
2000	17	50
3000	20	50
4000	22	50
5000	26	50
6000	24	55

By the time Major Scott's article on the suitability of howitzers for trench warfare was published in the fall of 1916, the hard-won experience of the first winter of the war had convinced the armies of Europe of the limitations of the light field gun. This realization, however, did not necessarily lead to the large-scale adoption of howitzers. Rather, whether an army took the German approach to field artillery or followed another road was a function of a combination of its prewar inclinations and the hard realities of industrial mobilization.

In October 1914, for example, the French War Ministry officially recognized its need to field artillery weapons more powerful than the 75mm field gun. However, rather than order the production of large numbers of weapons that corresponded to the German howitzers that had led the French Army to this understanding, the War Ministry formed heavy batteries of obsolete siege weapons—guns and howitzers of the late-nineteenth-century "de Bange" system. Although a serviceable 155mm howitzer was already in production for the French Army and a first-class 105mm howitzer, originally designed for export to Bulgaria, was available from the Schneider works, the War Ministry preferred to concentrate on the production of more field guns.[6]

The roots of the French disdain for howitzers ran back to the introduction of the 75mm quick-firer. The many virtues of this weapon encouraged the development of a school of thought that argued that the 75mm light field gun should be the only weapon used in both division and corps artillery regiments. When presented, in the years immediately preceding the outbreak of war, with the fact of German light howitzers, members of this school went so far as to claim that the Germans acquired howitzers only to compensate for the inferiority of their 77mm field guns.[7]

The position of the French anti-howitzer school was well summarized in an elegant little brochure written in 1911. The core argument was that the 75mm field gun was superior to a light field howitzer for all tasks that the field artillery was likely to encounter. Because of its higher rate of fire and its flat trajectory (which resulted in a more efficient pattern of flying bullets), the field gun was a better means of firing shrapnel. Against enemy batteries, the field gun was just as efficient a means of hitting field pieces. Even when the enemy batteries were masked, the field gun was inferior to the howitzer only when the slope behind which the enemy was hiding was steeper than nine degrees.[8]

The pro-howitzer forces received a boost from reports coming from the battlefields of the Balkan Wars (1912–1913). The first thing that French observers noted was the regularity with which field gun batteries in defilade were able to destroy field gun batteries set up in the open, while dug-in batteries were practically invulnerable to shrapnel. The second thing was that howitzers were appreciated less for the high angle of their fire than for the explosive power of their projectiles. The lesson that was generally drawn from the reports, however, was not that the French Army needed howitzers but that it needed weapons capable of firing projectiles heavier than that of the 75mm field gun. The immediate result of French study of the Balkan wars thus was not the procurement of additional howitzers but the formation of five heavy artillery regiments equipped with a mixture of modern 155mm howitzers and obsolete weapons—155mm and 120mm guns as well as 120mm howitzers.[9]

The French parliament, which would eventually have to vote the funds to buy light howitzers, had long remained neutral in the technical debate. On the eve of the war, however, when a combination of the German threat and the experience of Balkan armies convinced the War Ministry to ask for funds for light field howitzers, the deputies threw in their lot with the anti-howitzer forces. In particular, they chose to acquire a stock of *plaquettes*—cheap devices that, when attached to 75mm shells, reduced their ballistic efficiency. Because 75mm shells so modified had a curved trajectory, the advocates of the *plaquettes* argued that they represented a cheap alternative to the far greater expense of buying modern light howitzers.[10] As a result of these events, the only modern howitzers in the French service at the beginning of World War I were the 155mm heavy field howitzers assigned to three of the five army-level heavy artillery regiments.[11]

Of the nations that would be France's allies in World War I, only Italy and Belgium shared her minimalist policy. Like France, these states limited their acquisition of howitzers to a heavy model issued only to armies. (In the case of Belgium, however, this was more the result of an inability to decide on the ideal caliber for a light field howitzer than any lack of appreciation for its virtues.)[12] Other first- and second-rate powers, including Serbia and Greece, which were armed primarily with French weapons, attempted to acquire light field howitzers in calibers ranging from 100mm to 122mm.[13]

The experiences of the Russo-Japanese War of 1904–1905 made the Russians very appreciative of the peculiar virtues of light field howitzers. The same financial problems that prevented the reorganization of the light field gun batteries, however, prevented the acquisition of considerable numbers of howitzers. Only on the eve of World War I was the Russian Army able to provide each army corps with a battalion of twelve 122mm light field howitzers.[14]

As is often the case, one of the more complete resurrections of the howitzer came from the armies that had never really buried it. By 1911, the British Army, which had used large numbers of 5-inch (127mm) howitzers in South Africa, had eighteen modern 4.5-inch (114mm) howitzers in each division of the British Expeditionary Force.[15] There was, however, no corps artillery in the British service, and the army artillery of the six-division expeditionary force consisted exclusively of 60-pounder (127mm) guns of the Royal Garrison Artillery. The divisional howitzers were thus the only howitzers in the British field forces at the outbreak of war.[16]

Of all the major armies of the period immediately before World War I, only that of Germany had modern howitzers as organic parts of both divisions and corps. On the eve of World War I, about a fourth of the artillery of German active divisions—954 pieces out of a total of 3,300—was composed of 105mm light field howitzers.[17] Mobilization, which increased the number of divisions in the German Army without a proportionate increase in the number of modern artillery pieces in service, somewhat diluted this high concentration of light field howitzers. Thus, when Germany went to war in 1914, there was one light field howitzer to every five light field guns.[18]

To supplement these light field howitzers, the Germans of 1914 could dispose of no less than 416 150mm heavy field howitzers—weapons that were equivalent in performance to the French 155mm field howitzers.[19] Although they belonged to the siege artillery branch, the heavy field howitzers were organized into fully mobile batteries, four of which formed a battalion attached to each active army corps. (There was, in the German Army of 1914, no corps-level artillery commander. Consequently, the heavy field howitzer battalion of each corps was attached to the artillery brigade of one of the two component divisions.)[20]

The German light howitzer owed its existence to a consensus among German artillery officers on the need to combat enemy artillery and infantry protected by hasty field fortifications. As early as the Russo-Turkish war of 1878, German observers had noticed that field guns had almost no effect on field fortifications, even when the field guns fired high explosives instead of the usual shrapnel. After experimenting with reduced-charge shells for field guns and 120mm howitzers, the German Army settled, in 1898, on a 105mm howitzer. In 1909, a new version of this howitzer, improved by means of a modern recoil mechanism, was introduced.[21]

When light field howitzers were first introduced into the German field artillery, the War Ministry intended them to replace one of the eight field gun battalions then assigned to each army corps. By 1905 or so, analysis of reports from the Greco–Turkish War (1897), Second Anglo-Boer War, Boxer Rebellion, and Russo-Japanese War had convinced the German authorities of the increased value of light field howitzers. The number of light field howitzers (and, in consequence, the number of light field howitzer battalions) was therefore doubled. Each active German division thus went to war with a battalion of eighteen light field howitzers of its own.[22]

Germany's position as the leading user of heavy howitzers, on the other hand, was largely the result of a doctrinal battle between various agencies of the German army. Count Alfred von Schlieffen, who became chief of the General Staff in 1891, favored equipping the field army with heavy artillery because his campaign plans for war against France required the quick reduction of French and/or Belgian fortresses.[23] The siege artillery branch, led by a series of energetic inspectors, actively cooperated with Schlieffen. Their orthodox efforts were focused on altering the mounts of heavy howitzers and long-range guns originally designed for installation in fortresses. Less orthodox methods included hiring civilian teamsters and renting privately owned horses to move their gargantuan weapons on field maneuvers. (Many German heavy batteries, which were originally assigned to fortresses or the siege train, had no organic transport.)[24]

Opposition to equipping the German field army with heavy artillery was led by the corps commanders. Directly responsible to the Kaiser for both the peacetime training and the wartime employment of their corps, these officers were very much concerned with maintaining what they called the "tempo" of operations. In the campaigns of 1866 (against Austria) and 1870 (against France), the German Army's victories were largely due to their superior operational mobility. Part of that advantage must be credited to the German railroad network and its skillful exploitation by the "demi-gods" of the Elder Moltke's Great General Staff. The other part—and the part nearest to the hearts of the corps commanders—consisted of keeping the divisions that detrained at the railheads as unencumbered as possible.

Large numbers of heavy artillery pieces, the German corps commanders felt, would lengthen march columns and cause traffic problems at bottlenecks. The heavy horses required to pull the heavy guns would put a strain on the supply of fodder that was already needed to feed the horses of the rapidly expanding field artillery and cavalry. Even the prodigious thirst of the big horses was seen as a problem. During one field exercise a corps commander claimed that his whole organization was impeded by the need to stop at every village to draw water for the "elephants" that pulled the big guns.[25]

In the end, the partisans of heavy artillery convinced the Kaiser that fortifications were a greater threat to mobility than traffic jams. In a speech on the occasion of a field exercise in 1900, the Kaiser made his opinion clear when he commanded that the 105mm howitzers belonging to the field artillery henceforth be referred to as "light field howitzers" and that the 150mm howitzers crewed and commanded by siege artillery personnel be designated "heavy field howitzers."[26]

True to their origin as siege artillery, the German heavy field howitzers were provided with a high-explosive shell. Used with a delay fuse (*Verzögerungszünder*), this shell was designed to penetrate concrete roofs of permanent fortresses before exploding. Although its primary purpose was to destroy material targets, the blast effect of the high-explosive shell was devastating against soldiers who were unfortunate enough to be caught in a confined space when it exploded.[27]

For use against troops in the open, the German field howitzers, both light and heavy, had initially been provided with shrapnel rounds. In addition to this, the light field howitzers used a "unitary shell" (*Einheitsgeschoß*) that sacrificed part of its high-explosive filling in order to make room for a small number of shrapnel bullets. This projectile, introduced in 1905, could be equipped with a powder-train time fuse (*Brennzünder*) to provide air bursts, an impact fuse (*Aufschlagzünder*) for surface bursts, and a delay fuse for subsurface bursts. Introduced in 1905, the "unitary shell" was the only type of round carried in the caissons of most German light field howitzer batteries in the opening campaigns of 1914.[28]

Like many peacetime attempts to standardize weapons with divergent natures, the German "unitary shell" proved to be a failure. The addition of bullets made it as expensive as a shrapnel shell while taking space away from the high-explosive filling. The result was a shell that was particularly disappointing as a high-explosive round. Once active campaigning began in August 1914, this shortcoming became obvious and the "unitary shell" was soon replaced by traditional high-explosive and shrapnel shells.[29]

This defect notwithstanding, their howitzers—both 105mm and 150mm—gave the Germans a huge advantage in the early days of trench warfare. With the Russians busy with the Austrians, the Belgians reduced to defending the remaining sliver of their territory, and the British frantically trying to rebuild their tiny army, the job of holding the trenches across no-man's-land from the Germans fell to the French. This, in turn, meant that the Germans had a near monopoly on the use of howitzers.

Having howitzers meant that the Germans were able to inflict serious damage on entrenched French troops while the French artillery could do little more than harass the occupants of German field fortifications. The initial impact of this disparity was tremendous. French troops facing systematic bombardment by German howitzers often abandoned their shallow trenches.[30] Fortunately for the French, the Germans, short of both shells and reserves, lacked the means either to bombard as often as they liked or to turn their local successes into victories of greater significance.

The lesson of the practical value of howitzers was not lost on the German leadership. The first divisions that the German Army raised after the war began—the reserve divisions formed in October 1914—were short of cavalry, machine guns, transport, and artillery. The ratio of light field howitzers to field guns, however, was raised from the prewar standard of 1:3 to an unprecedented 1:2. The next series of divisions, raised in December 1914, had an even higher ratio of howitzers to guns. In addition to having one light field howitzer for every field gun, these divisions had, for the first time in German military history, an assigned battalion of eight 150mm heavy field howitzers.[31] By March 1915, the German War Ministry had settled on an ideal divisional artillery consisting of a single field artillery regiment of two field gun battalions and one light howitzer battalion. While it took two years of adding light howitzer battalions to reserve divisions and subtracting field gun battalions from the older active divisions, this eventually resulted in a standard ratio of one light howitzer to two field guns.[32]

Heavy artillery, including heavy field howitzers, was not made a permanent part of most German divisions until late in 1917. From the very beginning of the war, however, each passing month saw more heavy artillery made available for temporary attachment to German divisions. The German field armies began the war with 148 batteries of heavy artillery. The bulk of these, 104, were the heavy field howitzer batteries attached to active army corps. The rest were 210mm heavy howitzer, siege mortar (280mm, 305mm, and 420mm), and 100mm heavy gun batteries that had originally been attached to armies that were expected to have to deal with significant enemy fortifications. By the end of the second year of the war, the number of German heavy artillery batteries at the front had increased to 1,380.[33]

The French response to this explosive growth in German heavy artillery was to launch a series of programs to build a heavy artillery force of their own. For the first two years of the war, however, their only means of doing this was to take obsolete weapons out of storage and form them into batteries. While these pieces fired shells big enough (95mm to 155mm) to qualify them as heavy artillery, they were inferior to the bulk of German heavy artillery on two counts. First, they lacked modern recoil mechanisms. This greatly reduced their rate of fire. Second, they were guns rather than howitzers. As a result, despite heroic efforts to build up this long-neglected arm, the French heavy artillery of 1914, 1915, and to a certain degree 1916, was always at a disadvantage when dealing with its German counterpart.[34]

If the French had followed their prewar doctrine and tried to keep their field guns as far forward as possible, this would have resulted in disaster. The extent of that disaster can be gauged from a prewar experiment in which officers of the German siege artillery branch discovered that a battery of four heavy field (150mm) howitzers firing 80 to 100 rounds at a simulated French field gun battery would easily knock that battery out of action. A target battery located within a rectangle that was about 100 meters wide and 400 meters deep, for example, would lose 30 to 50 percent of its personnel and 60 to 65 percent of its guns, carriages, caissons, and other matériel.[35]

That this did not happen was due to the rapidity with which the French dropped their prewar beliefs in favor of moving the bulk of their artillery to the rear. Though the actual distance varied with the pecularities of the terrain, this usually translated into battery positions that were 2,000 to 3,000 meters behind the forward trenches of the infantry. Given that the Germans were doing the same thing, the result was batteries that, rather than firing at each other at ranges of 2,000 meters or less, were separated by 4,000 to 6,000 meters. The nature of the terrain of northeastern France being what it is, this meant that there was at least one hill, ridge, wood, or other terrain mask between the opposing artilleries.

As predicted in a number of articles appearing in professional journals before the war, this situation made it very difficult to locate enemy batteries. Firing blind offered no solution. A battery sheltered behind a relatively small bump in the ground might be located right behind it, 3,000 meters behind it, or anywhere in between. The semipermanent nature of the gun positions used in trench warfare, moreover, made batteries less conspicuous on the ground, and thus harder to spot from a church tower, hill, or aircraft. Not only was there time to provide camouflage, but there was much less need to encumber the guns and their crews with the telltale impedimenta of horses, caissons, and equipment wagons.

The other belligerents were similarly hampered in their attempts to knock out enemy artillery. The almost universal adoption of indirect fire and the continuing tendency for all armies to keep their batteries far to the rear made obsolete all preexisting ideas about counterbattery fire. At the same time, the scientific communities of the more advanced nations, many of whose members were serving in uniform, set to work to develop techniques for solving this problem. In the meantime, the artillerymen of Europe were in the position of being very harmful to the infantry but not very dangerous to each other.

This relationship had two major consequences. The first was a great increase in the difficulty of liaison between infantry and artillery. This resulted in a great deal of what we would now call friendly fire—French shells falling among French soldiers, German shells falling among German soldiers.[36] The second was a reversal of the traditional relationship between counterbattery fire and fire in support of the infantry. With counterbattery fire now no more than a stab in the dark, the chief means of depriving the enemy of their guns was to overrun them with one's own infantry.[37]

The irony of this last phenomenon was that the light howitzers acquired with an eye to counterbattery fire were an important accessory to the infantry eager to get at the enemy's guns. With their greater accuracy and heavier shells, howitzers made it more likely that the attacking infantry would be able to rush across no-man's-land and enter the enemy trenches before the enemy artillery could respond. If the rush succeeded, the attackers had little to fear from the defender's artillery. Unsure of the exact location of friend and foe, they were as likely to hit their own infantry as they were to hit that of the attackers. On the other hand, if the attacking infantry failed to engage the defenders in a timely fashion, it would find itself on the receiving end of a hail of shrapnel shells.

Because of this, the objective in the first year of trench warfare was to attack the most forward trench. Though defending batteries might (and certainly did) inflict casualties upon attackers, and considerable resources might still be devoted to counterbattery fire, the trench closest to no-man's-land, filled with the greater part of the defender's infantry, was the "center of gravity" of the defense. If it fell, the whole position was lost. If it held, there was little to fear from an attack.

As long as infantrymen insisted on fighting this way, the job of the artillery was simple. At the very least, it needed to pin the defenders within their trenches until the attacker's infantry was upon them. The greater the destruction that accompanied this pinning, the greater the degree to which the pinning would be effective and the longer the suppressive effect would last. For this reason, it is not surprising that the army that was the first to master this sort of fighting was the one that had entered the war with the largest force of heavy artillery and the highest proportion of howitzers.

NOTES

1. For examples, see Gascouin, *L'Évolution de l'artillerie pendant la guerre* (Paris: Flammarion, 1920), pp. 70–93.

2. This opinion is shared by the famous French artillery expert, General Hérr. Frédéric Georges Hérr, *L'Artillerie, ce qu'elle a été, ce qu'elle est, ce qu'elle doit être* (Paris: Berger Levrault, 1924), p. 26. For a description of a German artillery battalion in action in 1914, see A. Seeger, "Our Baptism of Fire," *Field Artillery Journal* 5, no. 4 (Oct.–Dec. 1915): 659–673. For the best description of the encounter battles of 1914 in English, see the series of articles by Arthur Higgins Burne in *The Fighting Forces*: "The Battle of Rossignol," Oct. 1931; "The Battle of Virton," Apr. 1931; "The Battle of Ethe," Oct. 1929.

3. These factors were noticed by the intelligence section (Deuxième Bureau) of the French General Staff before the war. Hérr, *L'Artillerie*, p. 14.

4. E. D. Scott, "Howitzer Fire," *Field Artillery Journal* 6, no. 4 (Oct.–Dec. 1916): 525–26.

5. Scott's figures were derived from fire on a standard trench built in accordance with the 1914 edition of U.S. Army Field Service Regulations and located on a forward slope. Had the trench been on a level field or a reverse slope, the accuracy advantage of the howitzer would have been even greater. E. D. Scott, "Field Artillery Fire," *Field Artillery Journal* 6, no. 3 (July–Sept. 1916): 400.

6. Hérr, *L'Artillerie*, pp. 17, 31–33.

7. In particular, the anti-howitzer school pointed out the German need to attack, at long range, French field guns in defilade positions. They did not, however, see a corresponding need for the French to attack German field guns should they be placed in defilade positions. Hérr, *L'Artillerie*, pp. 15–16. The contemporary French literature on this controversy is extensive, particularly in the journals *La France militaire* and *Revue d'artillerie*.

8. Sauterau de Part, "Note sur les programmes d'obusiers légers et artillerie lourde mobile," dated Dec. 1911, SHAT, carton 4b22.

9. G. Bellenger, "Notes sur l'emploi de l'artillerie dans la campagne des Balkans," *Revue d'artillerie*, Nov. 1913, pp. 85–100; Frédéric Georges Hérr, *Sur le théâtre de la guerre des Balkans, mon journal de route* (Paris: Berger-Levrault, 1913), p. 96; Hérr, *L'Artillerie*, p. 20. For the distribution of heavy artillery to the French armies in 1914, see the series on "Plan 17" in *Tactical Notebook* (July–Nov. 1992).

10. The invention of these *plaquettes* is often ascribed to a certain Captain Malandrin. In fact, they had long been used on French firing ranges to reduce the chances of richochets. Malandrin simply advocated their use on the battlefield. Hérr, *L'Artillerie*, pp. 18–19.

11. U.S. War Department, Office of the Chief of Staff, "Study on the Development of Large Calibre Mobile Artillery and Machine Guns in the Present European War" (document no. 509), reprinted in *Field Artillery Journal*, 6, no. 2 (Apr.–June 1916): 290.

12. Nippold, "Die Feldartillerie der Feindmächte vor, während und nach dem Krieg," in *Das Ehrenbuch der deutschen Feldartillerie*, ed. Albert Benary (Berlin: Verlag Tradition Wilhelm Kolk, 1930), p. 121. In 1911, the Belgians had gone so far as to adopt, on paper, a 95mm light field howitzer. The procurement of this weapon was delayed, however, pending the testing of a competing 105mm howitzer. As a result, the only howitzers available to the Belgian Army on mobilization in 1914 were twelve 150mm

heavy field howitzers that had been taken from a fort and hastily made mobile with requisitioned horses. Pontus, "L'Artillerie issue de la guerre," *Bulletin belge des sciences militaires*, June 1921, pp. 122–23; and "I.G.A.," "Développement de l'artillerie lourde au cours de la campagne 1914–1918," *Bulletin belge des sciences militaires*, Sept. 1921.

13. "Schneider-Geschütze in den Armeen," *Kriegstechnische Zeitschrift für Offizere aller Waffen*, 1915, pp. 53–58.

14. Nicholas N. Golovine, *The Russian Army in the World War* (New Haven: Yale University Press, 1931), pp. 32–34; and Aleksei A. Brussilov, *A Soldier's Notebook 1914–1918* (Westport, CT: Greenwood Press, 1976), p. 15.

15. Shelford Graham and Dominick Bidwell, *Firepower: British Army Weapons and Theories of War 1904–1905* (Boston: George Allen and Unwin, 1985), p. 13.

16. A. A. Scarisbrick, "The Organization and Deployment of the British Expeditionary Force," *Journal of the Royal Artillery*, Sept. 1989, pp. 110–12. The Royal Garrison Artillery was the British counterpart of the German *Fußartillerie* and the French *artillerie à pied*. Like the latter organizations, its officers were more technically oriented than the field artillerymen of the Royal Artillery and Royal Horse Artillery.

17. Edgar Graf von Matuschka, "Organizationsgeschichte des Heeres, 1890–1918," in *Deutsche Militärgeschichte in sechs Bänden 1648–1939*, ed. Militärgeschichtliches Forschungsamt (Munich: Bernhard and Graefe Verlag, 1983), vol. 3, pp. 227, 242; and Hermann Cron, *Geschichte des deutschen Heeres im Weltkriege 1914–1918* (Berlin: Karl Siegismund, 1937), pp. 144–45.

18. Reserve divisions rated one regiment of two battalions of light field guns (thirty-six guns). *Landwehr* (second-line reserve) divisions rated only two batteries of light field guns (twelve guns). Matuschka, "Organizationsgeschichte des Heeres," p. 227.

19. Ibid., p. 244.

20. The German siege artillery (*Fußartillerie*) was made separate from the field artillery in 1872. Ibid., p. 176. The designations "light field howitzer" for the howitzers of the field artillery and "heavy field howitzer" for the mobile howitzers of the siege artillery were introduced by Kaiser Wilhelm II as a means of reducing the distinction between the two branches. Georg Bruchmüller, *Die deutsche Artillerie in den Durchbruchschlachten des Weltkrieges* (Berlin: E. S. Mittler und Sohn, 1922), p. 4.

21. Hollweg, "Zweck und Bedeutung der Einführung des neuen deutschen Feldhaubitzenmaterials," *Jahrbücher für die deutsche Armee und Marine* 114, no. 1 (Jan. 1900); Wilhelm Rohne, "Über die Bedeutung der Artillerie im nächsten Kriege," *Vierteljahresheft für Truppenführung und Heereskunde*, no. 4 (1913): 642–44; "Taktik der Feldartillerie. 1874–98," in *Das Militärwesen in seiner Entwickelung während der 25 Jahre, 1874–1898*, ed. Pelet-Narbonne (supplement to *Von Löbell's Jahresberichte über das Heer-und Kriegswesen* 1898), p. 629; and "Renseignements Divers," *Revue d'artillerie*, Nov. 1912, p. 9.

22. Rohne, "Über die Bedeutung der Artillerie im nächsten Kriege," and "Die Neuordnung der deutschen Feldartillerie," *Jahrbücher für die deutsche Armee und Marine*, no. 2 (Feb. 1898).

23. von Freytag-Loringhoven, *Generalfeldmarschall Graf von Schlieffen: Sein Leben und die Verwertung seines geistigen Erbes im Weltkrieg* (Leipzig: Historia-Verlag Paul Schraepler, 1920), pp. 48–51. For an overview of these plans and how they developed, see Gerhard Ritter, *The Schlieffen Plan: Critique of a Myth* (New York: Praeger, 1958), pp. 17–37.

24. Georg Bruchmüller, *Die deutsche Artillerie*, pp. 2–10.

25. Matuschka, "Organizationsgeschichte des Heeres," pp. 175–76; and Bruchmüller, *Die deutsche Artillerie*, p. 5.

26. Bruchmüller, *Die deutsche Artillerie*, p. 4.

27. Matuschka, "Organizationsgeschichte des Heeres," p. 173.

28. Ibid.

29. Ibid.

30. For examples see *Das Ehrenbuch der deutschen schweren Artillerie*, vol. 2, pp. 101–12; "V.," "Impressions d'Allemagne. L'Armée sur pied de guerre," *Revue militaire suisse*, Aug. 1915, pp. 343–44; and Alexandre Percin, *Le Massacre de notre infanterrie* (Paris: Albin-Michel, 1923).

31. Cron, *Geschichte des deutschen Heeres*, pp. 146–47. For more on this subject, see "German Divisional Artillery," *Tactical Notebook*, Oct. 1992.

32. Ibid.

33. Cron, *Geschichte des deutschen Heeres*, pp. 154–58.

34. Hérr, *L'Artillerie*, p. 31–32, 41.

35. Ibid., p. 10.

36. Friendly fire is a subject worthy of its own book. For an extensive treatment of friendly fire in World War I, see Percin, *Le Massacre*.

37. General Percin claimed that in the course of World War I, four times as many French guns had been captured by the Germans than were destroyed by their counterbattery fire. Ibid., p. 112.

4

Artillery Conquers, Infantry Occupies

In addition to convincing the armies of Europe of the wisdom of the German Army's precocious fondness for howitzers, the onset of trench warfare on the western front forced all concerned to rethink the way that artillery fit into the larger battle. As is often the case with such revolutions, the people and institutions that were the quickest to adapt to the new conditions were those that had long been inclined toward the solution. Nevertheless, the dead hand of the past lay heavy on the armies that had become stuck in the mud of Flanders and on the chalk hills of Champagne. The way they adapted to trench warfare often reflected the way they had prepared for mobile warfare.

On the French side, one of the first officers to push for a change in artillery tactics was Philippe Pétain, who successively commanded an infantry regiment and an infantry division during the mobile campaign of 1914. Long an advocate of the systematic preparation of attacks by artillery fire, he was unpopular with the "red trouser" school of thought that was so prominent in the French Army of the time. As early as 1900, his reading of the fighting in South Africa had led him to favor the detailed study of the enemy positions and the assignment of particular units to deal with particular pieces of terrain. In the fall of 1914, this approach gained him a number of minor victories that, at a time when the French Army was suffering a large number of defeats, brought him both fame and promotion.[1]

Before the onset of winter, Pétain's views had become official. A memorandum promulgated by Joffre on November 28, 1914, recommended a formula for attacks that included the designation of a limited objective (several trenches); painstaking reconnaissance, to include aerial reconnaissance, of the objective; a search for positions from which the Germans could fire against the flanks of an attack; the designation of troops that are to attack and those that are to protect, by fire, the flanks of the attack; the use of small columns of infantry, each of which is to be reinforced by pioneers equipped with ladders and bangalore torpedoes for breaking through barbed wire obstacles; and the establishment of time-tables for each unit's attack. The artillery was to fire on the enemy trenches until the infantry was to attack. At that time, it was to lift its fire to form a barrage behind the enemy's first line. Additional artillery was to fire on positions that permited the Germans to fire on the flanks of the attack.[2]

The German counterpart to Joffre's recipe for systematic attacks developed along the same general lines. Differences in ingredients, however, gave the resulting method a very different flavor. German possession of trench mortars, as well as the skill and number of German pioneers, relieved the artillery of any need to worry about the problem of barbed wire. The German philosophy of command and control, with its faith in the competence of regimental officers and consequent emphasis on voluntary cooperation between units, reduced the need for instructions. The collegial relationships between ranks that made such a philosophy possible also served to make the planning process an iterative one. That is, rather than a detailed plan being drawn up by staff officers and then promulgated down the chain of command, the German planning seems to have included much frank talk between commanders of all ranks.[3]

The first German attack in which the deployment from the line of march was replaced by a carefully prepared attack launched from trenches was the capture of the north bank of the Aisne River near the town of Vailly on October 30, 1914. In this attack, the rapid appreciation of the situation by commanders riding at the front of columns was replaced by a reconnaissance effort that lasted a week and included aerial photography. The feeding in of batteries as they became available was supplanted by the deliberate assignment of particular units to particular sectors and particular sets of targets, with an organization that was custom designed. The most radical change, however, was the drawing up of a timetable that called for certain types of fire to be used against certain targets at certain times.[4]

Much remained, however, of the old system. Though the formation conducting the attack was a corps (the 3rd Corps of the 1st Army), there was no attempt to establish a corps artillery headquarters. Instead, the commanding officer of the field artillery brigade of one of the two divisions belonging to the corps coordinated the artillery effort for the whole attack. As a result, the additional heavy artillery that was given to the corps for the attack—three batteries of 150mm howitzers, one battalion of 210mm howitzers, and two batteries of 100mm heavy guns—was attached directly to the field artillery brigades. The artillery brigade commanders, as well as their subordinate commanders, established observation posts from which they could see the targets at which their guns and howitzers were firing.[5]

These observation posts, and the telephones that connected them to the guns, allowed the German technique for deliberate attacks in trench warfare to retain some of the flexibility of their method for conducting hasty attacks in mobile warfare. The central idea of the new German method—what might be called the leitmotif—was timing. All fire on the enemy's forward trenches had to lift at the same time. Within a few moments—before the enemy had time to recover from the effects of the bombardment—the infantry had to rise as one man from its trenches and rush into those of the enemy.

This simple idea was complicated by the fact that slightly over half of the German batteries at Vailly (representing 65 percent of the pieces) were equipped with guns. As most of these were located two or three kilometers behind the German lines in positions that were uphill from the French trenches, the lack of ballistic accuracy posed a problem. That is, even if all firing data were perfect, many of the 77mm and 100mm shells fired on the French trenches would fall on nearby German trenches. The German infantry was therefore required, in places where their trenches were particularly close to those of the French, to withdraw from their most forward trenches during the bombardment. This, of course, increased the interval between the time the German artillery fire lifted and the German infantry were safely on the other side of no-man's-land.[6]

The solution was to "train" the French infantry to react more slowly to the lifting of artillery fire. This was done by alternating intense bombardments with periods of absolute calm. After the first bombardment, the French infantry could be expected to rush from their dugouts to man their fighting positions. After four false alarms, they could be counted on to treat the cessation of fire as little more than an tiresome drill. (The fact that each resumption of the bombardment led to casualties among the troops in their firing positions was an added bonus.)

Lest the timetable that provided the structure for the attack turn into a straitjacket, the field artillery brigade commanders retained the right to redirect the fire of their batteries according to the requirements of the moment. This was the realization of the ideal, often mentioned in the litera-

Table 4.1
German Timetable for the Attack at Vailly, October 29–30, 1914

07:00–08:00 PM 29 October, 1914	Bombardment
08:00–10:00 PM " " " " " "	Pause
10:00–10:30 PM " " " " " "	Bombardment
10:30–12:00 PM " " " " " "	Pause
12:00–01:30 AM 30 October, 1914	Bombardment
01:30–04:00 AM " " " " " "	Pause
04:00–04:30 AM " " " " " "	Bombardment
04:30–06:30 AM " " " " " "	Pause
06:30–08:00 AM " " " " " "	Bombardment/Assault

ture of the German artillery on the eve of World War I: that of the artillery brigade commander massing the fire of batteries spread over a larger area.[7] (Given that subordinate artillery commanders—of regiments, battalions, and even batteries—also had their observation posts, they may have retained the right, central to the German field artillery tactics of 1914, to depart from the fire plan in order to take advantage of opportunity or prevent catastrophe.)

In addition to the fixed observation posts, the field artillery had yet another set of eyes in the form of forward observers, officers and senior NCOs provided with field telephones and located in the most forward infantry lines. Part of the work of these forward observers was technical. They could observe the fall of shells whose explosions might be invisible to a battery commander two or three miles away. The bulk of their work, however, was tactical. They were in the most forward infantry lines in order to cooperate with the attacking infantry.[8]

The fire used by the Germans at Vailly was of three basic types. The fire block (*Feuerblock*) resembled what the Allies soon came to call a "standing barrage." It was a wall of falling shells placed along the long axis of a trench for the purpose of forcing the defenders of that trench to take shelter in their dugouts. The "box barrage" (*Abriegelungsfeuer*) was a similar pattern placed behind a trench to prevent either its reinforcement or its orderly evacuation. Concentrations (*eng zusammengefasste Artilleriefeuer, zusammengefasste Massenfeuer*) served to attack more traditional targets like enemy batteries that had been located and enemy troops moving in the open. (Because they required merely the designation of a point upon which all batteries would fire rather than a scheme for distributing the fire of many batteries, concentrations were the simplest kind of artillery fire to use and thus gave brigade commanders means of intervening in emergencies.)[9]

Whether it was because they realized that their observation posts did not provide a view of the entire battlefield, because they lacked faith in the primitive telephones connecting forward observers to their batteries, or simply because they retained habits from the days of mobile warfare, the artillery brigade commanders detached a small number of field gun batteries from their battalions and ordered them to advance with the attacking infantry. These batteries were not, as they would be later in the war, formally attached to infantry regiments. Rather, like the batteries pushed forward into the firing line during the mobile phase of World War I—and, indeed, during the Franco-Prussian War—these units were to cooperate with the infantry by what General Percin had called "liaison par le bas" and "liaison par la vue."[10]

This provision of firepower and flexibility notwithstanding, the new attack method brought with it an unprecedented limitation on the freedom of action of the German infantry. Prior to Vailly, German attacks had been pushed to what might be called their natural limits. Commanders were guided less by the seizure of a particular terrain feature than by the need to take advantage of momentary opportunities, move around an exposed flank, come to the rescue of a neighboring unit, or pursue a beaten enemy. In his order for the attack at Vailly, the commanding general of the 3rd Army Corps forbade his subordinates to push beyond the banks of the Aisne. Once they reached the water's edge, the infantrymen of the 5th and 6th Infantry Divisions were to start digging a new trench system.[11]

The reason for this restriction was fear of counterattack. German troops on the south bank of the Aisne would not only be hard to reinforce but also would be attacking with far less artillery support than when the attack began. The problem was not so much one of range as of command and control. Once they had left the heights on the north bank of the river, the German infantry would be largely invisible to the observation posts of their own artillery. Once they crossed the river, the forward observers would have been hard-pressed to get messages—by telephone or messenger—across the Aisne. If another formation—early plans called for the participation of a second army corps of equivalent size—had been available, the Germans might have been able to set up a second line of guns and howitzers, with a new system of observation posts and forward observers, to support a second attack. As it was, the 3rd Army Corps had only enough combat power for a single push.[12]

The attack against Vailly was a success, the first enjoyed by the German Army since its defeat at the Battle of the Marne in the middle of the previous month. The German infantry was particularly successful in those sectors where it had been the most punctual. Where they attacked immediately after the lifting of the standing barrage, the German infantry tended to take the first line of French trenches with few losses. Where, however, the exploitation of this fire was delayed, the Germans took far heavier losses from French soldiers who had had the time to recover their wits and restore their weapons to working order.[13]

Two and a half months after the taking of the north bank of the Aisne near Vailly, the 5th Infantry Division, one of the divisions of the 3rd Army Corps, repeated the trick by taking similar positions on the Vregny Plateau, a piece of high ground just northeast of the city of Soissons and a few kilometers west of Vailly. The terrain here was somewhat more difficult—some of the German infantry brigades would be attacking uphill. This problem was mitigated by greatly increasing the ratio of artillery to infantry. This was made possible by the separation of the operation into two distinct attacks carried out by two different infantry brigades on two successive days.[14] The six infantry battalions that attacked at noon on January 12 were thus able to cooperate with thirty-two batteries—almost three times the allotment of a division. On the next day, the seven battalions of the other brigade enjoyed a similar level of support.

As at Vailly, the organization of the German artillery at Vregny was tailored to the operation. Heavy artillery batteries as well as additional field batteries from other divisions were attached to units of two field artillery regiments belonging to the 5th Infantry Division to form temporary tactical units. These teams of batteries (what the French would call *groupements*) were assigned missions in accordance with their location and the particular capabilities of their weapons.[15] Of the thirty-two batteries organized this way in the sector of the 5th Infantry Division, about half were howitzers of some sort. The 18th Field Artillery Regiment, which controlled about half of the artillery available to the 5th Infantry Division, commanded the fire of four heavy field howitzer (150mm) batteries, four light field howitzer (105mm) batteries, one "long cannon" (100mm) battery, and six light field gun (77mm) batteries.[16] Assuming that each battery could count on the services of all of its authorized pieces, there were forty howitzers and forty guns—one high-angle-of-fire weapon for each flat-trajectory weapon.

A similiar arrangement was used by the artillery of the neighboring 7th Reserve Division, a reinforced battalion that supported the attacks of the 5th Division. This battalion (the 1st Battalion of the 7th Reserve Field Artillery Regiment), armed with a mixture of obsolete 150mm "ring cannons" and modern field pieces, was augmented with a battery each of 100mm "long cannons" and 150mm heavy field howitzers. Located on the German-held heights northwest of Soissons, the mission of this team was to suppress the fire of French batteries south and southwest of Soissons, cut communications between the French front and rear, and prevent French reserves from moving forward.[17]

The attack of January 12 went well for the Germans. A morning's worth of registration and attacks on fixed installations (dawn to 10:00 AM), one hour's concentrated fire on the French trenches (10:00 AM to 11 AM) and twenty minutes of hand-to-hand fighting by four infantry battalions sufficed to put the first trench firmly in German hands. Subsequent French positions were dealt with in the same way. First, artillery fire was concentrated on the trenches. Under cover of this fire, the infantry moved up and, as the fire was lifted, rushed into the trenches with fixed bayonets.[18]

In most cases, this treatment was enough to induce the French to surrender. Certain parts of the trench system, however, had to be subjected to additional (and unplanned) treatments of concentrated artillery fire. The forward observers moving with the infantry made good use of their field telephones to arrange for these ad hoc concentrations. In less than an hour, the Germans succeeded in capturing the French position. They also managed to induce 2,000 Frenchmen to surrender.

The real prize, however, was a French artillery observation post. Without its reports, the French artillery became noticeably less efficient.[19] Its capture greatly facilitated the second phase of the German attack. This advantage was necessary, for the attack was hard enough without the French artillery fire. The Germans took the first French trench line with relative ease. Once they entered the woods, however, they were locked in a series of small unit engagements all afternoon and did not emerge victorious until after dark.[20]

In keeping with recent instructions on field fortifications, the French had fortified their positions on the Vregny Plateau with three successive lines of resistance.[21] These trenches, however, were not very deep, nor were they provided with any sort of bombproof dugouts. Thus, while the German fire would have to be spread over three positions, the French soldiers defending the plateau would have to crouch for over five hours with nothing more than their blue serge képis to protect them from the rain of howitzer shells.[22]

It is thus not surprising that these three French lines of resistance fell easily. The German artillery fire succeeded in shaking many of the French defenders. In many cases, the French simply dropped their rifles and ran away at the sight of the advancing rows of German riflemen;[23] thus the heavy rain and the resultant mud were more of an obstacle to the advance of some German units than the enemy. By 4:30 PM, some German units had made it all the way to the south edge of the Vregny Plateau. Behind the third French position was a maze of communications trenches that proved, in places, a far tougher nut to crack than the forward infantry positions. Here, in the woods, the Germans found batteries of 75mm field guns and sharpshooters from two battalions of *chasseurs alpins* (alpine light infantry).

Without much help from their own artillery, whose observers were hindered by the rain that started to fall in the afternoon,[24] the German infantry succeeded in taking these positions only at great cost. One company of the 52nd Infantry Regiment lost all of its officers.[25] The 1st Battalion of the 8th Life Guards Regiment lost half of its company commanders,[26] and Battalion Schultz, a temporary unit that captured two batteries of French artillery, had 5 officers and 25 enlisted men killed, and 105 enlisted men wounded.[27] These losses notwithstanding, the assaulting German infantry cleared the entire objective by nightfall. One detachment even pushed beyond the plateau to enter the north end of Soissons. The booty was enormous: 5,650 Frenchmen marched off the Vregny Plateau into captivity, dragging behind them 35 field pieces and 6 machine guns.[28]

To the Germans, their capture of the high ground near Vailly was a seminal event that set the stage for further developments in position warfare. For the French leadership, the loss of the Vregny Plateau was of greater significance. From the very beginning of the war, General Joffre had been trying to wean his army from the suicidal habit of sending masses of infantry into the attack without having dealt with the Germans' ability to massacre those masses. Each successive memorandum called for more attention to detail, greater cooperation between the infantry and artillery, and a more rapid exploitation of the effects of artillery fire by the infantry. On January 2, General Joffre promulgated a note ordering the adoption of a method of attack very similar to the one the Germans had used at Vailly and would use at Vregny. On January 15, he issued a supplement to the note that made explicit reference to the battle at Vregny and said, in essence, "Do you believe me now?"[29]

From its very beginnings, the French technique of attack fostered by Joffre's proddings differed greatly from the German techniques that had provided so much of the initial inspiration. Because the French heavy artillery was far less numerous than that of Germany and still consisted largely of slow-firing weapons of the De Bange system, the French found it far more difficult to match the intensity of the German bombardments. All other things being equal, the French could deliver the same number of shells as the Germans. Because, however, these shells had to pass through the tight bottleneck of obsolete tubes, it took far more time to deliver them. Thus deprived of the ability to suppress, shock, and demoralize, the French had no choice but to attempt the systematic destruction of German positions. This made their bombardments longer still. At a time when German bombardments rarely lasted more than twelve hours, French bombardments routinely lasted for days.

The most obvious disadvantage stemming from these long bombardments was the loss of surprise. Once the French started firing in earnest, the Germans had plenty of time to react. That they often did not do so effectively can be blamed, on the tactical level, on the German policy of concentrating most of their infantry in the most forward trench and, on the operational level, on the shortage of reserves. As a result, the French attacks with limited objectives often succeeded in tearing pieces out of the German defensive system.

Once this was achieved, however, the French weakness in modern heavy artillery manifested itself in a new problem. The ground so recently taken by the French often formed a salient—an indentation in the German line that was subject to artillery fire from three of the four cardinal points of the compass. Unless the salient was a wide one (wider than the maximum effective range of the German artillery pieces in the area), all of the captured ground would be vulnerable to such fire. Of course, the French could respond with fire of their own. Only rarely, however, could such fire hope to compete with that of the more modern, more numerous, and, because of the salient, more advantageously positioned, German heavy pieces. The French therefore concluded that any attack they made had to be carried out on a wide front.[30]

The major French offensives of 1915—the attack in Artois in May, and the double attack in Artois and Champagne in September—were carried out in accordance with these beliefs. In the bombardment that preceded the first Artois offensive, 340 heavy pieces fired for 6 days in order to prepare a front of 18 kilometers. In the September offensive in the same region, both attacks were aimed at the famous Vimy Ridge: 400 heavy pieces fired for 5 days on a front of 15 kilometers. In the Champagne offensive, 872 heavy pieces (in addition to 1,100 75mm guns and numerous trench mortars) took part in the battering of a front of 35 kilometers that lasted 3 days.[31]

Of these three attacks, the September attack in Artois was an abject failure. In most cases, the French failed to get beyond the wire in front of the German forward position.[32] The other two attacks made some progress but failed in their ostensible purpose of breaking through all three German positions. In both of the latter cases, the French had little trouble crossing no-man's-land and taking the first German position. Moreover, because the Germans held fast to their policy of putting the bulk of their infantry into that position, the taking of the first German position brought a huge haul of prisoners, many of whom were so affected by the bombardment that they were unable to put up any resistance. Likewise, because much of the German field artillery was within 2,000 or 3,000 meters of their forward position, the French were able to capture a number of guns.

Once beyond the German forward position, however, the French ran into trouble. In the first Artois offensive, this was because not all units progressed at the same rate. One hour after the assault began, two corps that formed the French main effort had covered the four kilometers that separated the German first position from their first objectives on Vimy Ridge. To the south, however, two other corps had a great deal of difficulty breaking through the German first position. As a result, the German reserves, both infantry and artillery units, were able to concentrate their efforts against the more successful French corps and the attack came to a standstill.[33]

Table 4.2
Major French Offensives of 1915

Offensive	Frontage (kilometers)	Length of Preparatory Fire	Number of Heavy Pieces Firing (French)	Depth of Penetration (kilometers)	Prisoners Taken	Artillery Pieces Captured
Artois, May	16	six days	340	3-4	7,500	24
Champagne, September.	35	three days	872	3-4	25,000	150
Artois, September	15	five days	420	0	-	-

In the Champagne fighting, the Germans could take more credit for undermining the French offensive. Behind their first position, they had dug a series of supplementary positions, each about 3,000 meters behind the one in front of it. As most of these positions were on the rear slopes of the many chalk hills of Champagne, they were far harder for the French artillery to locate and bombard.[34] As a result, the German batteries were in the enviable position of being able to fire on the enemy without the enemy being able to reply effectively. Even when the French were able, largely with the aid of airplanes, to locate the German batteries, they had no way of observing their fire. Thus, while the volume of French artillery fire ensured that some shells fell on the German batteries, the French were generally unable to make use of their huge superiority in numbers systematically to locate, focus on, and destroy German artillery units.[35]

Neither the failure to advance as one man nor the inability of French artillery effectively to knock out German batteries located on reverse slopes would have been a problem if the Germans had not had two or three days in which to scrape together units from all parts of the western front and send them to the threatened areas. When bombardments lasted for three to six days, strategic surprise was out of the question. The Germans did not know the exact day or hour of the attack, but they knew which railway station would be closest to the fighting and which sectors could be stripped of reserves in order to build a counterattack force.

On the eastern front, the immense spaces and the limitations of the Russian rail network made the reinforcement of a threatened sector a matter of weeks rather than days. This enabled the Germans to succeed where the French would fail. Ironically, the first battle of this sort was launched with the goal of rescuing Germany's embattled ally, Austria-Hungary.

The place chosen by the German and Austro-Hungarian General Staffs for this battle was a fifty-kilometer-wide portion of the foothills of the Carpathian Mountains, between the Polish towns of Gorlice and Tarnow.[36] Located at the juncture of Hungary, Poland, Romania, and the Ukraine, the Carpathians formed a natural barrier between the Austro-Hungarian and Russian empires. Whoever controlled the mountains—and in particular, the four passes that connected the Polish plain with the Hungarian plateau—was in an excellent position to dominate the enemy's heartland. While the Russians were succeeding—at great cost in lives—in the battles for the passes, the Austro-German plan was to take the indirect approach. After breaking through between Gorlice and Tarnow, the combined forces were to swing behind the passes, thereby cutting off the Russians.

The mission of performing this strategic surgery was assigned to the Eleventh Army, a recently formed force composed of both German and Austro-Hungarian units. The chief of staff of this polyglot formation was the same Colonel Hans von Seeckt who, while on the western front as chief of staff of the 3rd Army Corps, had planned the attacks at Vailly and Vregny. (The main differences between the attack that Seeckt planned to carry out at Gorlice–Tarnow and his recent victories on the western front were those of scale and purpose. Involving ten times the number of troops and artillery pieces that Seeckt had employed at Vregny, the attack was aimed not merely at capturing an enemy position but also at completely rupturing the Russian lines. The tactics, however, were essentially the same.)

In two of the four corps of the Eleventh Army, the command of the artillery was in the hands of the field artillery brigade commanders. These officers commanded, in addition to their field batteries, the heavy batteries assigned to the divisions. One of the two field artillery brigade commanders in each corps was put in charge of coordinating the use of artillery

Table 4.3
Artillery of the Austro-German 11th Army

	Field Guns	105mm Howitzers	Mountain Guns	Mountain Howitzers	150mm Howitzers	210mm Howitzers	305mm Howitzers	100-120mm Guns	Total Guns	Total Howitzers	Total Field Pieces	Total Heavy Pieces	Totals for Formation
Guard Corps	72	24	0	0	20	0	4	0	72	48	96	24	120
XXXXI Reserve Corps	48	48	0	0	16	8	0	8	56	72	96	32	128
Combined Corps Kneußl	48	0	8	4	16	16	0	4	60	36	60	36	96
AH VI. Army Corps	84	12	0	0	16	4	0	16	100	32	96	36	132
Totals for the Eleventh Army	252	84	8	4	68	28	4	28	288	188	348	128	476

within that corps up to the moment when the infantry began its assault. That is, organizing the preparatory bombardment was the responsibility of the generals commanding corps. Once the preparation was done, however, the divisions regained full control of both their field artillery and a portion of the attached heavy batteries.[37]

One corps, Combined Corps Kneußl, a formation whose mission on the first day of the attack consisted mainly of capturing a particularly difficult hill, centralized the control of most of its artillery. General Kneußl's plan for fulfilling this mission called for one task force (composed of four infantry battalions from a Bavarian division specially trained in mountain warfare) to take the hill while the rest of his infantry protected exposed flanks. To support the taking of this crucial hill, Kneußl placed the bulk of his artillery, both attached heavy batteries and field artillery, under the control of a single officer, a colonel of the siege artillery branch. This officer was to control the corps artillery throughout the attack, ensuring that it was available to cooperate with the troops forming the main effort of the corps. The infantry charged with less important missions had to make do with the support of sixteen field and mountain guns.[38]

The remaining corps, the XXXXI Reserve Corps, split the responsibility for controlling artillery fire between the corps and division commanders. The corps artillery commander, who was also the commander of the field artillery brigade of one of the divisions, was, as in other corps, responsible for the preparatory fire. Once the attack began, the divisions regained control of their field artillery while the heavy artillery remained formed into a groupment under the direct control of the corps artillery commander. The rationale for this arrangement was economy of force. The corps artillery would shell obvious targets so that the division artillery brigades could be free to react to the immediate requirements of the battle.[39]

Even though there was, for the first time in a major German offensive in World War I, an officer assigned as artillery commander (*Artillerie Kommandeur*) of the 11th Army, the artillery instructions promulgated by the headquarters of the 11th Army were minimal. The main points provided in the written order for the attack were the mandatory pauses in the preparatory bombardment (to allow patrols to check the extent of damage and pioneers to clear barbed wire and other obstacles) and a reminder that each corps was responsible for its own counterbattery effort. More detailed artillery instructions were promulgated by a separate order written by the 11th Army's artillery commander.[40]

At the level of corps and divisions, cooperation between infantry and artillery was achieved by the location of the command posts of the commanding generals of infantry divisions and the commanders of their field artillery brigades in the same place. The Russian practice of building strong points and trench lines on forward slopes combined with fine weather and German field glasses to give the Germans a nearly complete view of the first Russian line and, in places, the Russian battery positions behind it. When, on the second and third days of the offensive, the advancing Austro-Germans ran into the second and third Russian lines, they benefited from the same advantage. There were thus many occasions where the artillery commanders in their command posts were as aware of what was going on as the infantry commanders on the spot.[41]

Once the attack moved to the far side of the hills, the chief form of cooperation between the infantry and the artillery came in the form of batteries moving forward with the infantry.[42] Some of these—mostly field gun batteries—were actually attached to the infantry regiments. The majority remained under the command of the artillery battalion, regimental, and brigade commanders.[43] So that the heavier batteries that stayed behind would not fire on friendly infantry they could not see (because of woods or intervening terrain), German infantry battalions were equipped with signal flares.[44]

Little use seems to have been made of the telephone as a means of connecting the attacking infantry with the supporting artillery. The divisions involved in the attack, many of which had spent the winter of 1914–1915 behind the lines, had little experience in position warfare and therefore may have had little knowledge of the practice.[45] The relatively great distances involved in the operation—there was as much as a kilometer and a half of no-man's-land separating the Russian positions from the forwardmost German and Austro-Hungarian trenches—may also have made the use of field telephones more difficult. While not critical to the outcome of the battle, the lack of rapid communications between the attacking infantry and the main body of the artillery would make itself felt on the first day of the battle.

The bombardment began at nine—a short while after sunset—on the evening of May 1. At first the guns, howitzers, and trench mortars fired at their sustained rate; rounds were shoved into the breechblocks and lanyards pulled at a slow and steady pace that kept the artillery pieces from overheating and the crews from exhaustion. Twice during the night—from ten to eleven on the evening of May 1 and from one to three in the early morning of May 2—the German artillery ceased firing. In addition to giving the German and Austro-Hungarian artillerymen an opportunity to rest, it gave patrols a chance to ascertain the damage, confused the Russians as to the nature of the bombardment, and enticed Russian machine gunners to open fire, thereby revealing the exact locations of those rare and dangerous weapons.[46]

Between four and six on the morning of May 2—the exact time varied from corps to corps—the German artillery focused its attention on the forwardmost Russian line and increased its rate of fire. Between 9 and 9:30 AM, the tempo of the bombardment increased again to the maximum rate that the guns and the gunners could tolerate. One hour later—again the exact time depended on the corps commander—the fire shifted to targets behind the forward Russian trenches and the German infantry rushed forward in thick skirmish lines.[47]

In most places, the Russians responded to the approaching wall of bayonets by fleeing. The sheer weight of the bombardment—the heavier pieces fired 200 shells each and the light field howitzers fired 300—had convinced many Russians that there was no point in resistance. (The unwillingness of many Russian officers to share the rigors of the bombardment with their men may also have played a role in the rapid collapse of Russian resistance in some areas.) The experience of Queen Augusta Regiment of the Guard Corps was typical. Formed in three waves, it crossed no-man's-land at a cost of two or three casualties. Four and a half minutes after it had crossed the line of departure, this unit was in undisputed possession of the first Russian trench and hundreds of Russian soldiers who had thrown away their weapons.[48]

Two neighboring regiments, however, suffered terribly. Of the 3,000 or so men who advanced in the ranks of the Kaiser Alexander Regiment, which had the misfortune to attack a sector defended by Siberian riflemen, 12 officers and 290 men died, and an equal number were seriously wounded.[49] The Queen Elizabeth Regiment experienced similar damage.

Particularly hard hit was the 12th Company, which ran into Russian machine guns that had survived the bombardment. Sixty-six members of that company died in the first few minutes of the assault, and thirty-seven were wounded. After the battle, the regimental surgeon noted that most of the dead had been hit by at least two bullets each.[50]

Fortunately for the Austro-German offensive, the sectors where the Russians surrendered en masse greatly exceeded those where the attackers were delayed or massacred. As a result, the breakthrough of the first Russian position on May 2 was followed by the rupture of the second and third Russian positions on May 3 and 4. (These breakthroughs were, as a rule, a repetition, on a smaller scale, of the attack of May 2.) By May 5, the Germans and Austro-Hungarians were in open country, and the tactical victory was turning into an operational breakthrough. The Russian position in the Carpathians collapsed and the Austro-Hungarian forces that had been there were freed to march into Russian territory. When the marching was over, 140,000 Russian prisoners were in the hands of the Central Powers, almost all of Poland had been cleared of Russian troops, and the danger of a Russian invasion of Hungary was completely eliminated.

Gorlice–Tarnow was arguably the greatest German victory of the war. The lesson that many, both in Germany and elsewhere, drew from it, however, was misleading. The British and the French were convinced that a breakthrough leading to a resumption of mobile warfare was within their grasp. The senior German soldier of the time, Erich Falkenhayn, drew a different conclusion. Believing, largely for operational reasons, that a breakthrough on the western front was not possible, he was nonetheless convinced that Germany's superiority in artillery could knock France out of the war.[51]

Falkenhayn first promulgated this vision in mid-December 1915, at a meeting of army commanders and their chiefs of staff. A strong blow against the French Army in the west, he argued, would put stress on the "internal weaknesses" of the French nation and convince the French people of the uselessness of continuing the war. Falkenhayn therefore asked each army commander to explore suitable areas for attack within his sector.

In the course of follow-up conferences during the last two weeks of December 1915 and the first week of January 1916, Falkenhayn repeatedly expressed his belief that the goal of the upcoming German attack should not be the seizure of any particular piece of terrain. It was not to be another attack with limited objectives. Neither was it to be a breakthrough. Rather, the goal of Falkenhayn's proposed attack was to be direct attrition—the "bleeding" (*Ausblutung*) of the French army.

In the second week of January, after a number of consultations with General Schmidt von Knobelsdorf, the chief of staff of the German 5th Army, Falkenhayn chose the fortress complex of Verdun.[52] Located at a sharp bend of the Meuse River, in what might be called the foothills of the Vosges Mountains, Verdun seemed to serve Falkenhayn's purpose admirably. The area around the fortified zone formed a slight indentation—what World War I soldiers called a "salient"—in the German lines. This salient, and the slight advantage its possession would give to the French if they attempted to envelop the German position north or south of Verdun, provided an argument of "military necessity" to any general who wanted an excuse to fight over the area. Far more important to the French, however, and therefore to Falkenhayn, was the symbolic value of Verdun.

Verdun's heavy guns, whose domination of the valley of the Meuse had been the original justification for fortifying the area, had been withdrawn from the citadel. And the outlying forts had been all but vacated to provide the garrisons for trenches, blockhouses, bunkers, and other, more modern, field fortifications. Nonetheless, Verdun was still a fortress. Its loss to the Germans, in the third year of a war where the loss or gain of a few hundred yards was cause for banner headlines, would be considered by all but the most astute military observers to be a major defeat. This perception would be exacerbated when the French public was reminded, as it inevitably would be, of the history associated with Verdun—particularly its role as a "frontier post" in the expansion of France toward the Rhine.

From a purely military-technical viewpoint, the fact that Verdun was a salient, surrounded on three sides by German forces, facilitated the execution of Falkenhayn's strategic conception. Falkenhayn assigned the actual work of "bleeding" the French nation to the 1,612 artillery pieces of the 5th Army.[53] About a third of these were light (7.7mm) field guns and light (105mm) field howitzers organic to the infantry divisions. The rest were considerably heavier weapons of the "foot artillery," long-range guns of calibers up to 230mm and high-angle-of-fire weapons of calibers up to 420mm. The peninsular nature of the French position made it possible for this huge artillery park to concentrate its fire while the individual batteries remained reasonably dispersed.

Falkenhayn's confidence in the German heavy artillery was well placed. The terminal effect of the German shells, most of which were larger and fired at higher angles, was superior to that of French shells. The rate of fire of German pieces, most of which had been built in the decade prior to the battle, was greater than that of the generally older French pieces. And, most significantly, the German artillery greatly outnumbered the French artillery in the sector. This overwhelming superiority in artillery gave Falkenhayn every reason to assume that the 5th Army would be able to gain permanent fire superiority over the French artillery while having enough firepower left over to repel French counterattacks and repeatedly bombard French infantry positions.

In Falkenhayn's conception, the role of the German infantry was subsidiary to that of the artillery. It would maintain contact with the French, forcing them to bunch into suitable targets for the artillery. It would protect artillery forward observers. And it would, by threatening to occupy the citadel of Verdun, entice the French to send as many men as possible into the meat grinder. However, whether or not the German infantry succeeded in taking that citadel, Falkenhayn emphasized on a number of occasions, was secondary to the attrition of the French forces.[54]

This vision, however, was not shared by Falkenhayn's most important subordinate at Verdun, the commanding general of the German 5th Army. Crown Prince Wilhelm, the eldest son of Kaiser Wilhelm II, heir to the thrones of both the German Empire and the Kingdom of Prussia, was both personally and professionally disinclined to conduct the operation according to Falkenhayn's concept. As he confessed in his memoirs, Wilhelm not only wanted to take the fortress but also intended to avoid the battle of attrition that Falkenhayn sought.[55]

Wilhelm's confidence in the 5th Army's ability to take the fortress complex of Verdun was a direct result of recent experience. In the course of 1915, Wilhelm had acted as the protector and chief booster of two experimental units that were solving many of the tactical problems of trench warfare. Assault Battalion "Rohr," the first storm troop unit, had developed a tactical style that used closely coordinated heavy weapons—machine guns, trench mortars, grenade launchers, and field artillery—to support the deep penetration of ten- to twenty-man assault squads armed primarily with hand grenades. The Guard Reserve Pioneer Battalion, composed largely of reservists who had been firemen in civilian life, was experimenting with a number of primitive flamethrowers.[56]

The crown prince's close connection with these two units and his firsthand knowledge of their achievements gave him a perspective on trench warfare that differed greatly from Falkenhayn's. Whereas Falkenhayn was apt to see position warfare as a condition that made decisive infantry action impossible, the crown prince had seen the difference that the techniques developed by Assault Battalion "Rohr" and the Guard Reserve Pioneer Battalion could make. In a number of operations in the Vosges Mountains in the late summer and fall of 1915, German infantry trained and led by detachments from one or both of these experimental units had repeatedly succeeded in wresting trench systems from the elite French *chasseurs alpins*.

Wilhelm's view of the way to run the offensive at Verdun seems to have been shared by his infantry commanders. The divisions destined to take part in the battle—most of which had been on the western front throughout 1915—approached the operation as they would any other attack with limited objectives. Units were pulled out of the trenches, given a few days to rest, and then put through training programs that focused on close-combat skills. As had often been the case with state-of-the-art infantry units in 1915, the training programs often culminated with dress rehearsals of company, battalion, regimental, and, in at least one case, division attacks on full-scale replicas of the terrain over which they were scheduled to fight. The artillerymen likewise made the natural assumption that they were still in the business of taking ground. Emboldened, perhaps, by the example of Gorlice–Tarnow, they frequently bragged that they could cause the collapse of French resistance by fire alone. The infantry, they were often quoted as saying, would be able to goose-step into the citadel of Verdun.[57]

The German offensive at Verdun began early on the morning of February 21. At 8:12 AM, Crown Prince Wilhelm gave the order for the artillery to open fire. Except for the customary pauses to allow patrols to ascertain the damage, the bombardment lasted all day. The patrols usually reported seeing caved-in trenches, destroyed barbed wire obstacles, and groups of French soldiers running to the rear. The patrols also reported that they had received little or no fire from the enemy positions; the only German casualty of the day was an artillery liaison officer hit by a splinter from a short round. In some cases, the patrols took prisoners. Pilots of reconnaissance aircraft confirmed the reports of widespread destruction. They described railroad tracks that had been torn up by the shells of the German heavy artillery and reported that fires had broken out in the town of Verdun.[58]

On the second day, the mission of the artillery changed from destruction to suppression. Between eight AM and midday, each of the nine infantry divisions of the 5th Army conducted a series of attacks with limited objectives to capture the forwardmost French position in front of its sector. Because of the high proportion of high-angle-of-fire weapons in the German arsenal, the assault troops of the first wave, thoroughly rehearsed in the rear, were able to lean into the barrage to a degree that had not been possible in earlier battles, risking the occasional casualty from a short shell in order to be able to exploit fully the effects of the fire.[59] Because of this practice, the improvised storm troops often found that they were able to take possession of a trench within a few seconds of the barrage being lifted.

The French, still trying to gather their wits after being on the receiving end of thirty to fifty shells per hour from every German artillery piece, were often caught in their dugouts and therefore unable to offer any coordinated resistance.[60]

Against the forwardmost trenches of the French lines, these tactics were generally effective. Every German division reached its objectives on the second day of the operation, and a few units, commanded by officers who took advantage of unexpected weaknesses, were able, after a pause of a few minutes to request permission from the 5th Army chief of staff, General Schmidt von Knobelsdorf,[61] to push a few hundred meters beyond their assigned objectives.

The promise made by German artillery officers that the infantry would be able to goose-step into the citadel of Verdun, however, was not fulfilled. The twenty-four-hour bombardment had certainly torn up the ground forward of the German line and caused unprecedented destruction. That same bombardment, however, served also to arouse in the survivors a fanatic spirit of resistance that could be overcome only in close combat.

On the third day of battle, the German attacks began to acquire characteristics that totally severed the link between Falkenhayn's intent and the actions of his subordinates. The clearest documentary evidence of this divorce between strategy and tactics is provided by the brief order given by the commanding general of the 6th Infantry Division on February 23. In instructing his three infantry regiments to take the French positions in a woods known as the Herbebois, he admonished them to attack "without regard to casualties."[62]

As the Bradenburgers who filled the ranks of those regiments, many of whom were veterans of the fighting at Vailly, pushed further into the woods, they met stiffer and stiffer resistance. French reinforcements had arrived the previous evening and had taken up positions in shell holes and piles of rubble. With no trenches to provide certain boundaries between opposing forces and with the skeletons of trees hindering the observation of artillery liaison officers, the German infantry found itself relying more and more on its own resources the further it pushed into the woods.

The type of fighting experienced by the men of the 6th Infantry Division in the Herbebois was to become the pattern for most of the fighting at Verdun. As each day passed, however, the task of taking ground grew more difficult. The deep penetrations made by some German units early in the offensive soon became a thing of the past as the French put a machine gun in every shell hole and a rifleman behind every tree stump. During the week of February 21–27, the Germans had advanced by leaps and bounds. The high point of that week was February 25, when three companies of the 6th Infantry Division captured the almost undefended Fort Douaumont, ten kilometers beyond the line of departure that they had crossed on February 21. After February 27, however, the pace of German progress slowed markedly. The primary tactical event was still the attack with limited objectives, but the scale was drastically reduced. During the first week of the battle, a German attack could push the German lines a kilometer or more forward. During March, April, and May, however, daily progress began to be measured not in thousands, but in tens, of meters.

On July 11, Crown Prince Wilhelm ordered his divisions to cease all offensive actions. The British were attacking on the Somme, and all available resources would be needed for the defensive battle there. In terms of attrition, Falkenhayn had achieved his immediate strategic objective of bleeding the French: 400,000 Frenchmen who were in the ranks of the French Army at the beginning of the battle were dead, wounded to the point where further military service was impossible, or prisoners of war. It had not been the German artillery alone that achieved this, however, but the German infantry as well. And to achieve such gains, they had to expose themselves to the fire of the *French* artillery, which was just beginning to supplement its field guns with howitzers. As a result, for every three Frenchmen rendered *hors de combat*, the Germans had lost two soldiers.

The reason was not due to any failure of German tactics, which had made a great deal of progress since the early months of the war, but to Falkenhayn's inability to execute his strategy of attrition. Beginning with Crown Prince Wilhelm and his chief of staff, the leaders of the 5th Army never fully subscribed to Falkenhayn's concept for the battle. The operations order drafted by Schmidt von Knobelsdorf and signed by Wilhelm converted the operation into a series of attacks with limited objectives whose ultimate goal was the elimination of the French salient.[63] While these leaders of the 5th Army realized that artillery was to do most of the work and that they should economize their infantry,[64] they failed to pursue the objective of using the threat of loss of ground to force French infantry to expose themselves to the fire of the German howitzers. Thus, on the second day of the battle, Schmidt von Knobelsdorf enthusiastically gave permission for some units to push beyond the first day's objective, even though that advance did nothing to further Falkenhayn's strategy.

Given Falkenhayn's inability to communicate with Crown Prince Wilhelm and Knobelsdorf, it is not surprising that, four echelons of command below Falkenhayn's High Command and three below Wilhelm's 5th Army, division commanders, like that of the 6th Infantry Division, reverted to the terrain-dominated fighting of 1915 and ordered the seizure of the day's objective, "cost what it may." The same can be said for regimental and battalion commanders. Even more than the division commanders, these officers had spent a year specializing in the taking of ground. Although they did it well, tactical skill could not take the place of strategy.

Though great progress was made in small unit tactics, the German Army as a whole learned nothing from Verdun. Falkenhayn's idiosyncratic strategy of attrition was thoroughly discredited. In an army whose others leaders were, from the start, disinclined to pursue such a strategy, this was not much of a lesson. Likewise, the observation that attacks with limited objectives made sense only when they helped the Germans economize on the forces needed to hold a particular section of the front taught little to an organization that had been doing just that for more than a year.

The French, on the other hand, drew a great deal of inspiration from the battle. Though the French Army had failed to come out ahead on the numbers, and though the key factor in making the Germans break off their attacks was the Franco–British offensive on the Somme, many Frenchmen could convince themselves that they had won a battle of attrition. Ten months later, when the failure of yet another attempt at breakthrough had brought their army to the point of collapse, the French adopted their own strategy of attrition (*usure*). For a high command plagued by mutinies and desperate to draw some pressure off hard-pressed allies, such an approach bought the time needed to form the American divisions required for a renewed attempt at a breakthrough.

The means chosen to implement this strategy was attacks with limited objectives whose overall purpose was similar to the German minor operations of 1915. The Germans sought to seize terrain that would allow them to economize on the forces needed to hold what was, at that time, a secondary sector. The French, taking a leaf from Falkenhayn's concept, sought to use their local attacks to force the Germans to choose between losing important ground and using up resources that they could not replace.[65] Thus the approach to modern combat that had begun with the German attack on Vailly in October 1914 had gone full circle. Having started as an economy-of-force measure by an army that was seeking victory elsewhere, it had promised decision. When that decision proved out of reach, it was revived as an economy-of-force measure by an army that planned to seek victory at another time.

NOTES

1. Jacques Szaluta, "Marshal Petain Between Two Wars, 1918–1940: The Interplay of Personality and Circumstance" (Ph.D. thesis, Columbia University, 1969), pp. 69–70, 81–82.

2. France, Armée, Grand Quartier Général des Armées de l'Est, État-Major, 3ème Bureau, "Note pour les commandants d'armée," Nov. 28, 1915, SHAT, carton 24N1279.

3. Arthur Bullrich, "Die Schlacht bei Vailly am 30.X.1914 als Ausgangspunkt für die Erfolge bei Gorlice entscheidener neuer taktischer Grundsätze," unpublished typescript found in the papers of Hans von Seeckt, U.S. National Archives, Microfilm Series M132, roll 20, stuck 91, pp. 7–9. A translation of this article, with maps and explanatory notes, was published in *Tactical Notebook*, Nov. and Dec. 1992.

4. Ibid., pp. 6–10.

5. This was the 5th Artillery Brigade of the 5th Infantry Division. Ibid., p. 10. The use of observation posts was greatly facilitated by the nature of the terrain. Most of the positions that the Germans were firing on were downhill from their own locations.

6. III. Armeekorps, Generalkommando, Ia, "Korpsbefehl," dated October 28, 1914. Included as an appendix to Bullrich, "Die Schlacht bei Vailly."

7. den Erfordernissen des Augenblicks." Bullrich, "Die Schlacht bei Vailly, p. 9.

8. III. Armeekorps, Generalkommando, Ia, "Korpsbefehl."

9. Bullrich, "Die Schlacht bei Vailly," pp. 9, 15.

10. Ibid., p. 9.

11. III. Armeekorps, Generalkommando, Ia, "Korpsbefehl."

12. The army corps originally scheduled to follow up the attack of the 3rd Army Corps, the 2nd Army Corps of the 2nd Army, had to give up one of its divisions for the eastern front shortly before the attack. Bullrich, "Die Schlacht bei Vailly," pp. 5–6.

13. Ibid., p. 19–20.

14. Germany, Reichsarchiv, *Der Weltkrieg, 1914–1918* (Berlin: E. S. Mittler, 1925–1944), vol. 7, pp. 23–25, and "sketch d" of the maps and charts accompanying the volume; and Ernst von Schönfeldt, *Das Grenadier Regiment Prinz Karl von Preussen (2. Brandenburgisches), Nr. 12 im Weltkriege* (Berlin: Gerhard Stalling, 1924), pp. 41–43.

15. *Der Weltkrieg*, vol. 7, p. 25.

16. Alfred von Rosenberg Lipinsky, *Das Artillerie-Regiment "Generalfeldzeugmeister" (2. Brand.) Nr. 18 1914–1918* (Oldenburg: Gerhard Stalling, 1922), pp. 44–46.

17. Rudolf Werneburg, *Königl. preußisches Reserve-Feldartillerie-Regiment Nr. 7* (Oldenburg: Gerhard Stalling, 1926), p. 87.

18. Ibid.; Schönfeldt, *Das Grenadier Regiment Prinz Karl von Preussen*, p. 41; and *Der Weltkrieg*, vol. 7, p. 24.

19. Lipinsky, *Das Artillerie-Regiment "Generalfeldzeugmeister,"* pp. 47–48.

20. Schönfeldt, *Das Grenadier Regiment Prinz Karl von Preussen*, p. 41; and *Der Weltkrieg*, vol. 7, p. 24.

21. France, Armée, Grand Quartier Général des Armées de l'Est, État-Major, 3ème Bureau, "Note au sujet des organisations défensives," Jan. 3, 1915, SHAT, carton 24N1279.

22. At this time, these were mostly what the Germans called "all-purpose shell" (*Einheitsgeschosse*), a projectile that contained more high explosive than a shrapnel shell of the same caliber but had a better fragmentation effect than a high-explosive shell. Georg Bruchmüller, *Die deutsche Artillerie in den Durchbruchschlachten des Weltkrieges* (Berlin: E. S. Mittler und Sohn, 1922), p. 15 (hereafter referred to as Bruchmüller, *Durchbruchschlachten*).

23. Friedrich von Rabenau, ed., *Hans von Seekt, Aus Meinem Leben* (Leipzig: Hase und Koehler, 1941), p. 85.

24. Werneburg, *Königl. preußisches Reserve-Feldartillerie-Regiment Nr. 7*, p. 89.

25. Martin Reymann, *Das Infanterie Regiment von Alvensleben (6. Brandenbg.) Nr. 52 im Weltkriege 1914/1918* (Berlin: Gerhard Stalling, 1923), p. 50.

26. H. Schöning, *Leib-Grenadier Regiment König Friedrich Wilhelm III (1. Brandenberg) Nr. 8* (Berlin: Gerhard Stalling, 1924), p. 122. The regimental histories of the 52nd Infantry Regiment and the 8th Life Guards do not separate the enlisted casualties for the assault on the Vregny Plateau from those incurred during the French attack of January 8 and the subsequent counterattack.

27. Schönfeldt, *Das Grenadier Regiment Prinz Karl von Preussen*, p. 44.

28. Rabenau, *Hans von Seekt*, pp. 85–88.

29. France, Armée, Grand Quartier Général des Armées de l'Est, État-Major, 3ème Bureau, "Note pour les armées," Jan. 2, 1915 and "Note au sujet de la conduite des attaques (suite à la note no. 923 du 2 janvier)," Jan. 15, 1915, SHAT, carton 16N1676.

30. Pascal Lucas, *L'Évolution des idées tactiques* (Paris: Berger-Levrault, 1923), pp. 56–57; Frédéric Hérr, *L'Artillerie* (Paris: Berger-Levrault, 1924), pp. 34–35.

31. Lucas, *L'Évolution*, pp. 81–84; and Hérr, *L'Artillerie*, pp. 36–38.

32. My French sources are understandably discreet about this attack, preferring to damn with faint praise than to describe the debacle explicitly. I therefore relied on the British official history for a summary of the operation. Sir James E. Edmonds, ed., *History of the Great War: Military Operations, France and Belgium, 1915* (London: Macmillan, 1928), vol. 2, *Battles of Aubers Ridge, Festubert, and Loos*, pp. 267–70, 364– 48.

33. Lucas, *L'Évolution*, pp. 65–67.

34. The best description in English of these positions and how they came to be built is in G. C. Wynne, *If Germany Attacks* (Westport, CT: Greenwood Press, 1976), ch. 5.

35. For anecdotal accounts of German batteries in the Champagne battle of September 1915, see Verein Ehemaliger Offizere des Westfälischen Fußartillerie-Regiment Nr. 7, *Das westfälischen Fußartillerie-Regiment Nr. 7 im Weltkriege 1914–1918* (Oldenburg: Gerhard Stalling, 1932), pp. 391– 402; Wilhelm Lindner, "Bayer. Battr. 493 (3./bayer. Fußa. Batl. 8), 'die jungen Leute,' " in Franz Nikolas Kaiser, *Das Ehrenbuch der deutschen schweren Artillerie* (Berlin: Verlag Tradition Wilhelm Kolk, 1934), pp. 121–22; Fritz Schneider, *Das Feldartillerie-Regiment von Scharnhorst (1. Hannoversches) Nr. 10 im Weltkriege* (Hannover: Verein der Offiziere des Ehemaligen Feldartillerie Regiments von Scharnhorst, 1930), pp. 159–86; and Kurt Bischoff, *Im Trommelfeuer. Die Herbstschlacht in der Champagne, 1915* (Leipzig: Buchhandlung Gebrüder Fändrich, 1939), pp. 39–63.

36. These towns, still known by the same names, are currently within the borders of Poland.

37. These were the Guard Corps and the Austro-Hungarian 6th Corps. Oskar Tille von Kalm, ed., *Gorlice* (Berlin: Gerhard Stalling, 1930), pp. 36–39.

38. Ibid., pp. 36–37.

39. Ibid., pp. 36–39.

40. Ibid., pp. 35–36.

41. *Der Weltkrieg*, vol. 7, p. 370.

42. von Kalm, *Gorlice*, pp. 25–26, 192.

43. Walter Luyken, *Das 2. Garde-Feldartillerie-Regiment im Weltkriege* (Berlin: Wilhelm Kolk, 1925), pp. 73–77; and von Blücher, "Drauf," in Albert Benary, ed., *Das Ehrenbuch der deutschen Feldartillerie* (Berlin: Verlag Tradition Wilhelm Kolk, 1930), pp. 299–300.

44. Konrad Krafft von Delmensingen, ed., *Das Bayernbuch von Weltkrieg 1914–1918*, (n.d.) p. 145.

45. German heavy artillery batteries were, on the other hand, fully conversant with the use of forward observers connected by telephone to the battery commander's observation post. For a detailed description of how they were used, see *Das Ehrenbuch der deutschen schweren Artillerie*, pp. 363–65.

46. Once located, the Russian machine guns were fired upon, over open sights, by pairs of German field guns that had been placed in the forwardmost German trenches for that express purpose. The degree to which machine guns were available to the Russians in the first position can be gauged by the fact that the whole 11th Army captured only thirty-seven in the first day of the attack. von Kalm, *Gorlice*, p. 201.

47. Richard von Berendt, *Das 1. Garde Fußartillerie Regiment im Weltkrieg* (Berlin: Gerhard Stalling, 1928), pp. 140–42; Scheel, *Das Reserve Feldartillerie Regiment Nr. 70* (Berlin: Gerhard Stalling, 1923), pp. 16–19; and Herrmann Köhn, *Erstes Garde Feldartillerie Regiment und seine reitende Abteilung* (Berlin: Gerhard Stalling, 1928), pp. 148–51.

48. Karl von Unger, "Gorlice-Tarnow," in Ernst von Eisenhart-Rothe and Dr. Martin Lezius, *Das Ehrenbuch der Garde, Die preußische Garde im Weltkriege 1914–1919* (Berlin: Wilhelm Kolk und Verlag Oskar Hinderer, n.d.), pp. 176–79.

49. Babendieck, "Staszkowka und die Lipier Höhe," in Ernst von Eisenhart-Rothe and Dr. Martin Lezius, *Das Ehrenbuch der Garde* (Berlin: Wilhelm Kolk und Verlag Oskar Hinderer, n.d.), pp. 187–93.

50. Paderstein, "Erinnerungen an Staszkowka," in Ernst von Eisenhart-Rothe and Dr. Martin Lezius, *Das Ehrenbuch der Garde* (Berlin: Wilhelm Kolk und Verlag Oskar Hinderer, n.d.), pp. 181–82.

51. Crown Prince Wilhelm, *Meine Erinnerungen aus Deutschlands Heldenkampf* (Berlin: E. S. Mittler und Sohn, 1923), pp. 157–60.

52. Ibid.

53. Germany, Reichskriegsministerium, *Die Operationen des Jahres 1916 bis zum Wechsel in der obersten Heeresleitung* (Berlin: E. S. Mittler, 1936), p. 61. This work, the tenth volume in the official series *Der Weltkrieg 1914–1918*, prepared by former members of the Historical Section of the German General Staff who were hidden after the Treaty of Versailles in various civil bureaus, is hereafter referred to as *Der Weltkrieg 1914–1918*, vol. 10.

54. Crown Prince Wilhelm, *Meine Erinnerungen*, p. 160.

55. Ibid., p. 161.

56. For a detailed treatment of these units, see Bruce Gudmundsson, *Storm Troop Tactics: Innovation in the German Army, 1914–1918* (New York: Praeger, 1989), chs. 2, 3.

57. Cordt von Brandis, *Der Sturmangriff. Kriegserfahrungen eines Frontoffiziers* (n.p., 1917), p. 3; see also the various regimental histories of the German infantry units involved in the first few days of the battle.

58. Ludwig Gold, *Die Tragödie von Verdun* (Berlin: Gerhard Stalling, 1926), vol. 1, pp. 53–54.

59. I have yet to find a source that tells me how close "right up" to a barrage is. I would guess that any closer than thirty or forty meters from the point of impact would result in the attacking infantry being hit by a large number of splinters. In a German

training film from the early days of World War II, pioneers are shown advancing so close behind a barrage that clumps of earth thrown up by the exploding shells fall on them.

60. Reports of these largely bloodless victories filtering back to the French High Command led to speculation that the German infantry had "infiltrated" the French positions. That idea is ridiculed in an unsigned article, "Die deutsche Taktik bei Verdun," *Militär-Wochenblatt*, no. 66/67 (1916): 1610–12.

61. When Crown Prince Wilhelm, who was generally considered to be less than a serious soldier, took over command of the 5th Army, the Kaiser gave him strict instructions to heed the orders of Schmidt von Knobelsdorf: "Was er dir rät, mußt du tun!" ("Do what he advises").

62. Quoted in Adolphe Goutard, "Verdun 21 février–4 mars 1916: Le Contraire d'une ruée," in *Verdun 1916. Actes du colloque international sur la bataille, 6–7–8 Juin 1975* (Verdun: Association Nationale de Souvenir de la Bataille de Verdun, Université de Nancy II, 1975), p. 85.

63. Krafft von Delmensingen, *Der Durchbruch*, p. 344.

64. "During this bombardment the attack troops of the corps . . . are to be deployed so as to limit to the greatest degree possible damage to the infantry." Crown Prince Wilhelm, *Meine Erinnerungen*, p. 258.

65. France, Armée, Grand Quartier Général des Armées du Nord et du Nord-Est, État-Major, 3ème Bureau, "Directive no. 1," May 19, 1917, SHAT, carton 16N1686.

5

The Great Divorce

While the first two years of trench warfare saw a huge expansion of the artillery establishments of all major belligerents, this growth coincided with an increased separation—in outlook as well as in space—between the artillery and the infantry with which it was supposed to cooperate. Some developments—such as telephones, signal flares, and forward observers—mitigated this tendency. Others, such as growing interest in the problem of counterbattery fire, increased it. A third set of developments, generally referred to at the time as "trench artillery" managed to do both at the same time, reducing the gap between the infantry and its "hip pocket" means of fire support while making it easier for the "real" artillery to continue its march away from the most forward trenches.

The process of separation had begun before the war, with the introduction of indirect fire techniques. The blow that this development struck against the already difficult task of getting infantry and artillery to cooperate on the battlefield was sometimes softened by the practice of using, as observers, officers who had a sense of the tactical situation and what artillery could do to affect it. That is, having the artillery commander, connected to his battery by a telephone, forward with the infantry was almost as good as having the guns themselves near the firing line.

From the very beginning, however, the general practice was not to have the artillery commanders forward with the infantry. Instead, artillery battery, battalion (and, at least in the case of the Germans), regimental, and brigade commanders tended to command from observation posts located on high ground roughly halfway between the guns and the supported infantry. (The case of the Russian artillery battalion commander who, during the Russo-Japanese War, sat on a hill and commanded the fire of his three batteries by telephone is an early example.) The artillerymen who were actually with the infantry tended to be either lieutenants (in the French and British armies) or noncommissioned officers (in the German Army) who, because of their relatively low rank, were often reduced to the role of conduits for technical information rather than tactical decision makers.

For the latter task, both the Germans and the French eventually introduced the artillery liaison officer. This was an artillery lieutenant whose permanent relationship was with the supported infantry battalion rather than any particular artillery unit. Provided with various means of communication (telephones, messengers, carrier pigeons, signal lamps, and, toward the end of the war, radio), the artillery liaison officer was not to "spot" for a particular battery but, rather, to "gather in" whatever artillery was needed by the supported infantry battalion. That is, the liaison officer made connections with a number of artillery units in the area and then, in cooperation with the infantry commander, made requests of the most appropriate ones for various kinds of fire.[1]

In the German Army, the position of artillery liaison officers was strengthened in 1917 when the divisions holding positions adopted the institution of the battle troop commander (*Kampftruppenkommandeur*). This was an officer, usually the captain commanding a front-line battalion of infantry, who was put in charge of all resources in his particular sector. That is, he commanded, in addition to his battalion and various trench mortar, heavy machine gun, infantry gun, and other units stationed in his sector, any unit that was sent into his sector to help him, including artillery. This had the effect of converting the requests of the artillery liaison officers into commands.[2]

While the Germans also employed mobile artillery liaison officers, provided with the same resources and empowered with similar authority, in their offensives of 1918, the chief means of ensuring cooperation between attacking infantry and its supporting artillery during World War I was the timetable. From the simple one used at Vailly in October 1914, schedules soon developed into complex documents that governed not merely the timing of fires but also their location. When the task of the attacker was complicated by the replacement of a single defensive trench with a series of trenches and then a defended zone, the standing barrage that stood on top of the forward trench and then moved forward to a line behind the enemy's first trench turned into a "creeping" or "rolling" barrage—a series of standing barrages that moved forward at a prescribed rate.[3]

Although great pains were often taken to calculate the ideal rate of progress for such a barrage, chances were that it would not match the pace of the infantry. If the infantry was held up early in the attack, as it often was during the British attacks on the Somme in July 1916, the barrage would move on without them. This effectively destroyed the "combined arms effect" that the barrage had been established to provide. If, on the other hand, the infantry moved forward faster than expected, as the German Alpine Corps did in their attack on the village of Fleury during the battle around Verdun, they might find that their way was blocked by their own artillery.[4]

Because creeping barrages were the work of many batteries, they were the creatures of artillery officers at relatively high echelons—mostly division and corps—whose fixed observation posts possessed far surer means of communication with the gun lines. So that the infantry might signal to these observation posts that the barrage was too slow or (in the rare cases when such signals were permitted) too fast, infantry officers commanding battalions and regiments were provided with a variety of signal flares and/or rockets.

The same means were also used in trench warfare to request the firing of defensive barrages. These standing barrages were fired just in front of a trench that was under attack, with a primary purpose of stopping the attack and a secondary one of catching many enemy infantrymen moving in the open. In such cases, the pyrotechnic signals seem to have worked fairly well, particularly at night, when many of the smaller operations of trench warfare—raids, patrols, and small-scale attacks—took place. In the large offensives, however, where attacks were carried out in the daytime, the rockets had to compete with both sunshine and a very large number of exploding shells.

Given this problem, it is not surprising that the most famous student of the phenomenon of friendly fire, the French general Alexandre Percin, noted that the onset of trench warfare brought no decrease in the number of French soldiers killed by their own artillery during World War I.[5] On the one hand, position warfare led to increased certainty about where friendly territory ended and enemy territory began. On the other hand, the sheer volume of fire that could be delivered onto a small piece of ground, with the resultant smoke, dust, fire, and noise—not to mention the cutting of telephone cables—often rendered impossible the clear identification of friend or foe or the recognition of signals.

At the same time that it was becoming more difficult for artillery to intervene in the infantry battle, technical developments made it easier for it to participate effectively in the counterbattery battle. Here, as in so many other technical developments, the pioneers were able to build on the work of a full generation of officers of the various siege artillery branches. For these latter specialists, the idea of hitching their guns to teams of horses or gasoline-powered tractors was far more of a novelty than indirect fire. Indeed, in fortress warfare, indirect fire from cannon placed in defilade had been used since early modern times. This, combined with the relatively longer ranges of heavy pieces and the fact that terrain in the vicinity of fortresses tended to offer many places to hide siege pieces, produced the possibility that the defenders of a fortress might be fired on by artillery they could not see.

One solution to this problem was to conduct extensive acoustic studies of the neighborhood of each fortress. Armed with this knowledge, the artillery officers of a fortress would then be able to estimate the location of a "mystery gun" by virtue of the relative strength or weakness, as well as the apparent location, of its report. Because of its dependence on specific knowledge of terrain, this technique was obviously impractical for use by field artillery. Once trench warfare set in, and artillery units (particularly heavy artillery units) tended to stay in one place for a long time, the practice—known in English as "sound ranging"—was revived.[6]

Soon after the transition to position warfare in the west, another technique, known as "flash ranging," was introduced. This technique was based on the mapmaker's technique of triangulation. Observers located a known distance apart would record the azimuth (compass bearing) that connected their position with the flash of a firing artillery piece. They would then compare notes and construct a triangle with the distance between them as the base and the location of the flash as the apex. This triangle allowed the observers to put the offending cannon on the map.

The third method used to locate enemy artillery pieces was observation from the air. Observers in both heavier-than-air aircraft and balloons had the ability to look over intervening terrain masks and see what was hiding there. The advantage of the balloons was that they stayed in one place, thus allowing the observer to study a piece of terrain over time. The airplanes, on the other hand, could range further into enemy territory.

While all three techniques were in use as early as the winter of 1914–1915, it was a while before the problems were worked out. These fell into two main categories. The first was "clutter"—when artillery pieces fired at the same time, it was difficult to establish which signature belonged to which field piece. The second problem was communications. Observers in sound- and flash-ranging stations had to find a means of telling each other when they saw a flash or recorded a report. Observers in aircraft had to find ways of talking to the people on the ground. All three sorts of observers had to develop a language that they could use to communicate with each other and with the artillerymen who were to put their data to good use.

By the middle of 1917, a combination of familiar communications means (radio and telephone), as well as a variety of apparatus that bore a stronger resemblance to ninth-grade science projects than weapons of war, had solved these problems. Even before the problems were solved—indeed, as early as the fall of 1915—the armies on the western front were setting aside a portion of their artillery for counterbattery fire. By early 1916, the Germans at Verdun were able to accurately locate some, but not all, of the French batteries. Thanks to their ready supply of howitzers as well as their fondness for ruthless concentration of fire, the Germans were able to annihilate many of the batteries they located.[7]

This ability to locate hostile batteries did not turn into a general massacre of batteries because batteries that did not fire were almost impossible to locate. Likewise, when all batteries fired at once, it was far harder to distinguish the signature of any particular group of artillery pieces. An artillery commander could thus greatly reduce the risk of counterbattery fire by adopting two simple policies. One was to keep most of the guns silent during routine operations. The second was to ensure that guns that did fire in a regular basis did so in unison.

The only drawback to these policies was that it made the artillery far less flexible when it came to cooperating with the infantry. Batteries that fired only in large numbers (for missions such as defensive barrages) might prove useful when the enemy was attacking in force. They were not an effective means, however, of knocking out the single machine gun that was holding up an attack. As a result, the counterbattery battle not only pulled resources away from the support of the infantry but also denied the infantry the full use of what was officially earmarked to cooperate with it.

The weapons that arose to compensate for this failure were of a wide variety of types. They ranged from crude inventions assembled, quite literally, in junkyards to modifications of existing equipment to purpose-built devices, from clumsy spigot mortars to sleek high-velocity guns. Their common characteristic was providing the infantry of the forward trenches with artillery of their own, and they were generally referred to as "trench artillery."

Thanks largely to their habit of keeping a close eye on contemporary conflicts, as well as their willingness to learn from them, the Germans had a head start in the employment of trench artillery. From their observations of the siege of Port Arthur, they realized that some means of quickly clearing lanes in barbed wire obstacles was an important adjunct to modern siege warfare. They therefore introduced, in various sizes, a species of mortar known as the *Minenwerfer* (mine thrower). Because of its connection with siege warfare, this weapon was to be manned by the men of the "fortress pioneer" (*Festungspioniere*) battalions then being formed for the task of quickly reducing enemy fortresses in the course of campaigns of rapid maneuver.[8]

The first model *Minenwerfer* was introduced, under a thick veil of secrecy, in 1910. Built by the innovative Rheinische Metallwaren und Maschinenfabrik (Rheinmetall), this 250mm weapon fired a 97-kilogram bomb to a maximum range of 400 meters. The next model to be introduced showed that, even in the infancy of the new class of weapons, the German pioneers saw it as something more than a one-job weapon. Rather than being designed solely to clear barbed wire obstacles, this second model was viewed as a means of combating similar weapons in enemy hands. This "counterbattery" *Minenwerfer* had a longer range but a smaller charge. With a caliber of 170mm, it shot 51-kilogram *Minen* to 750 meters. By 1914, 116 of these had been provided to the German border fortifications.[9]

In the first weeks of the war, the fifty or so 250mm *Minenwerfer* in the hands of the fortress pioneers contributed to the rapid reduction of the French and Belgian fortifications that stood in the way of the advancing German armies. The full value of these weapons was not demonstrated, however, until the armies stopped moving and mobile warfare gave way to trench warfare. The heavily wooded Argonne in northeastern France was one of the first regions where the French and German armies bogged down. In the short-range fighting that ensued, the German artillery found itself unable to cooperate properly with the German infantry. At short ranges, the relatively flat trajectories of the German field guns prevented them from reaching many hollows where the French troops had sheltered. At longer ranges, the German artillery was outclassed by the French 75mm field guns. The German solution was to pull some 170mm *Minenwerfer* out of the fortresses and use them as short-range artillery pieces.[10]

It did not take long for the German infantry in the Argonne to see the value of these new weapons. In addition to the advantages brought by high-angle fire, the *Minenwerfer* were valued because they were close enough to the infantry to be able to communicate directly with them. At a time when traditional artillery pieces were moving further and further to the rear, this ease of liaison was greatly appreciated. This appreciation was soon turned into a program to vastly increase the numbers of *Minenwerfer* in the German Army because of a special relationship between the local German commander in the Argonne, Crown Prince Welhelm of the 5th Army, and the military industrial complex in Berlin. The crown prince had special access to his father the Kaiser, and his staff had a very good working relationship with the General Staff officer working on heavy artillery and other siege warfare equipment, Lieutenant Colonel Max Bauer. Bauer, in turn, had a very good relationship with both Krupp and Rheinmetall, the firms capable of designing and building additional *Minenwerfer*.[11]

The French on the receiving end were also quick to appreciate the *Minenwerfer*. As early as September 1914, the French authorities began to seek to obtain their own version of the German weapon. An immediate, though not necessarily ideal, solution was found in the museums and depots of the French Army. During the reign of Louis Philippe (1830–1848) and its immediate aftermath, French foundries had produced a number of small bronze muzzle-loading mortars. Provided with bags of black powder propellant, these smooth-bore pieces quickly proved to be a handy and popular way to toss improvised projectiles into enemy trenches.[12]

Substantially heavier bombs could be thrown by the conversion of a slightly more modern piece, the 80mm mountain gun of the De Bange system. Deprived of much of its carriage (including the wheels), this obsolete weapon became the basis for what we would now call a "spigot mortar"—a weapon in which the bomb was placed over the barrel rather than within it. The resulting contraption was known as the *lance-mines Gatard* (Gatard minethrower), a name that referred to both the inventor (Gatard) and the German *Minenwerfer* that inspired it. Because the size of the barrel was no longer a limiting factor, the *lance-mines Gatard* could be provided with projectiles of various sizes. The standard bombs weighed 58, 78, or 102 kilograms and contained, respectively, 18, 25, or 30 kilograms of explosive.[13]

Despite these and many other improvisations, the French were still outclassed by the German *Minenwerfer*.[14] The French authorities therefore turned to a certain Major Duchêne, an officer of engineers who had, in the years before the war, made himself somewhat unpopular by his advocacy of trench mortars. The weapon that resulted from Duchêne's work was the 58T, a spigot mortar firing a winged bomb containing six kilograms of high explosive.[15]

The 58T (also called, after its inventor, the *appareil Duchêne*) was made from items that could be spared from the manufacture of "real artillery." The steel tubes of 58mm diameter that formed the barrels of the device were originally intended for the recoil mechanism of 105mm guns. The 150mm diameter cylinders that formed the body of the projectiles were originally intended for the shells of an obsolete 150mm siege mortar. The explosive that filled these shells—perchlorate of ammonia—though widely used for civilian purposes, was too unstable to be fired from traditional artillery pieces.[16]

Largely because of the use of these already available elements, the first seventy examples of the 58T were sent to the front on January 18, 1915. The place chosen for the combat trials of this weapon was the Argonne Woods, where the threat from German *Minenwerfer* was considered the greatest. Reports from these trials were so favorable that the 58T was made (in February 1915) the standard equipment of the "official" trench mortar units then being raised. In keeping with the leitmotif of improvisation from elements "surplus" to the artillery, these units, christened *artillerie de tranchée* (or, less formally, *les crapouilloteurs*), were made up of individuals that the 75mm batteries could spare. Needless to say, not all of these were men who regularly displayed the martial virtues appreciated by French battery commanders in 1915.[17]

Despite this rapid progress, the French were still far behind the Germans. Beginning in December 1914, the German Pioneer Corps began to form detachments of *Minenwerfer* that were independent of the fortress pioneer battalions. By the spring of 1915, there were enough of these to provide each army corps with one medium detachment of about six medium (170mm) *Minenwerfer* and one heavy detachment of two heavy (250mm) *Minenwerfer*. By the middle of 1916, most divisions had their own *Minenwerfer* companies of three heavy and six medium trench mortars. In the same period, light *Minenwerfer*—76mm weapons with recoil mechanisms—had been designed and put into production. These first supplemented and later replaced the large number of "homemade" light bomb throwers that the pioneers had built in their mobile workshops. By the end of 1916, most divisional *Minenwerfer* companies had twelve of these weapons.[18]

With this increase in numbers, the *Minenwerfer* became an integral part of the most important German combat technique of this period—the attack with limited objectives (*Angriff mit begrenzten Ziele*). Unlike traditional German infantry attacks, which were geared to the destruction of enemy units within the framework of the tempo and geometry of a larger battle, attacks with limited objectives had the sole purpose of gaining small pieces of terrain. In most cases, this meant advancing 100 or 200 meters in order to take a piece of high ground that made possible observation over important parts of the battlefield.[19]

Conducted by an infantry battalion, regiment, or brigade, an attack with limited objectives was supported by all the guns, howitzers, and *Minenwerfer* that could bring their fire to bear on the piece of terrain in question. With greater range but reduced ability to communicate with the infantry, the artillery proper tended to support these attacks by firing at targets on the enemy side of the objective—guns, assembly areas for reserves, command posts, and the like. The *Minenwerfer*, on the other hand, fired on targets closest to their own infantry.

In general, this *Minenwerfer* fire was of two types. Before the attack, the *Minenwerfer* would fire slowly, to destroy specific installations—observation posts, strong points, machine gun nests, and the like—systematically. A few moments before the attack, the rate of fire would increase to provide what some Germans called a "fire bell" (*Feuerglocke*), a standing barrage on top of the forwardmost firing trench. When the German infantry went over the top and began running toward the enemy trench, this fire would be shifted to targets behind the forward trench.[20]

In cases where adequate preparations—isolation of the trench to be taken, rehearsal of the infantry plan, and stockpiling of ammunition—had been made, German attacks with limited objectives were generally successful.[21] Part of the credit for this success must be given to the assault techniques of the infantry and the pioneers. The key reform here was the replacement of linear tactics—many infantrymen getting up at the same time and trying to take the whole enemy trench at one time—with the *Schwerpunkt und Aufrollen*, infantry using a limited number of covered avenues to reach "break-in points" in the enemy trench and then, once they were in the trench, fanning to the left and right.

The *Schwerpunkt und Aufrollen* technique greatly reduced the vulnerability of the attacking Germans to enemy fire. It also greatly reduced the problem posed by barbed wire and other obstacles. That is, instead of having to deal with the entire enemy trench, the Germans had to deal only with particular lanes leading up to it. As a result, it was possible to clear barbed wire with a few Bangalore torpedoes or *Minenwerfer* rounds. Similarly, instead of suppressing all enemy firing positions, the attacking Germans had only to suppress those positions that could fire on the chosen avenues.

The rest of the credit for the success of German attacks with limited objectives in 1915 belongs to the *Minenwerfer*. Without it, the Germans would have been unable to knock out the few machine guns whose ability to enfilade no-man's-land prevented unprepared attacks. At a time when friend and foe were often entrenched within 100 meters of each other, heavy howitzers and siege mortars could not fire on the enemy front-line positions without risking harm to the most forward Germans. The shells fired by light field howitzers were often too light to easily penetrate the cover behind which the machine guns were hiding. Only *Minenwerfer* combined the necessary accuracy with the necessary explosive power to ensure the rapid destruction of these weaons.[22]

Because they were so dependent upon the *Minenwerfer*, German attacks with limited objectives seem also to have been limited by them. The early *Minenwerfer* could not shoot very far. The heavy model (250mm) could reach to 476 meters. The medium model (170mm) could hit targets at 750 meters. As a result, any advance of the German infantry beyond their first enemy trench would often have to be done without the participation of *Minenwerfer*. At the same time, the weight of the *Minenwerfer* and their ammunition, as well as the fact that they were not designed for rapid displacement, made it nearly impossible to move the trench mortars forward in time to support the rapid exploitation of a successful attack.[23]

To solve this problem, the same Colonel Bauer who had done so much to promote the *Minenwerfer* became, in the winter of 1914–1915, interested in the problem of how to provide the German infantry with small artillery pieces that could accompany them once they got beyond the first enemy trench. Bauer's first answer was to provide an experimental pioneer unit with relatively portable 37mm guns that had been designed by Krupp as secondary armament for fortifications. While these guns proved to be worse than useless (not only were their shells ineffective but their pronounced muzzle flash made them easy to target), the concept of a portable cannon that could accompany the infantry in the assault lived on. By the winter of 1915–1916, Assault Battalion Rohr, the lineal descendent of Bauer's experimental unit, had made the use of such weapons an integral part of their tactics. The particular weapon that they settled on was the standard Russian 76.2mm field gun, modified by cutting down the barrel, lowering the carriage, and removing the long-range sights.[24]

The Germans also used infantry guns for defensive purposes. As soon as trench warfare was set, a small portion of the field guns of each division was kept in the front lines and used, along with 37mm "pom-pom guns" and small-caliber pieces designed for fortress and naval use as flanking guns (*Flankengeschütze*). That is, they were used as single pieces sited to fire on attacking infantry from the flank. Lest they become targets for the attacker's artillery, flanking guns were hidden behind hills or other terrain masks. Because such positions offered limited fields of fire, flanking guns fired at comparatively short ranges.[25] It was therefore not long before the Germans realized that their field guns were overqualified for such work. A much smaller piece with a shorter barrel, lower carriage, and simplified sighting equipment would not only do all that was asked of a flanking piece but also be easier to hide. In other words, the sort of weapon used by Assault Battalion Rohr would also make an excellent flanking piece.

As a result of this realization, the German Army raised, in 1915, 1916, and 1917, a total of fifty batteries of what soon came to be known as infantry guns (*Infanteriegeschütze*).[26] These were equipped with a variety of weapons derived from light field guns—77mm pieces whose barrels were so worn that they were too inaccurate to use as field artillery, 75mm Skoda mountain guns provided by Austria-Hungary, and, toward the end of the war, *Infanteriegeschütz* 18, a weapon that had been designed as an infantry gun. As machine guns took over the greater part of the job of serving as flanking guns, the Germans tended to see their infantry guns as a means of attacking point targets with steel-capped, high-explosive shells. At first, the prime targets tended to be machine guns protected by steel shields and sandbags. Later, infantry guns proved useful as a means of knocking out the crude tanks of 1916, 1917, and 1918.[27]

German infantry gun units did not play a larger role in World War I largely due to competition from the light *Minenwerfer*. First introduced as a baseplate-mounted weapon that would be easier to move and to hide than the medium and heavy versions, this 75mm weapon soon proved to be far more versatile than its larger brothers. Thanks to the relatively light weight of its shell (4.6 kilograms), its low muzzle velocity, and its recoil absorption system, the light *Minenwerfer* could be used for direct as well as indirect fire. In 1917, the Germans capitalized on this capability by mounting the light *Minenwerfer* on a small carriage and providing it with armor-piercing rounds.[28] The Germans now had a small field piece that could serve, according to the situation, as an infantry gun, a light mortar, or an antitank weapon.

In contrast to the Germans, who settled on infantry guns of field gun caliber, and the British, who never displayed any sustained interest in the idea, the French Army adopted, in 1916, a significantly lighter, tripod-mounted infantry gun with a caliber of 37mm. Much better designed than the Krupp 37mm that the Germans rejected early in the war, this Puteaux gun was conceived as a means of knocking out German machine gun nests with short-range, direct fire. For the Western allies, however, the main answer to the German infantry guns, as well as the German light *Minenwerfer*, was the Stokes mortar.

The direct answer of almost all modern mortars, the 81mm Stokes was, for the time, revolutionary in its simplicity. In the age of the quick-firing gun, the Stokes was completely devoid of any device to absorb recoil. Instead of a trigger, it depended on a fixed firing pin to fire each bomb as it hit the bottom of the tube. And rather than bother with wheels, this weapon intended to accompany the infantry everywhere it went was designed to be broken into man-portable loads, the heaviest of which was 23 kilograms. Despite this simplicity (or, rather, because of it), the Stokes mortar was able to fire thirty rounds, each of which was the explosive equivalent of the 75mm field gun shell, each minute, to a distance of 450 meters.[29]

From its introduction in December 1915 until the end of the war, the Stokes mortar was the mainstay of British trench artillery. The officers and men who served the Stokes mortars were, like the French trench artillerymen, the castoffs from "proper" units. Unlike the *crapouilloteurs*, the British mortarmen had not, for the most part, been trained as artillerymen before being exiled to trench mortar units. This fact, combined with the bureaucratic nature of contemporary British command and control, led to a situation where the particular virtues of this weapon were rarely appreciated, let alone exploited.[30]

The Stokes seems to have done better in the hands of the French. The continued strength of the now ubiquitous *Minenwerfer*, as well as the greatly increased use of storm troop tactics, convinced the French authorities that their infantry needed such a weapon, more powerful than a rifle grenade and easier to move than the 58T. The first weapon designated for this task was the 75mm Jouhandeau-Deslandres, a conventional mortar that had been designed to fire 75mm field gun shells rejected by quality control. During the Nivelle offensive, sixteen of these weapons were provided to one of the attacking divisions. Attached, as sections of four pieces, to each of the four infantry regiments of the division, these mortars proved themselves a useful means of attacking machine gun nests.[31]

At 105 kilomgrams, the Jouhandeau-Deslandres was far too heavy to keep up with rapidly advancing infantry. By 1917, moreover, with the French armaments factories in full production, its ability to use "irregular" 75mm field gun shells was far less important than it had been in the past. Finally, the relatively long ranges at which the Jouhandeau-Deslandres could fire (1,700–2,000 meters, depending on the shell) were of little use in tactical situations where the targets were far closer. (The growing German fondness for placing machine guns and infantry strong points on rear slopes led to situations where the French would not discover an appropriate mortar target unless they were relatively close to it.)[32]

Given these considerations, it is not surprising that despite the foreign provenance of the Stokes, there was great interest in it as an alternative to French-made mortars. The battle of La Malmaison (October 23–25, 1917) served to confirm the opinions of the Stokes enthusiasts. In that offensive, twelve batteries of *crapouilloteurs* armed with Stokes mortars were able to accompany and cooperate with infantry units that penetrated the German position to a depth of five kilometers.[33] By the time of the armistice of November 11, 1918, Stokes mortars had been made part of the standard French infantry regiments.[34]

Despite the eventual triumph of the Stokes as the accompanying weapon of choice (most modern infantry mortars are its direct descendants), the evolution of the trench mortar into a weapon central to modern mobile warfare was not a smooth one. For most of the war, trench mortars contributed to great offensives, not as the "hip pocket" artillery of the infantry but as a form of battering ram to open the gates of the enemy fortress.

In the great offensives that started in 1915, the name of the game was fire superiority, getting as many guns as possible into action so that they could overwhelm the guns of the enemy. Thus, even generals who did not understand the advantage that trench mortars had when it came to cooperation with the infantry appreciated them as weapons that allowed them to make the most of their most limited asset, real artillery.[35]

Despite their short ranges, trench mortars could do this job because of the way defensive positions were organized. Until 1917 (for the Germans) or 1918 (for the French and British), most divisions defended with the bulk of their infantry in the forward line. This meant that the first enemy position, with its trenches and barbed wire, was not merely the first obstacle to be overcome by attackers but also the most important. It thus seemed sensible to make it the object of the heaviest possible fire from the greatest number of trench mortars.

Painfully aware of their lack of heavy artillery, the French were the first to use such grand batteries of trench mortars. By August 1916, they had, in addition to the 190 batteries assigned to divisions, 125 trench mortar batteries kept under the direct control of the Artillery Reserve of the Group of Armies. These served as the source for the bulk of the thousand-odd trench mortars that supported the French troops attacking on the Somme in July 1916 and the 1,922 trench mortars that took part in the Nivelle offensive of April 1917.[36]

Like the rest of the artillery employed, the French trench artillery that took part in the Somme and Nivelle offensives was given the mission of destroying, by means of systematic fire conducted over a number of days, the German field fortifications and the men in them. In contrast to the light field guns and heavy howitzers, the French trench mortars succeeded in their mission. Observers of the German positions opposite the concentrations of *crapouillots* were unanimous in their horror at the degree of destruction inflicted and their praise of the efficacy of the trench mortars.[37]

In keeping with their long-standing fondness for short, sharp bombardments, the Germans did not use their *Minenwerfer* to achieve the complete destruction of forward positions. They were not averse, however, to massing those *Minenwerfer* when the situation demanded. To that end, the Germans formed a "flying circus" of *Minenwerfer* units under the direct control of the Supreme Headquarters (Oberste Heeresleitung, O.H.L.). This reserve of *Minenwerfer* organizations included a number of independent battalions equipped with standard *Minenwerfer*, as well as a few units armed with experimental and "limited edition" weapons such as spigot mortars and weapons that used compressed air rather than explosive propellant.[38]

The most extreme case of massing *Minenwerfer* took place at the battle of Riga in September 1917. There, the main effort of the German operation was the crossing of a relatively broad river onto a peninsula that, by the standards of the western front, was not very heavily fortified. The problem was thus less one of supporting the infantry once it got into the enemy position than the effective suppression of any position from which the Russians could fire on the German boats and pontoon bridges. The vast majority of the *Minenwerfer* were therefore detached from the attacking divisions, added to the weapons of independent *Minenwerfer* units, and assembled into a *Minenwerfer* brigade of 100 heavy, 130 medium, and 320 light trench mortars.[39]

The employment of trench mortars as a mass or, more precisely, along a single line, was predicated on a linear target. As long as the bulk of the infantry of a defending division was crowded into forward positions, they would provide both the easiest and the most lucrative target for trench mortars. With the reform of German defensive tactics in 1917 and the French and British attempts of 1918 to replicate those reforms, the role of the infantry changed. Rather than filling a few forward trenches, the defending infantrymen were increasingly distributed among strong points of various sizes that were spread over a zone three, four, or even five kilometers deep. At the very least, this ensured that the bulk of the defenders' rifles, machine guns, and trench mortars were beyond the range of the attackers' trench mortars.

The Allied response (as described in Chapter 4) to this phenomenon was to slow the pace of the attack. The Germans, on the other hand, made their trench artillery as mobile as possible. Light *Minenwerfer* mounted on wheeled carriages were provided to infantry units at a rate of eight per battalion. Four of the medium *Minenwerfer* of each division were provided with horses and carts, and made directly subordinate to infantry brigade commanders.[40] Field gun batteries were detached from the division artillery and assigned to infantry regiments. Finally, infantry gun batteries, which had spent the bulk of the war without transport of their own, were provided with horses and caissons, and attached to divisions.

In some respects, the provision of all sorts of short-range artillery to infantry brigades, regiments, and even battalions brought the German Army back to the point where it had been in 1914, with a good portion of the artillery devoted to direct support, over open sights, of the infantry. The development of "infantry artillery" was not, however, merely retrogressive. Instead, it was part and parcel of a tactical paradigm shift that, boiled down to its essentials, consisted of breaking the battlefield into a far greater number of relatively small conflicts than had hitherto been the case.

Some of these conflicts could be resolved by the light machine guns, hand grenades, and grenade launchers of a single squad or platoon. Others required the intervention of heavier weapons—the machine guns and light *Minenwerfer* of battalion commanders, the accompanying infantry batteries belonging to regimental commanders, or the medium *Minenwerfer* at the disposal of infantry brigade commanders. This intervention could take one of two forms. Either the heavy weapons would join directly in the little engagement or would lessen the burden on an engaged unit by guarding its flanks with fire, shooting at enemy reinforcements, or combating enemy heavy weapons.

Ideally, the process by which these heavier weapons joined each fight would follow a certain logic. Units would call on the resources of higher echelons only if their own means did not suffice. The fragility of such an arrangement, however, is obvious. Once sent into battle, the crew of a mortar or infantry gun was as much a fighting unit as any infantry squad or platoon. The way in which such a gun crew cooperated with other units was as much a function of its immediate environment as it was of the echelon of command to which it belonged.

As had been the case in 1914, the guns and mortars working closely with the German infantry gave it a considerable edge over its counterparts in the enemy camp. They could not directly overcome the problems that had led to the establishment and preservation of position warfare— the vulnerability of troops moving in the open, the power of field fortifications, and the ability of a defender to fill a breech more rapidly than the attacker could widen it. These new weapons did, nonetheless, make a contribution to solving the "riddle of the trenches." In concert with other aspects of the new German infantry tactics, they greatly reduced the work of the "real" artillery. This liberated resources to work on the prerequisites—the silencing of the enemy artillery, the achievement of operational surprise, and the maintenance of the momentum of the attack—for a successful breakthrough.

NOTES

1. Lange, "Der Artillerie-Verbindungs-Offizier im Stellungskrieg," *Artillerie rundschau*, August 1929, pp. 152–56; Emil Popp, "A.V.O. (Artillerie-Verbindungs-Offizier)," *Der Luitpold-Kanonier*, 1931, pp. 5, 10; Pierre Arnoult, *Guerre d'artilleur. Liaisons de 75 (2 Mai 1917–11 Novembre 1918)* (Paris: Livres des Deux Guerres, 1939).

2. For more on the *Kampftruppenkommandeur*, see Graham Chamley Wynne, *If Germany Attacks, The Battle in Depth in the West*, (Westport, CT: Greenwood, 1976), pp. 312–15.

3. For detailed treatments of the evolution of defensive tactics during World War I, see Wynne, *If Germany Attacks*; Martin Samuels, *Doctrine and Dogma: German and British Infantry Tactics in the First World War* (Westport, CT: Greenwood, 1993); and Timothy T. Lupfer, *The Dynamics of Doctrine: The Changes in German Tactical Doctrine During the First World War* (Fort Leavenworth, KS: U.S. Army Command and General Staff College, 1981).

4. For more on the battle of Fleury, see Bruce Gudmundsson, *Storm Troop Tactics* (New York: Praeger, 1989), ch. 4.

5. Percin, *Le Massacre de notre infanterie*, pp. 30ff.

6. The German term for this technique (*Schallmeß*) provides a better idea of its essential element, the measuring (*Meß*) of a cannon's report (*Schall*).

7. Frédéric Hérr, *L'Artillerie* (Paris: Berger Levrault, 1924), pp. 30, 37, 43, 50. The verb used in the source is *annihiler*. It seems to refer to the physical destruction of the guns rather than the massacre of all the gunners, who, because they were able to take shelter in trenches and dugouts, were far harder to injure. For an anecdote in which six French guns were destroyed by German counterbattery fire without any of the French gunners being killed or wounded, see Arnoult, *Guerre d'artilleur*, pp. 41–42.

8. Paul Heinrici, ed., *Das Ehrenbuch der deutschen Pioniere* (Berlin: Verlag Wilhelm Kolk, 1932), pp. 32–41, and 482–84; and Westphal, "Von der 'Bombenkanone' zum Infanteriegeschütz," *Wehrtechnische Monatshefte*, July 1938, pp. 9, 306–08. In the 1880s and 1890s, the German field artillery had experimented with a number of small mortars as a means of solving the problems that were eventually resolved by the introduction of the 105mm light field howitzer. F. Mouths, "Zur Vorgeschichte der Minenwerfer," *Wehr und Waffen*, 1934, pp. 53–55. For more on the German fortress pioneers, see "The German Army in World War I: The Pioneer Corps," *Tactical Notebook*, Sept. 1992.

9. Westphal, "Von der 'Bombenkanone' zum Infanteriegeschütz," pp. 306–08; and Augustin, "Minenwerfer," in Max Schwarte, ed., *Die militärischen Lehren des großen Krieges* (Berlin: E. S. Mittler, 1920), pp. 157–59.

10. Westphal, "Von der 'Bombenkanone' zum Infanteriegeschütz," pp. 308–09.

11. Bauer wrote a very interesting account of his activities during World War I in *Der große Krieg im Feld und Heimat* (Tübingen: Osiander, 1921).

12. Pierre Waline, *Les Crapouillots*, (Paris: Charles-Lavauzelle, n.d.), pp. 36–38.

13. Ibid., pp. 39–41.

14. A detailed description of these improvisations can be found in "French Trench Artillery," *Tactical Notebook*, Oct. 1992; and Waline, *Les Crapouillots*, pp. 28–43. Photographs of some of these weapons can be found in Polster, "Minen- und Bomben-werfer Frankreichs," *Kriegstechnische Zeitschrift*, 1917, pp. 153–56.

15. The "58" referred to the caliber of the tube that fired the rod that supported the bomb. "T" referred to the fact that this was a weapon for the trenches (*les tranchées*). Waline, *Les Crapouillots*, pp. 45–49.

16. Ibid.

17. Ibid., pp. 49–52. The word *crapouillot*, used to describe the French trench mortars of World War I, seems to have been derived from the word *crapaud*, meaning "toad." Ibid., p. 37.

18. Augustin, "Minenwerfer," pp. 157–61; and Westphal, "Von der 'Bombenkanone' zum Infanteriegeschütz," pp. 308–09.

19. For more on attacks with limited objectives, see Wilhelm Balck, *Development of Tactics—World War*, trans. Harry Bell (Fort Leavenworth, KS: General Service Schools Press, 1992), ch. 7; and Gudmundsson, *Storm Troop Tactics*, chs. 3–6.

20. Augustin, "Minenwerfer," pp. 159–60.

21. This, at least, was the opinion of General Joffre.

22. Balck, *Development of Tactics*, pp. 173–75.

23. E. Hofmann, "Vom Minenwerfer zum Infanteriegeschütz (Rückblick einer Entwickelung)," *Wehrtechnische Monatshefte*, May 1939, pp. 204, 205, 207, 209. The figures are conveniently arranged in a table in Waline, *Les Crapouillots*, p. 241.

24. Gudmundsson, *Storm Troop Tactics*, pp. 45–53. The field guns seem to be those captured during the summer campaign of 1915, which began with the breakthrough at Gorlice–Tarnow.

25. German descriptions of flanking guns in this period do not give exact ranges. If the specifications for purpose-built infantry guns are any guide, however, they would rarely, if ever, have fired at targets over 1,000 meters away.

26. The infantry gun batteries were initially known as "close combat batteries" (*Nakhampfbatterien*) and were, for the most part, in addition to the platoons and batteries of guns attached to the assault battalions formed on the pattern of Assault Battalion Rohr.

27. Cron, *Geschichte des deutschen Heeres im Weltkriege 1914–1918*, pp. 151–53.

28. Hofmann, "Vom Minenwerfer zum Infanteriegeschütz," p. 208.

29. Waline, *Les Crapouillots*, pp. 175–76. The story of the invention and adoption of the Stokes mortar can be found in Ian Hogg, *Grenades and Mortars* (London: Ballentine Books, 1974).

30. Shelford Bidwell and Dominick Graham, *Fire-Power: British Army Weapons and Theories of War, 1904–1945* (Boston: George Allen and Unwin, 1985), pp. 124–30.

31. France, Ministère de la Guerre, Section Technique de Génie, "Artillerie d'accompagnement" (by Lieutenant Colonel Deslandres), Dec. 20, 1917. SHAT carton 4B24/3.

32. Ibid.

33. Waline, *Les Crapouillots*, pp. 176–77. These regimental Stokes mortars were served by the same infantrymen (*fantassins bombardiers*) who handled the 37mm Puteaux guns. For a brief discussion of the battle of Malmaison (referred to by the Germans as the battle of Laffaux-Ecke), see Pascal Lucas, *L'Évolution des idées tactiques en France et en Allemagne* (Paris: Berger-Levrault, 1923), pp. 156–58.

34. Piere Guinard, Jean-Claude Devos, and Jean Nicot, *Inventaire Sommaire des Archives de la Guerre, Série N 1872–1919, Introduction: Organization de l'Armée Française, Guide des Sources, Bibliographie* (Troyes, France: Imprimerie La Renaissance, 1975), p. 125.

35. Waline, *Les Crapouillots*, pp. 124–25, 138.

36. Ibid., pp. 135, 140.

37. Ibid., pp. 113–19, 135–40.

38. These were initially provided with two heavy, four medium, and six of the new light *Minenwerfer*. In April 1916, this was increased to three heavy, six medium, and twelve light *Minenwerfer*. Augustin, "Minenwerfer," pp. 161–62.

39. Lichnock, "Der Dünaübergang, 1. September, 1917," in Paul Heinrici, ed., *Ehrenbuch der deutschen Pioniere* (Berlin: Verlag Wilhelm Kolk, 1932), p. 326. For a detailed discussion of the battle of Riga in September 1917, see Gudmundsson, *Storm Troop Tactics*, ch. 7.

40. These medium *Minenwerfer* had to be dismounted to be fired. Augustin, "Minenwerfer," pp. 162–66. It is important to note that at this time, there was a single infantry brigade commander in the German infantry division. He directly commanded the three infantry regiments as well as attached heavy weapons, such as the medium *Minenwerfer*.

6

Bruchmüller

Of the hundreds of thousands of artillerists who plied their trade in World War I, only one, Georg Bruchmüller, has achieved lasting fame. In a war so vast that most generals do not merit even a footnote, a prematurely retired lieutenant colonel managed to earn a permanent place in the literature of that conflict. And while some of the credit for Bruchmüller's reputation is due to his skills as a writer and a certain fondness for self-promotion, the lion's share was the result of solid achievement.[1] That achievement, in turn, was based on a thorough knowledge of what artillery could and could not do.

After spending a year and a half in near obscurity as a siege artillery battalion commander and then the commanding officer of a field artillery regiment, Bruchmüller was recognized by the German leadership on the eastern front as a man with a special talent. By 1916, he had been turned into a one-man "flying circus," moving from place to place to organize short, sharp offensive bombardments that featured a very high ratio of tubes to both frontage and infantry. At the Witonitz bridgehead (November 1, 1916), for example, the three infantry regiments of the 121st Infantry Division were supported by 156 artillery pieces and 49 trench mortars that fired for 5 hours and 15 minutes before the infantry attacked. Five months later, 300 artillery pieces and 100 trench mortars supported the attack of the 1st Landwehr Infantry Division against the bridgehead at Toboly (April 3, 1917). That bombardment lasted five hours and forty-five minutes.[2]

In addition to these division-sized attacks, Bruchmüller organized larger enterprises. In East Galicia (July 1917) and Lake Narocz (April 1916), he directed the artillery that took part in two successful attacks of army corps.[3] At Riga (September 1917) he put together the bombardment that contributed to the victory of the thirteen divisions of Oskar von Hutier's 8th Army.[4] At Jakobstadt, twenty days after the battle of Riga and a few miles east of that town, he achieved a similar, though far less known, success.

After Jakobstadt, Bruchmüller moved west. There he repeated his role as a one-man "flying circus," going from one portion of the front to another to organize the artillery support for major offensives. Thus, he can take the credit for the success of the artillery preparations of all of the German tactical victories on the western front in the last year of the war: the counterattack at Cambrai (November 30, 1917), the "Kaiser's Battle" in Picardy (March 21–April 1, 1918), and the offensives at Armentiers (April 9–18, 1918) and on the Chemin des Dames (May 27–June 2, 1918).[5]

Bruchmüller's success in these battles has often been attributed to his use of the rolling barrage. While this technique was certainly a key tool in his bag of tricks, its use is not sufficient to explain Bruchmüller's first-class record. Neither the British on the Somme (July 1916) nor the French in the Champagne (Nivelle offensive, April 1917) had been able to make their rolling barrages work. Likewise, Bruchmüller's use of box barrages (*Abriegelungsfeuer*), standing barrages (*Sperrfeuer*), and other standard techniques of the time did not distinguish him from either his German colleagues or his Allied counterparts.

What made Bruchmüller a virtuoso was his ability to use these techniques at the right time and place. This ability, in turn, was dependent on his knowledge of factors other than the purely mechanical. For example, he knew enough about human psychology to realize that the key to the rolling barrage was the closeness with which the infantry followed it. He therefore worked hard on both the reliability of the artillery and the trust of the infantry. The former consisted of getting all batteries to read from the "same sheet of music," of making sure that the right sort of weapons and shell-fuse combinations were used for the rolling barrage, and ensuring that short rounds would be kept to the absolute minimum. The latter required that he convince the infantry that following fifty meters or less behind a curtain of exploding shells was a good idea.

Gaining the confidence of the infantry was probably the simpler of the two jobs. It was made all the easier by his reputation as a skillful gunner. "The troops," wrote General Max Hoffmann, the de facto commander of German forces on the eastern front for the last two years of the war, "also noticed that an attack that had previously been prepared by artillery under Bruchmüller's command was a sure thing, and they advanced with . . . confidence in the success of any undertaking that had been prepared by Bruchmüller and his staff."[6]

Bruchmüller also used his skills as a communicator. From the very first, he made it a practice to give lectures to the officers, including NCOs serving as platoon commanders, of the artillery and infantry units that would take part in one of his attacks. In these lectures he described in detail the artillery plan he had put together, the effect he intended the artillery fire to have on the enemy, and coordination measures such as signal rockets, liaison officers, and forward observers. These lectures were followed by extensive question-and-answer periods.[7]

Needless to say, if Bruchmüller's reputation had not been built on a solid foundation of competence, it would soon have faded. His talent for "knowing, as if by instinct, the exact quantity of ammunition that was necessary to discharge on any single point to render it ready to be stormed" was not the unexplainable gift of an idiot savant.[8] On the contrary, it was the result of years of studying one of the more neglected subfields of military science; terminal ballistics. During his years of peacetime service as an officer of the foot artillery, he made it his business to find out how many shells of a particular type would be needed to achieve a desired effect against a fortress. From that, it was a short step to learning how to deal with field fortifications.

Bruchmüller's knowledge of terminal ballistics led him to use particular weapons for particular purposes. Having discovered that, contrary to popular belief, the fragments from an exploding 210mm howitzer shell tended to fly backward, he made sure that such shells would be fired only on targets that were far from friendly infantry. Realizing that light field guns, because of their high rate of fire, could deliver far more gas shells in a given time than howitzers, he made them the prime counterbattery weapons. Knowing that field howitzers, both light and heavy, were less likely to fire short rounds than were guns, he used them as the principal means of providing the rolling barrage.[9]

This appreciation of the technical characteristics of the artillery matériel of the time led Bruchmüller to devise a scheme for task-organizing artillery that was radically different from what was rapidly becoming traditional in the armies of Germany's enemies. Whereas the latter had come to the conclusion that the light field guns of the division artillery should fire on targets of interest to the infantry, while the heavier pieces belonging to corps commanders should concentrate on the counterbattery battle, Bruchmüller reversed the relationship. He organized the majority of the light field guns into counterbattery task forces (*Artilleriebekämpfungsgruppen* or *Aka*) that answered directly to corps commanders, and put howitzers into the infantry support task forces (*Infanteriebekämpfungsgruppen* or *Ika*) responsible to divisions.

That Bruchmüller was able to do this was the result of the flexibility of the German artillery command system. Because there was no permanent corps artillery organization, there was no one to object to Bruchmüller's reversal of the "natural order of things." For the same reason, German artillerymen were used to task organization. In particular, three years of trench warfare had habituated them to the practice of making siege artillery battery and battalion commanders directly responsible to the division artillery commanders in whose sectors they were operating.[10]

A further stepping-stone toward Bruchmüller's organization was provided by the German institution of "floating" regimental headquarters. Some of these were the headquarters of the field artillery regiments that had been taken out of infantry divisions in the winter of 1916–1917. Others were the headquarters of siege artillery regiments whose component batteries and battalions had been assigned to different divisions, corps, and armies. In either case, they provided Bruchmüller with the framework for assembling separate battalions and batteries into groupments of various sizes.[11]

How this worked in practice can be seen from the example of the artillery organization of a single German army corps (1st Bavarian Corps) whose artillery took part in one of Bruchmüller's bombardments. At the time of the attack, 1st Bavarian Corps consisted of three divisions, with two (1st and 2nd Bavarian Infantry Divisions) in the first line and a third (30th Infantry Division) in the second. The artillery resources consisted of 4 divisional artillery commanders and their staffs;[12] 11 artillery (both field and siege) regimental staffs; 40 artillery (again both field and siege) battalion staffs; and 126 firing batteries.[13]

The artillery commander of the 30th Infantry Division commanded the counterbattery task force (*Aka*) and reported directly to the corps commander. The artillery commanders of the 1st and 2nd Bavarian Divisions each commanded one of the infantry support task forces (*Ika*) and reported to their respective division commanders. One of the regimental commanders commanded the long-range task force (*Fernkampfgruppe* or *Feka*). He, like the *Aka* commander, was directly subordinate to the corps commander.[14]

With the exception of the *Feka*, these task forces were further subdivided into two groupments (*Untergruppen*) under regimental headquarters and subgroupments (*Unterverbänden*) under battalion headquarters. The levels of subdivision corresponded to sectors into which the corps area was divided. The *Untergruppen* were composed of a variety of weapons, while the *Unterverbänden* were generally made up of weapons of a single type. The *Feka*, already the size of a groupment, was divided into two subgroupments.[15]

The *Aka* consisted, for the most part, of field artillery batteries. Some 100mm gun and heavy field howitzer batteries were also provided. The *Ika* consisted primarily of heavy field howitzers, supplemented by a few field artillery batteries and an occasional 210mm howitzer. The *Feka* consisted of long-range weapons: 150mm and 100mm heavy guns as well as some field guns.[16] (Given the general pattern, it is reasonable to assume that the field batteries attached to the *Aka* consisted mostly of older— M1896 n/A—field guns, that those attached to the *Ika* consisted largely of light field howitzers, and that those attached to the *Feka* were extended-range M1916 field guns.)

Six field gun batteries were not assigned to any of these task forces. Instead, each served as the accompanying battery for one of the six infantry regiments in the first line of attack. They were supplemented by two batteries of infantry guns, one of which was attached to each first-line division. The accompanying batteries were equipped with the older (but lighter) M1896 n/A field gun. The infantry gun batteries were equipped with special infantry guns, either purpose-built German weapons or modified Russian field guns.[17]

Their functional names notwithstanding, the artillery pieces of the various task forces were not restricted to a single mission. The number of pieces assigned to a given task varied according to the particular phase of the fire plan. That it, the guns and howitzers of the *Aka* were primarily, but not exclusively, concerned with the counterbattery effort. Likewise, the howitzers, siege mortars, and guns of the *Ika* were usually, but not entirely, devoted to directly supporting the infantry.[18]

The three hours and forty minutes of preparatory fire by the artillery of the 1st Bavarian Corps during the attack of July 15, 1918, for example, consisted of five phases. In the first phase, which lasted ten minutes, the *Ika*, reinforced by the trench mortars, pounded the enemy's forward position while the *Aka* attacked the presumed locations of enemy batteries. The projectile of choice was "blue cross," a mixture of high explosives and teargas. Weapons not provided with "blue cross" fired high explosives. While this was going on, *Feka* attacked command posts, telephone exchanges, headquarters, and barracks.[19]

In the second phase, of seventy-five minutes' duration, both *Ika* and *Aka* concentrated their fire on enemy battery positions, with an average of two German batteries firing on a single enemy battery. The chief projectiles for this task were "blue cross" and "green cross" (which contained diphosgene, a highly poisonous gas). The trench mortars, lacking the range to fire on enemy batteries, continued to pound the forward infantry positions and clear gaps in the enemy wire. *Feka* attacked distant targets.[20]

During the ninety-minute third phase, the *Ika* again attacked forward targets of interest to the infantry. Using high-explosive ammunition, its howitzers, siege mortars, and guns focused on enemy strong points and positions from which the enemy would be able to deliver flanking fire. Lest the enemy gunners recover from the concentrated gassing of the second phase, *Aka* continued to fire on enemy batteries with gas shells.[21]

The fourth phase was an exact repetition of the second, except that it lasted fifteen minutes rather than seventy-five. A minor result of this repetition was the refreshing of the gas around the enemy batteries. Its main purpose, however, was to make the enemy think that the attack was about to begin. If all went well, the enemy would respond to the lifting of fire from the forward positions by moving out of dugouts and into trenches.[22]

At that point, the enemy infantry would be hit for half an hour by the concentrated high-explosive shelling of the fifth phase. Even if the enemy had not taken the bait, the fire of the *Ika* and trench mortars on the enemy forward positions provided a wall of explosions behind which the German infantry could move into their jumping-off positions. To hinder the enemy's ability to observe the imminent infantry attack, some of the heavy field howitzers (the only German pieces provided with such projectiles) fired smoke shells. *Aka* maintained the volume of gas on enemy batteries while *Feka* shelled the distant targets that had been attacked throughout the morning.[23]

In the last ten minutes of the fifth phase (which was also the last ten minutes of the preparation and the last ten minutes before "H-Hour"), the German artillery fired the first round of the rolling barrage. Siege mortars, as well as medium and heavy trench mortars, switched to targets behind the enemy forward trench. About half of the guns of the *Aka* left their counterbattery duties to join in the rolling barrage. (This left about two German guns firing on each enemy battery position.)[24]

The main portion (*Hauptwalze*) of the rolling barrage consisted of high-explosive shells. This was the wall of explosions behind which the attacking German infantry was to follow as closely as possible. At times, a second barrage was placed on the enemy side of the main barrage. When this second barrage was 600 or more meters on the enemy side of the German infantry, it consisted of a mixture of "blue cross" and high explosives. When it was placed within 600 meters of the German infantry, it was entirely high explosives.[25]

Since neither the rolling barrage nor the weapons of the infantry could deal with all problems encountered during the advance, the rolling barrage was supplemented by ad hoc artillery fire. This fire could be organized either by mobile forward observers moving with (but not attached to) the infantry or the artillery liaison officers attached to each infantry regiment. The former were senior artillery NCOs linked by telephone to the fixed observation posts of their subgroupments. The latter were junior officers who used their telephones to link local forward observers into a network that could be exploited by their infantry regiment.[26]

The rolling barrage led the attacking infantry through the enemy position to a depth of six or seven kilometers—through one or two infantry positions as well as the area occupied by most of the enemy's field artillery. Once the German guns started to run out of range, a portion of them began to move forward. (In the case of 1st Bavarian Corps, 41 out of 126 batteries moved forward with the two attacking divisions. The others were retained by corps, army, and army groups as reserves or reassigned to other formations.)

Once this process was in motion, the Germans considered themselves to be out of the business of trench warfare and back in the business of mobile warfare. As a result, the *Ika*, *Aka*, and *Feka* were dissolved and the batteries returned to their parent battalions.[27] These battalions, in turn, were formed into new groupments whose organization reflected the peculiarities of the situation facing each division. In one of the offensives, for example, the commanding general of one of the armies recommended that reinforced artillery of each infantry division be divided into three groupments. A direct support groupment, consisting of two battalions of field artillery and some batteries of heavy field howitzers, would be attached to each of the two forward infantry regiments. A third groupment, made up of the remaining field batteries, as well as 100mm and 150mm long-range guns, and 210mm heavy howitzers, would remain under the direct control of the divisional commander.[28]

If all went well, the effect of a Bruchmüller bombardment was a mixture of neutralization, deception, and physical destruction. Taken singly, none of these effects were perfect. Even if the German artillery executed Bruchmüller's plan flawlessly, there would be enemy batteries and machine guns that continued to function, enemy commanders who were not fooled, and, in particular, enemy installations that remained intact. Taken as a whole, however, the various imperfect results of a Bruchmüller bombardment combined with each other and the work of the properly trained infantry to produce an overall effect that was all but irresistible.[29]

Because the attacking infantry was capable of reaching (and therefore destroying) enemy battery positions within the first few hours of the attack, neutralization of the enemy artillery was all that was required of the counterbattery effort. Similarly, the ability of the German infantry to knock out isolated machine guns with their own weapons (grenades, flamethrowers, grenade launchers, light machine guns, heavy machine guns, infantry guns, and accompanying guns) made neutralization (by means of the rolling barrage) a sufficient means of dealing with that danger.

The deception effort contributed to this neutralization effect by "training" the enemy troops, both gunners and infantrymen, to stay in their dugouts as long as possible. Enemy artillerymen who responded to the first ten minutes of fire by rushing to their guns would reach them just in time to be hit by the second phase of fire—the one in which most of the German tubes were firing against enemy battery positions. Enemy infantrymen who responded to the false "end" of the bombardment (during the fourth phase) by moving to their firing positions would similarly be exposed to concentrated fire within moments of their leaving shelter. Those who survived were far less likely to respond to the actual lifting of fire by an enthusiastic dash from the comparative safety of their shelters.

The destruction that took place in the course of one of Bruchmüller's bombardments was not, on the surface, different from what resulted from other bombardments of a similar scale. Other bombardments—those of the Germans at Verdun in February 1916, the British at the Somme in July of that same year, or the French in Champagne in April 1917—had aimed for the complete elimination of any significant resistance so that the infantry could concentrate on occupying the conquered ground and defending it against counterattacks. Because of this, failure to achieve perfection—usually in the form of a few surviving machine guns—had led to failure of the entire enterprise.

Bruchmüller, on the other hand, did not aim for complete destruction; incomplete destruction of enemy installations was sufficient for his purposes. Many enemy machine gun nests, dugouts, trench mortars, infantry guns, and artillery pieces must have been destroyed by direct hits during the course of a Bruchmüller bombardment. Such destruction left gaps in the enemy's defenses, an avenue of approach uncovered by fire, a bunker exposed on one side because another bunker was no longer in working order, a ravine no longer subject to mortar fire. Such gaps were all that the German infantry needed to start the process of unraveling the entire defensive system.

Ironically, the German inability to destroy all targets of interest may have helped their overall effort. The panic that often ensued when the

German infantry was pushing rapidly into the enemy rear areas would not have spread nearly as rapidly if the *Feka* had succeeded in destroying all command posts, headquarters, and telephone exchanges. At the same time, if the enemy command apparatus had been left intact, it might have been in much better shape to resist such confusion.[30]

Combined with the infiltration (storm troop) tactics of the German infantry, Bruchmüller's technique brought Germany close to victory on the western front. On five separate occasions, German divisions supported by his bombardments were able to do what no army on the western front had been able to do in the three years since trench warfare had set in—break through the enemy defensive position, destroy whole divisions, and set their gaze on the "green fields beyond."[31]

Despite such achievements, Bruchmüller's technique was not a panacea. For every maneuver there is a countermaneuver, and Bruchmüller's orchestration of artillery was no exception. In July 1918, in the wine-growing country east of the ancient city of Reims, the French 4th Army conducted a successful defense against a German "infiltration" attack opened by Bruchmüller's last bombardment. Quite appropriately, the undoing of the German attack was as musical as the attack itself. Bruchmüller's method was based on careful timing, on the neutralization of the enemy batteries while the German infantry was moving, on the German infantry following closely behind the rolling barrage, and on the German infantry reaching the enemy guns before the enemy system as a whole could recover from the shock and confusion of the first few hours of the attack. The French countermaneuver interfered with this rhythm and therefore deprived the attack of its power.

The French were able to do this because they radically changed the way they occupied the ground they intended to defend. The standard approach, from the very first days of the war, and still in use by the neighboring 5th Army (west of Reims), was to use the bulk of the infantry to form a main line of resistance at the forward edge of French-controlled territory. The approach used by the 4th Army resembled contemporary German defensive layouts in that the main line of resistance was located four or five kilometers behind the forwardmost French trench.

To prevent the kind of infiltration that had recently caused so much trouble for the British, this main line of resistance had been made continuous.[32] More important, this main line, located mainly on reverse slopes beyond the extreme range of all of the German trench mortars and some of the German field artillery, was much less susceptible to bombardment. (One need only recall the difficulties the Germans experienced in trying to hit French rear slope positions at Verdun and their subsequent conversion to a policy of putting their main line of resistance on the rear slope, to understand the value of a rear slope position.)

In the 3,000 or so meters immediately in front of the main line of resistance (and thus 1,000 to 2,000 meters behind the forwardmost trench), the forward divisions of the French 4th Army established a defended area of strong points manned by half-companies of infantry and machine gunners.[33] Because of the undulating nature of the terrain—a given section of the French position might sit atop two or three successive ridge lines running parallel to the French front—the strong points were positioned on both north (forward) and south (rear) slopes. Unlike the main line of resistance, the strong points were not intended to form an impenetrable wall. Instead, the strong points of the defended area had the mission of breaking up the German attack.[34]

A few hundred meters to the north was a second belt of strong points known as the "outpost line." Smaller than the strong points of the defended area, the strong points of the line of outposts were manned by a platoon or half-platoon of infantry and/or a handful of machine gunners. Like their larger counterparts these outposts had the mission of breaking up the German attack, of preventing the Germans the freedom of movement necessary to conduct a well-prepared attack against the main line of resistance.

To this end, the strong points of the line of outposts were placed on the rear slopes of the east–west ridges that dominated the local terrain. So situated, they would be much less vulnerable to German observation and fire. In particular, they would be nearly impossible for the German artillery to locate or knock out. The rear slope location also increased the chances that they would be able to catch the advancing Germans by surprise—with a *rafale* (hail of bullets) striking them in the flanks or rear. The French engineers who laid out these lines took care to ensure that they were mutually supporting. That is, the strong points were so laid out that any Germans trying to attack a strong point would find themselves in the sights of a French machine gun firing from another strong point.[35]

Forward of the line of outposts, what was once the forwardmost trench had been replaced by two- or three-man observation posts. In case of a determined attack, the duty of these observation posts consisted solely of giving the alarm—through the use of signal rockets, messenger pigeons, or telephone. Once this was accomplished, they were permitted to leave their posts and reach safety by any means at their disposal.[36]

The French 4th Army's new defensive tactics also changed the location of the French artillery. The standard practice had been to place the bulk of the field artillery within three or four kilometers of the forwardmost French

Figure 6.1
French Defensive Arrangements at Reims, July 15, 1918

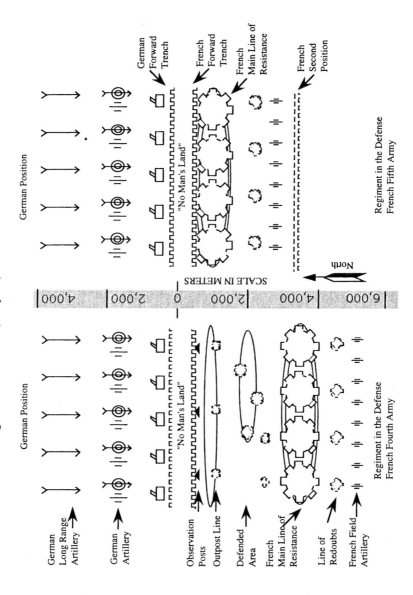

position. This allowed the French field pieces to reach four or more kilometers deep into the German position. In the 4th Army, however, the bulk of the field artillery was placed behind the main line of resistance. Thus, most French field guns were five or more kilometers from no-man's-land.

The cost of this new pattern of deployment was reduced effect against the German trenches. Very few field pieces could fire at targets further than a kilometer or so behind the German front lines. The benefit was that most French field pieces were now beyond the range of most German light field guns and field howitzers. The distance between the French field guns and the German balloon observers, ground observers, and sound and flash range detachments was now significantly greater than it had been before. Better yet, there was a good chance of two or three low ridge lines separating the French guns from the German counterbattery organization.[37]

Needless to say, had the Germans learned of this technique, they might have adjusted their own tactics accordingly. At the very least, they would have focused their bombardment on the main line of resistance rather than the forward line.[38] The success of the French defense, therefore, depended on convincing the Germans that the French 4h Army was conducting business as usual. That is, that the French would prefer, as they had for almost four years of trench warfare, to lose both men and guns rather than voluntarily give up territory.

Much of the work of keeping up appearances fell to a handful of French artillery units. While many batteries that had been located behind the forwardmost French line, as well as new batteries brought in from other areas, were being relocated to positions on or behind the new main line of resistance, the pieces that remained in the forward areas had to keep up a normal volume of harassing fire, fire in support of trench raids, and "revenge" fire in response to enemy raids. To fool the German sound and flash ranging detachments, these pieces (singly, in pairs, or as full batteries) would move between firing positions, making sure to fire from every abandoned battery position.[39]

A second key element of the French deception plan was to continue manning the front trenches as if their tactics had not changed. This, though easy enough to set in motion, placed two important limitations on the French. First, they had to have sufficient warning of a German attack to pull their infantry out of the front-line trenches before the German bombardment began. Second, the main line of resistance would have to be close enough to the front line so that the bulk of the infantry could be warned of the impending attack, pulled out of the front line, moved to the main line of resistance, and, in case the alarm was a false one, returned to the front line in the course of a single night. It was this second requirement that prevented the French from carrying out their original plan of placing the main line of resistance beyond the range of the German field artillery.[40]

As it turned out, this policy was well worth the trouble. While the dispositions of their infantry remained secret until the Germans overran the forward trenches, the French had not been able to hide the rearward shift of their artillery. German aviators, balloonists, sound and flash units, interrogators, and spies were well aware of the tendency for French artillery units in the Reims area to be located further to the rear than was usual. Fortunately for the French, the Germans did not see this movement as a symptom of a larger change in defensive tactics. The German reponse was thus limited to moving some of their longer-range guns (100mm heavy guns and model 1916 extended-range 77mm field guns) closer to the French lines.[41]

Advance warning of the German attack at Reims came from the French strategic intelligence service and the fact that routine harassing fire had hit (with spectacular results) some German ammunition dumps.[42] On July 7, 1918, General Henri Gouraud, the one-armed commanding general of the French 4th Army, issued an order of the day warning his troops of the impending attack, reminding them of their duty, and exhorting them to stand fast. This attack never materialized. At eight PM on July 14, a French raiding party returned with twenty-six German prisoners and the news that the German bombardment would begin at ten minutes past midnight on the morning of July 15; the assault troops would leave their jumping-off positions four hours and twenty minutes later.[43]

General Gouraud's response to this was to order the "counterprepara-tion."[44] At 11:30 PM, all of his batteries, including the ones that had remained both silent and hidden from view, went into action. For forty minutes the French shells fell on the forward German positions, while General Gouraud wondered whether the German attack had indeed been scheduled for that morning or if he had "shot his bolt" for little gain. At ten minutes past midnight, the German bombardment began.[45] Among the first salvos was a shell from a long-range heavy gun that hit the power station supplying Gouraud's command post with electricity. Despite the darkness, Gouraud was elated. His bet had paid off. "Never," he confided to his chief of staff, "has a cannon shot given me so much pleasure."[46]

As might be expected from fire that came from over 300 batteries on a front of over 50 kilometers, the effects of the French counterpreparation varied. Some divisions suffered heavily. Others were hardly touched. The most spectacular casualties were the handful of German munitions depots that blew up.[47] Less evident, from the point of view of observation posts, was the impact that the French fire had on German morale. Experienced soldiers of all ranks no doubt could tell, merely from the scale of the bombardment, that it was something other than routine harassing fire. From that knowledge it was but a single logical step to the realization that, instead of the Germans surprising the French, it was the French who were surprising the Germans.[48]

Perhaps the greatest damage to the attackers was done by the fire that fell on the jumping-off positions of the German infantry. In previous offensives, these forward trenches a few score meters from the enemy front line had provided a relatively safe haven for the German infantry. The closer they were to the enemy, after all, the less the chance that the enemy would risk firing the kind of intense, large-caliber bombardment that would do the most damage. East of Reims, however, the French front-line trenches were empty. As a result, the French bombardment was uninhibited by fear of losses from friendly fire.[49]

The effectiveness of the French counterpreparation was matched by the ineffectiveness of the German bombardment. The bombs of the trench mortars assigned to the closest French targets fell on empty trenches. The gas and high-explosive shells fired by the field guns and heavier pieces assigned to counterbattery duties exploded on battery positions that had long been vacated. (The wind was such that, in some sectors, more of the gas may have been breathed by the advancing Germans than the evacuating French.) The point targets to be destroyed by the fire of siege mortars were likewise abandoned.[50]

At 3:50 AM, the focus of effort of the German artillery switched from the counterbattery effort to the rolling barrage. At first this great curtain of fire, moving at its preset rate, seemed to be doing its job. The German infantry certainly had little difficulty breaking into the first French trenches. Once there, however, they found themselves faced with an uncomfortable dilemma. If they used the trenches for shelter, they had to deal with the mustard gas that had been left in the dugouts and the barbed wire obstacles blocking the communications trenches. If, however, they moved in the open, they were vulnerable to the French artillery fire, which grew stronger with every step forward that the Germans took.[51]

Beyond the first line of trenches, the Germans ran into the French line of outposts. The chief achievement of this thinly manned barrier was to separate the German infantry from their protective barrage. As the German infantry regiments used their ample firepower—platoons of infantry guns, batteries of accompanying field guns, light trench mortars, grenade launchers, machine guns, and, in a few lucky units, flame-throwers—to reduce the French strong points, the barrage moved on at its customary rate. As a result, the firepower designed to be a supplement to the rolling barrage became the chief source of fire support for the attacking Germans.[52]

The Germans encountered more of the same among the larger strong points of the defended area. Because of this, many German units failed to reach the French main line of resistance until after 8:30 AM, a full hour behind schedule. Between that time and noon, they launched a number of local attempts to storm, without the help of significant amounts of friendly artillery fire, the French main line of resistance. The results were predictable.[53]

Even with the new infiltration tactics that maximized the power of small units while minimizing exposure to enemy fire, the German attackers were fighting at an extreme disadvantage. Subject to the full power of the French artillery, as well the fire of trench mortars, machine guns, grenade launchers, and automatic rifles, they were nonetheless able to take some of the bunkers, dugouts, and stretches of trench that made up the French position. An immediate breakthrough, however, was out of the question.

As each hour passed, the German units—both infantry and artillery—that had been held in reserve to exploit the initial breakthrough moved closer to the French position. As they did, they took increasingly greater losses from the fire of the French artillery. These losses were magnified by the fact that the exploitation troops, expecting the path ahead of them to be relatively clear, often moved forward in closely packed march formations.[54]

After the failure of the initial attacks against the French main line of resistance, the Germans pulled back a few score meters and began to dig in. The German army commanders resolved to renew the attack around noon. The bombardment that preceded this attack, however, was fired by only a small portion of the German artillery; the attacking infantry was much depleted by a combat-filled morning. Faced with an intact French defensive system and a defensive barrage composed of shells fired from almost every French gun in the 4h Army's zone, this second attack failed to make any progress.[55]

A third attack, set for 7:00 PM, was preempted by a French counterattack. Though this attained little more than local success, it seems to have convinced the German authorities that their attack east of Reims had ended. A few German troops continued to move forward. Their task, however, was not to give fresh impetus to the attack but to begin transforming the hastily dug German trenches into a proper defensive system.

West of Reims, the German attack against the French 5th Army made a great deal of progress. Thanks to the combination of a Bruchmüller bombardment and infiltration tactics, they quickly broke through the French main line of resistance, wreaked havoc among the French battery positions, and threatened to turn their tactical victory into an operational one. The success of the 4th Army was so complete, however, that all Allied reserve divisions in the area could be focused against this threat. Consequently, the French not only were able to reestablish a strong defensive line behind the one that had collapsed but also had sufficient forces to launch a strong counterattack against the right flank of the attacking German 7th Army.[56]

This was the beginning of the first of the great Allied offensives that, five months later, would result in the German High Command's decision to sue for peace. Three days after the beginning of the German offensive at Reims, the French and Americans were attacking throughout the region. A few days later, the forces of the British Empire joined in what was now clearly a general offensive aimed at depriving the Germans of any chance of resuming their attacks.

In previous years, the Germans, who had proved themselves masters of mobile war in Russia, Romania, Serbia, and Italy, would have profited from such a return to mobile warfare. By the summer of 1918, however, the German armies were in no position to take advantage of the opportunity offered to them. Poor rations, influenza, poor-quality recruits, and dissatisfaction in the ranks, as well as an officer corps so depleted that most companies were commanded by reserve second lieutenants, robbed the German armies of the moral and material qualities that had made them so formidable four years earlier.

From the point of view of the artillery, the greatest obstacle to success in the open field was lack of horses. Even before the Reims battle, some batteries were so short of horses that they could not move all of their pieces at the same time.[57] None were in any position to provide teams to pull the extra field guns and light field howitzers that allowed many units to return to the peacetime standard of six field pieces per battery.[58]

Motor transport failed to provide much relief. French and German experiments with fully motorized artillery units led both sides to conclude that any field piece pulled by or carried in a World War I-era truck was completely road-bound. The Germans, moreover, could count on the services of far fewer trucks and drivers than the Western allies, and therefore had to satisfy themselves with six fully motorized field artillery regiments supplemented by the occasional motorized heavy battery.[59]

Whether the fault was lack of traction or lack of will, the German Army stopped fighting on November 11, 1918. When they did, they gave both themselves and their erstwhile enemies an opportunity to examine what had been learned in the past four years. As might be expected, the conclusions reached had as much to do with who was doing the looking as the facts that were being looked at.

NOTES

1. Bruchmüller wrote two books, *Die Artillerie beim Angriff im Stellungskrieg* (Charlottenberg: Verlag "Offene Worte," 1926) and *Die deutsche Artillerie in den Durchbruchschlachten des Weltkrieges* (2nd ed., Berlin: E. S. Mittler und Sohn, 1922).

2. Bruchmüller, *Die Artillerie*, pp. 15–19, 41–42.

3. For more on the battle of Lake Narocz, see Norman Stone, *The Eastern Front 1914–1917* (New York: Charles Scribner's Sons, 1975), pp. 230–31.

4. For a description of the battle of Riga, see Bruce Gudmundsson, *Storm Troop Tactics* (New York: Praeger, 1989), pp. 114–21.

5. Bruchmüller, *Die deutsche Artillerie*, pp. v, vi.

6. Max Hofmann, *The War of Lost Opportunities* (London: Kegan Paul, 1924), p. 135.

7. Bruchmüller, *Die deutsche Artillerie*, pp. 44–48.

8. Hoffmann, *The War of Lost Opportunities*, p. 135.

9. Ferdinand Meier, "Die Artillerie des Kgl. Bayer. I. A.K. bei der Juli-Offensive 1918," *Der K. B. Feld-Artillerist*, 1936, no. 7–8, 75, 88.

10. Cron, *Geschichte des deutschen Heeres im Weltkriege 1914–1918*, p. 159.

11. German "floating" headquarters were not restricted to artillery. Pioneer regimental staffs were occasionally used to coordinate the work of two or more pioneer battalions. As the war progressed, corps staffs, and to a lesser extent division staffs, were separated from their commands and used as the framework for new formations.

12. Divisional artillery commanders had evolved from the artillery brigade commanders of the first two and a half years of the war. The fourth divisional artillery commander was from an infantry division not engaged in the battle.

13. This example, ironically, is taken from the failed German attack east of Reims on July 15, 1918, the only Bruchmüller supported attack that failed to achieve tactical success. Other Bruchmüller attacks were organized in a very similar way. For details, see Bruchmüller, *Die Artillerie*, passim.

14. Meier, "Die Artillerie des Kgl. Bayer. I. A.K.," p. 75. As a rule, the command of the *Aka* was given to the artillery commander of the *Stellungsdivision*, the division in the attacking corps that had been in position before the assault divisions arrived on the scene. For Bruchmüller's extensive justification of this arrangement, see *Die deutsche Artillerie*, pp. 59–66.

15. Regimental and battalion staffs not placed in command of groupments or subgroupments were given various administrative tasks. One regimental headquarters was given the task of supervising ammunition supply. Two battalion headquarters were put in charge of salvage—making the most of leftover ammunition and spent shell

casings at emplacements once a battery had moved forward. Meier, "Die Artillerie des Kgl. Bayer. I. A.K., p. 75.

16. Ibid.

17. Ibid.

18. Ibid., p. 88. For a brief discussion of German gas shells, see Gudmundsson, *Storm Troop Tactics*, pp. 102–03.

19. This preparation was uniform for all corps of all three armies participating in the attack. Germany, Heer, Headquarters 7th Army, Ia—Chief of Artillery, no. 435–18, "Artillery Orders no. 3," dated June 26, 1918, document no. 128-A in U.S. Army, General Service Schools, *The German Offensive of July 15, 1918 (Marne Source Book)* (Fort Leavenworth, KS: General Service Schools Press, 1923).

20. Meier, "Die Artillerie des Kgl. Bayer. I. A.K.," p. 88.

21. Ibid.

22. Ibid.

23. Ibid.

24. Ibid.

25. Ibid.

26. Ibid., p. 90.

27. Ibid.

28. Germany, Heer, Headquarters, 1st Army, Ia., no. 3060, "Instructions for Employment of Artillery in the Ensuing Battles," dated July 14, 1918, document no. 324 in U.S. Army, General Service Schools, *The German Offensive of July 15, 1918*, pp. 417–18.

29. For more on the infantry side of this equation, see Gudmundsson, *Storm Troop Tactics*, passim; Martin Samuels, *Doctrine and Dogma: German and British Infantry Tactics in the First World War* (Westport, CT: Greenwood Press, 1992), passim.

30. There is no evidence in Bruchmüller's books that he actually aimed at such an outcome. Nonetheless, if the substantial British literature on the German attack that began on March 21, 1918, is to be believed and extended to the other Bruchmüller-supported offensives, confusion was a common response, particularly in the rear areas. See, among others, Martin Middlebook, *The Kaiser's Battle, 21 March, 1918* (London: Allen Lane, 1978); G. MacLeod Ross, "The Death of a Division, the 39th Division in March, 1918," *The Fighting Forces*, Apr. 1930; and G. E. Milward, "Memories of Cambrai and the German Counter-Offensive in March, 1918," *Journal of the Royal Artillery*, March 1985.

31. These tactical breakthroughs' failure to lead to victories of strategic significance was the fault of neither the new German infantry tactics nor Bruchmüller's system, but of the inability of the German armies rapidly to exploit the great holes that they had ripped in the Allied lines. See the "Conclusion" to Gudmundsson, *Storm Troop Tactics*, for a detailed explanation of this phenomenon.

32. Great Britain, Army General Staff, "Notes on Recent Fighting—No. 18," July 23, 1918. The British "Notes on Recent Fighting" were widely circulated and can be found in a number of libraries and archives, including the research library at the Carlisle Barracks in Carlisle, Pennsylvania, the Marine Corps Research Center in Quantico, Virginia, and the U.S. National Archives in Washington.

33. Great Britain, Army General Staff, "Notes on Recent Fighting—No. 18a," August 8, 1918.

34. In most cases, the task of breaking up the attacking German infantry formations required that these outposts be held at all costs. R. H. Lewis, trans., "Employment of the Artillery in the Defensive," *Field Artillery Journal* 10, no. 2 (Mar.–Apr. 1920): 120–21.

35. For more on this concept of mutual defense, see "Enfilade Fire," *Tactical Notebook*, Nov. 1991. This article was reprinted in the June 1992 issue of *Strategy and Tactics*.

36. C. Asplin, "Surprise in Defense, the Battle of Reims, 15th July, 1918," *Fighting Forces*, April 1939, p. 63.

37. This was, of course, a peculiarity of the terrain east of Reims. For a description of the ground, see Douglas Johnson, *Battlefields of the World War, Western and Southern Fronts: A Study in Military Geography* (New York: Oxford University Press, 1921), pp. 254–55.

38. Given the German habit of relying on *Minenwerfer* to bombard the forwardmost enemy trenches, this would probably require the replacement of a large number of those short-range weapons with heavy field howitzers. For more on the ranges of World War I artillery pieces and their effect on employment, see "Ranges of World War I Artillery," *Tactical Notebook*, Sept. 1992.

39. R. H. Lewis, translator, "Employment of the Artillery in the Defensive," p. 117.

40. Asplin, "Surprise in Defense," p. 60.

41. Meier, "Die Artillerie des Kgl. Bayer. I. A.K.," p. 91.

42. The story of the role played by the French strategic intelligence services is detailed in L. de Cointet, "Le Service des renseignements au G.Q.G. français du 13 juin au 15 juillet 1918," *Revue historique de l'armée*, spec. no. (1968): 27–40.

43. Ph. Gouraud, "La Victorie de Champagne de juillet, 1918," *Revue historique de l'armée*, spec. no. (1968): 65.

44. Technically, this was the interdiction phase of a series of phases that included a number of separate counterpreparations and dispositions. For details, see R. H. Lewis, trans., "Employment of the Artillery in the Defensive," passim.

45. The times given are French. German times were one hour later.

46. Gouraud, "La Victoire de Champagne," p. 66.

47. O. Meienborn and K. Probst, *Infanterie Regiment Nr. 466* (Oldenburg: G. Stalling, 1925), p. 140. At least some of the German munitions depots had been identified prior to the battle. Heinz von Bomhard, "Der 15. Juli 1918 beim Gegner," *Der K. B. Feld-Artillerist* no. 11 (Nov. 1931): 181.

48. Asplin, "Surprise in Defense," pp. 73–74. For the effect of the counterpreparation on a battle-hardened German artillery officer, see Herbert Sulzbach, *Zwei Lebende Mauern, 50 Monate Westfront* (Berlin: Verlag Bernard und Graefe, 1935), pp. 197–99.

49. Asplin, "Surprise in Defense," p. 74.

50. Ibid.; Meier, "Die Artillerie des Kgl. Bayer. I. A.K.," p. 91; and Meienborn and Probst, *Infanterie Regiment Nr. 466*, p. 141.

51. Ibid.

52. Because of the difficulties encountered in moving them over the heavily shelled ground, even these heavy weapons were sometimes in short supply. Asplin, "Surprise in Defense," pp. 74–75; and Meienborn and Probst, *Infanterie Regiment Nr. 466*, p. 141.

53. Asplin, "Surprise in Defense," pp. 74–75; and Meienborn and Probst, *Infanterie Regiment Nr. 466*, p. 142.

54. Asplin, Surprise in Defense," p. 74; and Meier, "Die Artillerie des Kgl. Bayer. I. A.K.," p. 91.

55. Meier, "Die Artillerie des Kgl. Bayer. I. A.K.," p. 91. Some German infantry units in a position to attack did not. While the author whose article provided both the bulk of the information and the original inspiration for this chapter ascribes this to the failure of

orders to get forward, it is possible that some German units were so depleted that their leaders declined to participate in what was clearly a futile gesture. Asplin, "Surprise in Defense," pp. 75–76.

56. Asplin, "Surprise in Defense," pp. 76–77.

57. See, for example, Walter Luyken, *Das 2. Garde-Feldartillerie Regiment in Weltkriege* (Berlin: Wilhelm Kolk, 1929, pp. 220–21.

58. Meier, "Die Artillerie des Kgl. Bayer. I. A.K.," p. 77; Duffour, "Extract from the Battle of France in 1918," in U.S. Army, General Service Schools, *The German Offensive of July 15, 1918*, p. 440; and Bruchmüller, *Die deutsche Artillerie*, p. 32.

59. Meier, "Die Artillerie des Kgl. Bayer. I. A.K.," p. 77; and R. H. Lewis, trans., "Employment of the Artillery in the Defensive," p. 119.

7

From One War to Another

One of the few propositions that most survivors of World War I could agree upon was that the conflict had been dominated by heavy artillery. When it came to deciding whether that dominance would reassert itself in the next war, however, the consensus broke down. Some saw the model for the future in the great artillery battles of 1918. Others took the opposite view, arguing that trench warfare had been an anomaly and that, as a result, the future of artillery belonged to light field guns moving in the company of hard-marching infantry and horse cavalry. Still others took a third view that saw heavy and light artillery, systematic bombardment and improvised exploitation, not as opposites but as complementary parts of the same system.

Of all the major powers to survive World War I, the French were the most satisfied with their artillery park. As a result, the artillery force they fielded in 1939 differed little from that of 1918: the only major changes were a slight increase in the use of trucks to pull or carry field pieces, the introduction of radio as a supplementary means of communication, and the replacement of some of the older heavy pieces with modern 105mm guns and howitzers. The basic organization of the division artillery—a light regiment of three battalions of 75mm guns and a heavy regiment of two battalions of 155mm (model 1917) howitzers—remained unaltered. Likewise, the artillery at the disposal of higher echelons changed little in the twenty years that separated the two world wars.[1]

The constrained fiscal environment of the 1920s and 1930s provides one explanation for French conservatism with regard to new guns and howitzers. Another was the fact that the artillery pieces on hand in November 1918 were, for the most part, less than a year or two old and had only recently displaced the weapons of the de Bange era that had provided the bulk of the French heavy artillery for most of the war.[2] The chief factor, however, in the continued French fondness for the weapons that were seen to have brought them victory was doctrine. The French military establishment spent the interwar period convinced that it had found, in the methodical attacks of 1918, the formula for slow but sure victory in the next war. Consequently, they never developed any sustained interest in weapons that had not been present at the creation of this formula.[3]

The French Army thus retained, throughout the interwar period and into the first year of World War II, a standard divisional artillery consisting of two regiments. The light regiment, lineal descendant of the original divisional field artillery regiment, consisted of four (later reduced to three) battalions of twelve 75mm field guns each. The heavy regiment had two battalions of twelve 155mm howitzers, usually of the improved model that had been introduced in 1917. Corps artillery consisted of a heavy regiment of four battalions, two of 105mm guns and two of 155mm guns. In many cases, these artillery organizations would be reinforced by battalions (with weapons ranging from 75mm field guns to 220mm howitzers) belonging to a central pool known as the Réserve Générale d'Artillerie.[4]

The Réserve Générale d'Artillerie had two functions, one strategic and the other more mundane. At the national level, it was one of the major means by which the French *général en chef* could concentrate the resources of the French Republic against a particular portion of the front. So that this movement could be done with rapidity, the bulk of the units assigned to this reserve were motorized. For operations of lesser significance, battalions belonging to the Réserve Générale d'Artillerie could be detached for assignment to particular divisions or army corps.[5]

As had been the case during the last two years of World War I, the battalions of the Réserve Générale d'Artillerie tended to be motorized. This was a response not merely to a shortage of horses and fodder but also to the need to move these units between far-flung battlefields on France's excellent network of paved roads. Because of this emphasis on strategic mobility, many of the motorized units (known as *artillerie tractée*) were provided with vehicles with very little cross-country mobility. A few of the lighter units, particularly 75mm field gun regiments, were provided both with trucks (for fast movement on roads) and small tractors (including, at mobilization, many requisitioned agricultural vehicles). These latter units carried both field pieces and tractors on the back of trucks, leading to their designation as *artillerie portée*.[6]

The model that the French Army of the interwar period chose for its "artillery battle of the future" was not the artillery ambush that had proved so useful at Reims. Instead, the French decided to study, praise, and emulate the battles in which, after two years of trying, the formula of "artillery conquers, infantry occupies" was finally made to work. The first of these battles (an attack by the 1st Army in Flanders) took place in the summer of 1916; the last, in the fall of 1918. The two definitive elements were very long, very methodical bombardments by unprecedented numbers of artillery pieces and the abandonment of any hope of exploiting the attack for purposes beyond the seizure of terrain, the attraction of reserves from other sectors, and the wearing down of the enemy.[7]

The slogan for this technique, often repeated in the interwar period, was "maneuver of fire" (*manoeuvre de feu*). The image evoked was of a modern "scientific" commander manipulating groups of explosions, as Napoleon or Frederick the Great might have maneuvered battalions of grenadiers. The reality was more prosaic. While the French artillery got very good at developing fire-control techniques that allowed batteries to shift their fire quickly from one target to another, the technical characteristics of their field pieces as well as the hierarchical nature of their command and control system limited the rapid shifting of fire to targets within a "fire fan" so narrow that it might better be described as a "fire sliver."[8]

To speed things up, the French Army introduced what would soon be recognized as a seminal development, the *poste central du groupe*. This was a small headquarters subordinate to the battalion commander that relieved batteries of much of the work of transforming tactical orders into technical reality. That is, rather than telling batteries what outcome was desired on a particular piece of the battlefield, the officer in charge of the *poste central du groupe* calculated firing data for all three of the batteries in his battalion.[9]

Like many innovations from this period, the *poste central du groupe* was a product of what the French called "*le Taylorisme*." Named for the American efficiency expert Frederick W. Taylor, this was, on both sides of the Atlantic, a systematic attempt to reduce the "waste" in routine operations by replacing dependence on the judgment of workers with standard procedures based on a thorough, scientific study of every detail of an operation. In the case of the *poste central du groupe*, the workers whose judgment was replaced by standard procedures were the battery commanders, who became less like the artisans of traditional French industry and more like the middle managers of an early-twentieth-century American corporation.

The great advantage of the *poste central du groupe* was that it allowed French battalions to mass the fires of their three batteries quickly on a single target. Assuming that the batteries had registered their guns on a common aiming point, the fire of all twelve pieces was brought to bear simultaneously. Compared with a traditional fire mission, where each battery registered in turn, this method promised to provide the kind of surprise and psychological impact that hitherto had been achievable only through timetables and other time-consuming coordination measures. The great disadvantage of the system was that it took battery commanders "out of the loop." No longer were they actors on the tactical stage. Instead, they were reduced to the level of technicians or even bureaucrats, blindly responding to the data provided to them by a voice on the other end of a telephone line.[10]

At a time when new weapons such as infantry tanks, 60mm and 81mm infantry mortars, and antitank guns had completely taken over the role of accompanying artillery, one of the results of this trend toward the centralization of fire control was to ensure that the physical and organizational separation between the infantry and field artillery that had begun with the "great divorce" of World War I would continue. As before, one of the chief casualties of this divorce was the tempo of operations, as progress of the infantry was deliberately kept to a snail's pace in order to allow time for high-level headquarters to coordinate the next move.

While the Germans of the interwar period were also hard at work developing techniques for quickly massing the fire of battalions and even larger artillery units, their experience, taken as a whole, was quite different. The men who created the *Reichswehr* were well aware that, thanks to the Treaty of Versailles, they lacked the means to fight a second World War I. They also followed a deliberate policy of trying to restore in the postwar German Army the virtues that had characterized the companies, squadrons, and batteries that had served the Kaiser. These two factors, combined with the fact that the biggest field piece permitted the *Reichswehr* was a 105mm light field howitzer, served to re-create the battery-oriented world of the prewar German field artillery. As before, the chief characteristics of this world were an emphasis on the authority of the battery commander, an interest in the maneuver of artillery units (as opposed to the movement of their fire), and a belief that the action of artillery would be part of a larger campaign in which rapid movement would be the rule.[11]

The rearmament of Germany following Hitler's seizure of power in 1933 saw a partial reversal of this trend. The repudiation of the Treaty of

Versailles restored heavy artillery to the German arsenal. The National Socialist love affair with the internal combustion engine promised a means of moving the new heavy pieces both to and on the battlefield. Finally, the great expansion of the German Army provided the means for fighting campaigns that were more than national delaying actions. The result was a new artillery organization, based on many of the ideas developed in World War I but otherwise completely reformed.[12]

The first casualty of this reformation was the shrapnel shell. The experience of World War I had shown, at least to the satisfaction of the German authorities, that shrapnel was inferior to high explosives for attacking troops under cover. Subsequent improvements in the design of high-explosive shells put the last nails into the coffin of the shrapnel shell by providing, in the form of more efficient splintering, a reasonable imitation of the sawed-off shotgun effect. While it would take the introduction of electronic variable-time fuses to improve on the terminal effect of properly fused shrapnel against troops in the open, the splintering effect of the improved high-explosive shells was good enough to make them the new *Einheitsgeschoß* of the German field artillery.[13]

Hard on the heels of the shrapnel shell was the weapon that had been built to fire it, the light field gun. Although there were many attempts to design a weapon that could serve as an all-purpose (antitank gun, field piece, and even antiaircraft gun) divisional cannon, the German authorities finally decided that the weight of explosive (and consequent splinter effect) needed for effective field artillery work was incompatible with the high muzzle velocity needed by a true antitank or antiaircraft gun. The German Army therefore ended up with an improved 105mm howitzer as the standard light field piece.[14]

Largely because of an anticipated shortage of gasoline, the German Army decided to retain horses as the principal means of pulling the 105mm howitzers. The only motorized artillery units were those too heavy to be efficiently pulled by horses (some 150mm howitzers, 100mm and 150mm guns, and 210mm howitzers) or those assigned to motorized or armored divisions. In contrast to the French, the German motorized artillery was provided with cross-country vehicles. This not only reflected the poor quality of roads on Germany's eastern borders but also facilitated the rapid deployment of heavy artillery units during fast-moving operations.

Like the French, the Germans of the interwar period had concluded that divisions needed heavy artillery in the form of a heavy field howitzer. This they provided in the form of a 150mm howitzer similar to, but much lighter than, the 150mm howitzers that had done such effective work in World

War I. Nondivisional heavy artillery was to take the form of 100mm guns, 210mm howitzers, and 150mm guns—all of which were improved versions of weapons familiar to German artillerists of the previous conflicts. Indeed, the chief modifications to German heavy artillery were the far greater use of motor transport to move it and the fact that, regardless of the caliber of the piece they served, all German artillerymen now belonged to the same branch.

If the numbering scheme of regiments is any guide, the German plan on the eve of World War II seems to have been to give each infantry division a divisional artillery of two regiments, one light and one heavy. The light regiment was to consist of three battalions of 105mm light howitzers, and the heavy regiment was to have two battalions of 150mm heavy howitzers. Given that each battallion was to consist of three batteries of four pieces each, there was a superficial resemblance to the French divisional artillery organization of the time. The provision of a single officer (the *Artilleriekommandeur* or *Arko*) with a small staff to command both regiments also resembled contemporary French practice.[15]

The resemblance broke down at the corps level. As had been the case for most of World War I, the German Army of the late 1930s had no corps artillery organization. Instead, any battalions not part of a division were kept in a general reserve, to be attached to armies, corps, and divisions as the situation dictated. When attached to divisions, these battalions could be attached to one of the regiments, subordinated to one of the battalions, or made directly answerable to the *Arko*. If a corps or army artillery needed to be improvised, it also could be commanded by an *Arko* who could be borrowed from a division or could be one of the "floating" *Arkos* that were provided for in the German tables of organization and regulations.[16]

To an even greater degree than the French infantry, the German infantry was well provided with "hip pocket" artillery of its own. Medium (81mm) mortars, 75mm and 150mm infantry guns, 37mm antitank guns capable of being used against bunkers and other point targets, and heavy machine guns equipped with long-range sights all contributed to the ability of the German infantry regiment to fight many of its battles with little or no outside help. Indeed, the only type of "hip pocket" artillery that the German infantry lacked was the infantry tank, the heavily armored "moving pillboxes" that played such an important part in French armored doctrine of the time. Given the generosity with which other infantry heavy weapons were supplied and the aggressive way they were used, the lack of these weapons seems not to have done much damage to the German infantry of the first half of World War II.

Despite this independence, the German infantry and artillery suffered much less than their French counterparts from the effects of the "great divorce." If the anecdotes from the 1939, 1940, and 1941 campaigns published in the German military press of the time are representative, German battery and battalion commanders were both willing and able to push their commands far forward and work directly with infantry battalions and regiments. While incidents where direct fire was used seem to have been the exception rather than the rule, cooperation, even during operations conducted at a very high tempo, seems to have been both close and flexible.[17]

Some of the credit for this belongs to the revival of the "horsey" tradition of the German field artillery during the 1920s and early 1930s. Part belongs to the increasing tendency for battery commanders to serve as their own forward observers, commanding either from forward observation posts capable of directly observing the infantry battle or, when this was not practical, moving as far forward as the most forward infantrymen. The bulk of the credit, however, must be laid at the feet of the organizational culture of the German Army. While not entirely immune to the siren song of Taylorism, the relationships among members (particularly officers) and between members and the organization as a whole were ones of voluntary cooperation rather than formal adherence to explicit rules.

This is not to say that the German Army of 1939 (or, for that matter, of 1914) was a utopian collective inhabited by "new socialist men," a sort of commune full of free spirits in jackboots. Its adherence to the form and substance of traditional military discipline was as strong as that of any contemporary army. What distinguished it from most other forces, and in particular from the French Army of the time, was the source of discipline. For most soldiers, discipline is something imposed from above, the bending of the individual will so that actions might conform not so much to the will as to the words of superior officers. For the Germans, the source of discipline was battle itself.

The implications of this difference were many. For the German artillery, it meant that batteries could have their cake and eat it too. In fast-moving situations, individual batteries could follow in the wake of the infantry to provide a small volume of very responsive fire. When things slowed down a bit, the batteries reformed into their battalions, battalions that were well drilled in a variety of techniques for massing the fire of their own batteries or combining their fire with that of other battalions. In the case of very heavy resistance, battalions and regiments could be formed into large groupments under the command of *Arkos*. These latter virtuosos could then, playing the role made famous by Georg Bruchmüller, orchestrate the kind of systematic bombardment needed to break through the resistance and restore a situation in which the batteries were, once again, on their own.

The virtues of the German artillery organization were made plain in the invasion of Poland that began in September 1939. In fast-moving situations, the German light batteries managed, despite poor roads that made many older German artillerymen nostalgic for the days of the light field gun, to keep up with the hard-marching infantry. The nature of most of the fighting in the campaign, which consisted largely of "retail" fighting to eliminate the many small groups of Poles who continued fighting long after all semblance of higher organization had disappeared, made this close cooperation particularly important. On those few occasions where Polish formations were able to put up coordinated resistance, the German ability to combine the fire of many batteries proved itself superior to the French-style fire control of the Polish artillery.[18]

The true cost of the French approach to artillery command and control was less evident at the tactical level than at the operational. For while it may have been less efficient on the battlefield, the slowing down of entire divisions, corps, and armies to permit it to function had a profound effect on campaigns. In particular, it hobbled the attempts of the French Army to come to the aid of Poland in September 1939 by launching, in accordance with an agreement drawn up between the French and Polish general staffs in May 1939 and French contingency plans written in July 1939, an invasion of Germany.[19]

The jumping-off point for the invasion was the valley of the Sarre (Saar) River, a convenient piece of reasonably trafficable terrain between neutral Luxembourg and mountainous Alsace. The target was Hamburg. The means of doing harm to the Germans was to be the methodical advance of thirty-odd divisions divided among the three armies of the 2nd Army Group.

The first phase of the Sarre offensive, as this operation soon came to be known, was the seizure of a portion of the no-man's-land between the Siegfried and Maginot lines. This was intended to serve as a means of protecting the right flank of formations conducting the next two phases of the attack.[20] At the end of these three phases, the French would have a base of operations from which their artillery could blast a hole through the Siegfried Line wide enough to permit the subsequent advance, in "bounds" of ten kilometers or less, toward the towns of Dillingen and Homburg, twenty kilometers behind the Siegfried line.

Given the relative strengths of the forces involved, this should not have proved difficult. Spread thinly behind the half-finished Siegfried Line, the

Germans had a few battalions of border guards, some antitank companies armed with obsolescent 37mm cannon unable to pierce the armor of the newer French tanks, and a handful of foot-mobile infantry divisions composed primarily of men considered too old or poorly trained to take part in a campaign of rapid maneuver.[21, 22]

The offensive, which was ordered on September 3, 1939, the day that France declared war, went well at first. Between September 4 and 12, units of General Gaston Prételat's 2nd Army Group leapfrogged slowly toward the Siegfried Line. Each division advanced in turn, its flanks secured by the presence of a neighboring division and its front covered by scores of 75mm field guns and dozens of 155mm howitzers in position to fire. In this way, some French divisions managed to advance eight kilometers in a single day. The force as a whole, however, crawled forward at a rate of one or two kilometers a day.

German resistance was light—most patrols fell back without firing on the French invaders. French casualties, mostly caused by land mines and booby traps, likewise was light. The chief determinant of the rate of advance was thus the French doctrine of methodical battle, a doctrine that subordinated all considerations to the ability to be able to protect, at all times, the entire infantry with a heavy curtain of artillery fire.

Sometime on September 10 or 11, the most forward French forces came into 155mm howitzer range of one of the forward outworks of the Siegfried Line. Eighty rounds were fired. No damage was detected.[23] At a time when the news from Poland gave little cause for hope, this was bad news for the French. The two chief assumptions upon which the Sarre offensive had been based—that German progress against Poland would be slow and that French progress through the Siegfried Line would be quick—had proved false. On September 12, the French High Command called off the offensive. On October 4, the French High Command, convinced of the danger of a German attack against the Maginot Line, ordered a complete withdrawal from the captured German territory.[24]

The French 2nd Army Group pulled out of Germany as it had entered. In the course of eleven days, the French units retreated cautiously, ensuring that at every moment their flanks were secure and that, until they reached the shelter of the Maginot Line, they remained under the protection of their own artillery. The Germans launched a few desultory attacks that did little to upset the French timetable. By October 14, the French 2nd Army Group was back in France. In six weeks, it had suffered about 1,800 casualties (killed, wounded, and prisoners).[25] It had failed, however, to keep a single German soldier out of Poland.

While the success of Germany's infantry divisions and corps and the failure of its French counterpart had much to do with the fall of Poland, the lion's share of the credit has been traditionally ascribed to Germany's armored divisions. These formed a veritable army within an army that, building on many of the traditions and concepts of its muscle-powered antecedents, fought a very different war with different tools and a much faster tempo of operations. In the years before the Polish campaign, when the German armored force was but a gleam in the eyes of its creators, there was much debate about what type of artillery, if any, these new organizations would need.

The two most prominent advance men for the phenomenon that we now know as blitzkrieg—J. F. C. Fuller and Basil Liddell-Hart—had experienced, firsthand, the failure of the British attempt to make artillery conquer so that infantry might occupy. Many in their audience had likewise seen the great battle of the Somme and similar fiascoes at very close range. It is thus not surprising that they often presented the tank as a weapon that would supplant, rather than serve alongside, the artillery piece.

The more complete versions of Fuller's and Liddell-Hart's visions for future warfare made provision for the retention of some forms of field and heavy artillery. Less radical than Fuller, Liddell-Hart favored field artillery that consisted primarily of self-propelled weapons whose chief (though not exclusive) projectile would release smoke. He did, however, contemplate the retention of a small proportion of towed artillery pieces in the field army.[26] Fuller, on the other hand, could imagine towed pieces being useful only to the besiegers of cities or extensively fortified areas. The guns and howitzers of the field army were to be self-propelled, with the former serving primarily as antitank weapons while the latter provided support. This support would consist primarily of firing smoke shells to blind the enemy and secondarily of shooting high explosives to deprive them of the cover afforded by built-up areas.[27]

The British tank enthusiasts were not alone in denigrating of the role that field artillery would play in armored warfare. On the other side of Europe, their German-language counterpart, the retired Austrian general Ludwig Ritter von Eimannsberger, came to essentially the same conclusions. In 1934, he published these conclusions in a book entitled *Tank Warfare (Kampfwagenkrieg)*.

Eimannsberger, born in 1878, had spent most of his professional life as an artillery officer in the service of the Hapsburg Empire. When that empire collapsed late in 1918, he entered the army of the Austrian Republic. If, however, *Tank Warfare* is any guide, the battles that fascinated him were not those involving the troops of the Double Monarchy but the great breakthrough battles of the western front of World War I. It was one of these battles, the British tank attack at Amiens on August 8, 1918, that provided the scenario for the operations of the ideal tank and motorized divisions that Eimannsberger designed.[28]

Both types of divisions were richly provided with what Eimannsberger called "infantry guns" (*Infanterie Kanone*): 47mm weapons capable of penetrating the armor of contemporary tanks as well as providing direct fire support for the infantry. Each battalion of motorized infantry or combat engineers had a company of six of these weapons. An additional regiment (nine companies of six guns each) or two of these guns was provided to each motorized infantry brigade. This resulted in a ratio of one company of 47mm antitank guns for each rifle company in the motorized division and four companies of 47mm antitank guns for each rifle company in the tank division.[29]

The generous allocation of antitank guns did not end with the infantry brigades. The artillery regiment of each division consisted of what might be called "triple purpose guns." (Eimannsberger called them *Tufkanone*, the word *Tuf* being an acronym for *Tank-und-Flieger*, "tank and aircraft"). These were 75mm towed guns mounted on cruciform platforms of the type later made famous by the German 88mm antiaircraft gun of World War II. With a 360° traverse and the ability to elevate the barrel to vertical angles close to 90°, these mounts allowed a high-velocity gun to be used against both tanks and aircraft. The gun crews and unit staffs were trained in field artillery procedures, making it possible to use the high-velocity guns as a partial substitute for traditional field artillery.[30]

The *Tuf* regiment of Eimannsberger's motorized division consisted of three battalions (of three batteries) of 75mm *Tuf* guns, one battalion of heavy (85 to 100mm) *Tuf* guns, and an observation detachment (*Beobachtungsabteilung*). The *Tuf* regiment of the tank division was smaller and more mobile. Lacking both the heavy battalion and the observation detachment, it had three 75mm *Tuf* battalions, one of which was equipped with guns on self-propelled, armored mounts.[31]

The *Tuf* regiment of the motorized division, with its observation detachment and heavy battalion, was marginally better prepared to provide massed indirect fire than the artillery regiment of the tank division. Both organizations, however, were designed to do most of their firing in the direct mode. Eimannsberger even went so far as to write that "the farther forward that they [the gun crews] go to fulfill their missions, the greater their honor."[32] Eimannsberger ended his discussion of the role of the artillery component of tank and motorized divisions by musing a bit about the merging of tanks and artillery into a single arm. The difference between a self-propelled gun optimized for direct fire against tanks and a tank provided with an antitank gun, after all, is often less than the difference between different types of tanks.

For a short period (culminating in the summer of 1942) the German expeditionary force in North Africa bore a striking resemblance to the formations described in the works of Fuller and Eimannsberger. The decisive arms of the opening battles of World War I—infantry and field artillery—all but disappeared. The infantry became so concerned about combating tanks that some infantry battalions had more antitank guns than the specialized antitank battalions. The field artillery was both greatly reduced in numbers and distracted from its now traditional mission of indirect fire by the additional task of serving as yet another means of combating tanks by direct fire. Indeed, as Fuller predicted, only the siege artillery retained any resemblance to its World War I counterpart.

The degree to which Fuller's ideas found concrete form in the Afrika Korps can perhaps best be illustrated by a detailed description of the mobile elements of the German 90th Light Division. From the time Rommel launched his 1942 offensive (in May) to the expansion of the formation after the fall of Tobruk (on June 21), the 90th Light Division consisted of seven truck-mobile battalions. Four of these were infantry battalions, two were antitank battalions, and one was a field artillery battalion.[33]

The four infantry battalions, described by the commanding general of the 90th Light Division as "entire arsenals," were expected to serve either as conventional motorized infantry or as antitank troops. For the former task they had a full complement of light machine guns, heavy machine guns, mortars, and infantry guns. For the latter duty, each squad was provided with one of the many 7.62cm field guns captured from the Russians in 1941.

A direct descendant of the Putilov guns of World War I, the Russian 7.62cm field gun had a high muzzle velocity, a flat trajectory, and a choice of projectiles. Firing an antitank shell, it was second only to the 88mm antiaircraft gun as a tank killer. Firing high explosives, it served as a first-class infantry gun and an only slightly obsolescent field gun. Indeed, it was a good enough antitank gun to equip one of the specialized antitank battalions of the 90th Light Division and a good enough field piece to arm the single field artillery battalion. (The second antitank battalion was provided with 50mm antitank guns of German manufacture). In other words, the 7.62cm field gun was the principal weapon of six of the seven combatant battalions of the 90th Light Division.

There remained, of course, substantial differences between the three types of unit in terms of armament, training, and organization. The infantry units retained a capacity to engage in close combat that the antitank and field artillery battalions never had. The field artillery battalion likewise retained some of its original character—it was the only unit with the means of organizing indirect fire.[34]

The degree to which the German authorities were pleased with this organization can be seen in the design for the only German formation "custom designed" (as opposed to cobbled together) for service in North Africa. This was the 164th Light Division, a motorized infantry outfit that was as richly supplied with antitank guns as either the 90th Light Division or the fantasy formations of Fuller and Eimannsberger. Its divisional artillery, however, consisted of a paltry five batteries—three of 105mm howitzers and two of 75mm mountain guns.[35]

In contrast to Eimannsberger and Fuller, the most influential German tank theorist of the interwar period, Heinz Guderian, believed that traditional field artillery had an important role to play in armored warfare. This opinion was based on two sets of insights. The first was prosaic. Guderian foresaw a number of tasks on the armored battlefield that could best be fulfilled by field artillery. The second bordered on the sublime. Retaining field artillery in the armored division fit in with Guderian's approach to military problems in general.

At the most basic level, Guderian thought that the motorized field artillery of an armored division would be employed to cooperate with the truck-borne infantry. It could fire smoke shells to blind enemy observers, interfere with the work of enemy antitank guns, and help tanks break contact. It might be used to attack enemy antitank guns and artillery positions with high explosives. It would be able to bombard villages, woods, reverse slopes, and other locations that might hide enemy forces. Finally, it could be used to isolate selected portions of the battlefield during attacks with limited objectives and similar undertakings.[36]

On a more philosophical plane, Guderian's belief that field artillery belonged in the armored division reflected his empirical approach to military theory. In contrast to those (like Fuller and Eimannsberger) who arrived at their opinions and designs by a process of deduction from a few key axioms, Guderian never forgot that he was involved in a practical business whose particulars were sufficiently complex to defy the most brilliant theories.

If, because of close terrain or artificial obstacles, the infantry of an armored division was attacking in front of the tanks of an armored division, the artillery support that they would need would differ little from the artillery support needed by other sorts of infantry. For this reason, the artillery component of divisions designed according to Guderian's ideas bore a closer resemblance to that of an infantry division than to that of divisions designed by Fuller or Eimannsberger. Indeed, the chief difference between the artillery regiment of a German armored division of the late 1930s and that of a German infantry division of the same period was that the artillery of the armored division was entirely motorized.[37]

If the detailed after-action report of the commander of one of the 105mm howitzer battalions of the 7th Panzer Division is any guide, life in the gasoline-powered German artillery of 1940 bore a close resemblance to that in the horse-drawn counterpart of 1914. In the course of a six-week campaign that took his battalion from Germany's border with Belgium to the Channel coast of France, this officer used, to say the least, a wide variety of techniques. He commanded the fire of masked batteries from high ground overlooking the Meuse, personally directed counter-battery fire from a pile of industrial refuse in a town near Lille, responded to calls for fire from an artillery liaison team attached to the motorized infantry of the division, and carried out an approach march of his battalion over open terrain by deploying in a wedge formation of the kind used by the German tanks of the time. From that formation, the battalion commander fought off an attack by British tanks (that thought that they were attacking German tanks) and destroyed fifteeen of them in the process. At another time, he organized a fire brigade consisting of four half-track prime movers pulling four 105mm howitzers to counter-attack against a group of French tanks.[38]

As if this repertoire was not sufficient, it was in this same division that General Rommel served as both commanding general and artillery forward observer. Riding in his command tank at the front of the main body of his division, he would often command, by radio message, that artillery fire (or, in some cases, bombs dropped by Stukas) be placed on certain points on the map. To eliminate the need for encoding these commands, he used a technique known as the thrust line—a line drawn between the same two landmarks on the maps of all parties concerned. Once established, the thrust line provided a reference by which any point on the map could be designated.[39]

NOTES

1. Robert A. Doughty, *Seeds of Disaster: The Development of French Army Doctrine, 1919–1939* (Hamden, CT: Archon, 1985), pp. 102–04. For a detailed treat-

ment of French divisional artillery of the interwar period, see "The French Infantry Division Artillery—the Light Artillery Regiment" and "The French Infantry Division Artillery—the Heavy Artillery Regiment," *Tactical Notebook*, March and April 1992.

2. For a detailed treatment of the process of replacing the de Bange weapons with newer pieces in the course of World War I, see Frédéric Hérr, *L'Artillerie* (Paris: Berger Levrault, 1924).

3. Doughty, *Seeds of Disaster*, provides a detailed treatment of the rationale for the doctrine of methodical battle, as well as the reasons that the French Army rejected the 105mm howitzer as the standard divisional piece.

4. This had begun, during World War I, as the Réserve Générale d'Artillerie Lourde (General Reserve of Heavy Artillery), but the inclusion of "spare" 75mm field gun regiments soon caused a change in nomenclature. Farsac, "Organisation de l'artillerie dans le corps d'armée," *Revue d'artillerie*, Oct. 1920, pp. 285–88.

5. Ibid., p. 286.

6. Toward the end of the 1930s, a few 75mm field gun and 105mm howitzer units were provided with cross-country vehicles. The 194mm G.P.F. and 155mm G.P.F.T. guns also had an all-terrain capability, the former by means of its caterpillar mount and prime mover and the latter by virtue of a cross-country truck. Stephane Ferrard, *Les Matériels de l'armée de terre française, 1940* (Paris: Charles-Lavauzelle, 1984), vol. 2, pp. 34–77.

7. Hérr, *L'Artillerie*, pp. 84–86.

8. The chief limit on the rapid shifting of fire of field guns and howitzers from one point to another was the difficulty of moving the trails of the guns. The British artillery of the time solved the problem by providing their 25-pounder field pieces with turntable mounts. Similar French turntable mounts were provided, at a rate of one per battery of 75mm field guns, only for antitank work.

9. I am unsure of the exact date of the introduction of the *poste central du groupe* in the French artillery. It is, however, associated with General Condé, who became inspector of artillery in 1934. Michel de Lombarès et al., *Historie de l'artillerie française*, (Paris: Lavauzelle, 1984), pp. 300–02.

10. For a detailed discussion of French fire-control techniques at the end of the interwar period, see O. Poydenot, "Fire Manoeuvre or the Application of Fire and Its Control in the French Artillery," trans. by T. G. G. Heywood, *Journal of the Royal Artillery*, Apr. 1938, pp. 76–89.

11. For an excellent, "present at the creation" view of the formation of the *Reichswehr*, see Ludwig Maercker, *Vom Kaiserheer zur Reichswehr* (Leipzig: R. F. Koehler, 1921). For a description of the *Reichswehr*'s operational doctrine, see James Sterling Corum, "The Reichswehr and the Concept of Mobile War in the Era of Hans von Seeckt" (Ph.D. diss., Queen's University, Kingston, Ontario, 1990).

12. From the very beginning, the *Reichswehr* had taken steps to preserve its heavy artillery knowledge base. See "Remarks on the Organization of the German Artillery," *Journal of the Royal Artillery*, Jan.–Feb. 1923, pp. 66–73. This is a translation of an article that had earlier appeared in *Revue d'artillerie*.

13. For an analysis of this question, see K. Fischer, "Neuzeitliche Artillerie—eine Schriftumsübersicht," *Wehrtechnische Monatshefte*, Feb. 1938, pp. 78–80.

14. Wilhelm Berlin and Huether, "Die Spitzenvertretung der Artillerie in der Obersten Führung des Heeres, 1938–1945. Ihre Aufgaben, Mittel, und Wirkungsmöglichkeiten," U.S. National Archives, Foreign Military Studies, Ms P-041, pp. 32–33.

15. During the first of the prewar expansions, the German Army formed a regiment of 105mm howitzers for each of its thirty-six infantry divisions. Each of these regiments bore the same number as its parent division. This done, the Germans began to form thirty-six regiments of 150mm howitzers, which were numbered by adding 36 to the division number. Rolf Hinze, *Die hannoversche Artillerie* (privately published by the author, 1977), vol. 1, pp. 34–35.

16. Germany, Oberkommando des Heeres, *Merkblatt für den Dienst im Stabe eines Artillerie-Kommandeurs* (Berlin: Ernst Siegfried Mittler und Sohn, 1938).

17. Many of these anecdotes, originally published in the *Militärwochenblatt* and the *Wehrwissenschaftliche Rundschau*, were translated and republished in the U.S. Army Command and General Staff College's *Military Review*.

18. Steven Zaloga and Victor Madej, *The Polish Campaign, 1939* (New York: Hippocrene, 1985), and the after-action reports of the following German units on file at the U.S. National Archives (Series T-78, Roll 861): Artillerie-Regiment 24, 17. Infanterie-Division; 23. Infanterie-Division; 24. Infanterie-Division; 27. Infanterie-Division; 31. Infanterie-Division.

19. Guy Rossi-Landi, *La Drôle de guerre. La Vie politique en France 2 septembre–10 mai 1940* (Paris: Armand Colin, 1971), p. 170.

20. To see how closely the operation followed the plan, compare the troop movements recounted in Henri Hiegel, *La Drôle de guerre en Moselle, 1939–1940* (Sarreguemines: Editions Pierron, 1983), pp. 225– 45 with map 8 in the back of that book.

21. For a description of the German units in the Sarre region, see ibid., pp. 220–21.

22. Ibid., p. 221.

23. Ibid., p. 225.

24. Ibid., p. 241.

25. Ibid., p. 235.

26. B. H. Liddell-Hart, *The Remaking of Modern Armies* (London: John Murray, 1927), pp. 22–23.

27. J. F. C. Fuller, *Armored Warfare* (Harrisburg, PA: Military Service Publishing, 1943), passim, esp. pp. 20–29. For a more complete view of the opinions of Fuller and Liddell-Hart, see Anthony John Trythall, *"Boney" Fuller: Soldier, Strategist, and Writer, 1878–1966* (Baltimore: Nautical and Aviation, 1989); Brian Holden Reid, *J. F. C. Fuller, Military Thinker* (New York: St. Martin's Press, 1987); and Brian Bond, *Liddell-Hart: A Study of His Military Thought* (London: Cassell, 1977).

28. For a detailed description of these divisions, see "The Unknown Prophet: General von Eimannsberger and the Panzer Division," *Tactical Notebook*, July and Aug. 1992.

29. Ludwig Ritter von Eimannsberger, *Kampfwagenkrieg* (Munich: J. F. Lehmans, 1934), pp. 160–67.

30. Ibid., pp. 134–36.

31. Ibid., pp. 160–67.

32. Ibid., p. 136.

33. Strictly speaking, this was not an expansion but a reabsorption of elements that had been separated from the division because of a shortage of trucks. When, as the result of the capture of large numbers of British trucks at Tobruk, vehicles became available, these elements—two infantry regiments and a few artillery batteries equipped with captured French weapons—rejoined the 90th Light Division, doubling its size and returning to it a slightly more conventional character. Ulrich Kleeman, "Streiflichter zur

Kriegsführung in Nordafrika," U.S. National Archives, Foreign Military Studies, Ms D104, p. 4–8.

34. Ibid.

35. Tables of organization for the 164th "Afrika" Division microfilmed at the U.S. National Archives, Captured German Records, Series T-78, Reel 861. For a detailed treatment of the history and organization of this formation, see the series "The 164 Light 'Afrika' Division," beginning in *Tactical Notebook*, July 1992.

36. Heinz Guderian, *Die Panzertruppen und ihr Zusammenwirken mit den anderen Waffen* (Berlin: E. S. Mittler und Sohn, 1943), pp. 34–43. Though the particular volume consulted was printed in 1943, internal evidence, as well as the fact that the 1943 run was the fourth printing of the book, indicates that *Die Panzertruppen* was little more than a reprint of the first edition of the book, published in 1937.

37. See Chapter 6 for a detailed discussion of German infantry division artillery. The division artillery of a "standard" German armored division at the beginning of World War II consisted of two 105mm howitzer battalions. After the Polish campaign, most armored divisions were provided with a third battalion, consisting of two batteries of 150mm howitzers and one of 100mm guns. Joachim Feist, "Formationsgeschichte der Artillerie in zwei Jahrhunderten," *Artillerie Rundschau*, no. 3 (1967); Berlin and Huether, "Die Spitzenvertretung der Artillerie," p. 38.

38. Kepler, "Artillerie nach Vorn" (unpublished ms), the Rommel Collection, U.S. National Archives, microfilm series T-84, Roll 277, beginning with frame 26.

39. B. H. Liddell-Hart, ed., *The Rommel Papers* (New York: Harcourt, Brace, 1953), p. 15. For examples of how the thrust line worked, see Russel H. S. Stolfi, *A Bias for Action: The German 7th Panzer Division in France and Russia, 1940–1941* (Quantico, VA: Marine Corps Association, 1991).

8

Artillery Alone

Though doctrine and tactics played their roles, the German victory over Poland in 1939 can easily be dismissed as a matter of technology and numbers—a large modern force equipped with the latest weapons defeating a smaller, less well-equipped army—the defeat of France in 1940 permits no similar excuse. In terms of conventional ways of calculating military power—whether it be counting heads, divisions, tanks, planes, or guns—the antagonists were roughly equal. The bulk of the credit for the German victory must thus be laid not on the size or modernity of the German forces but on the way they were employed. The same can be said for the stunning German victory over the bulk of the Soviet Army in the summer and fall of 1941. While this victory was incomplete, it was even more of a triumph for the German high-tempo warfare than the six-week campaign against the Western allies. The forces defeated were larger, the obstacles overcome were more numerous, and the territory captured far greater than had been the case in 1940.

The fruit of the partial victory of 1941, like its counterpart of 1914, was stalemate. Once again, the army that had staked its hopes on its talent for mobile warfare was stuck in a long series of field fortifications. This time the line was longer and the forces available were significantly smaller. As the war dragged on, moreover, and German casualties, particularly among the infantry, began to mount, the problem of defending a line stretching from the Arctic Circle to the Black Sea with fewer and fewer troops became ever more pronounced.[1]

For three years, the German Army staved off the inevitable collapse of its position on the eastern front by a combination of expedients. One was the fire brigade—those few units that were entirely gasoline powered were pulled out of the front line and used as mobile reserves. The other was an increased reliance on massed artillery fire. As Hitler persistently refused to allow his generals the flexibility they needed to make full use of the first expedient, the defense of German positions in the east tended increasingly to rest on the shoulders of German artillerymen. Time and again Soviet forces would succeed in breaking through the thin crust of machine gun posts and antitank guns that passed for a main line of resistance, only to find themselves driven to ground by the concentrated fire of German howitzers.[2]

The essence of the German technique for massed fire is perhaps best expressed by the motto used by the artillerymen of the *Großdeutschland* Division—"many tubes, few rounds, suddenly on a single point."[3] The use of a single point as the target greatly simplified fire control. A concentration could be brought down by means of a code word and a map reference. The inevitable minor inaccuracies—uncorrected because the first rounds fired were for effect—served to prevent all the shells from landing in exactly the same place. The small number of rounds fired allowed the Germans to maximize effect while using a minimum of ammunition. Most important of all, the suddenness with which the concentration fell made it far more likely that the enemy would be caught unprotected.

The role played by German artillery in holding the line for three years is even more remarkable when the relative weakness of the German artillery park is taken into account. The rapid expansion of the German Army in the first few years of World War II had prevented it from reaching the original goal of giving three 105mm howitzer and two 150mm howitzer battalions to each infantry division. Upon mobilization in September 1939, the second battalions of the divisional heavy regiments were pulled out of their divisions and attached to the general reserve of artillery. After the French campaign many of these battalions, almost all of which were motorized, were assembled into regiments for new divisions—infantry, armored, and motorized—that were being formed for the invasion of the Soviet Union.

As a result, most German infantry divisions were provided with three 105mm and one 150mm battalion formed into a single regiment, though some less favored infantry divisions had to make do without the heavy battalions. Armored divisions, some of which had gone through the 1939 and 1940 campaigns with only two 105mm battalions, were, in the fall of

1940, almost all provided with a heavy battalion. (This was either a 150mm battalion or a mixed battalion with one 100mm gun battery and two 150mm howitzer batteries.)

In 1943, the authorized strength of the artillery regiments of German infantry divisions on the eastern front was reduced by cutting the number of pieces in each battery from four to three. Needless to say, there was often a large gap between the number of guns authorized and those present for duty. Thus, German divisions in action during the last two years of World War II were often reduced to twenty-seven or fewer pieces.[4] By contrast, an American division could count on its thirty-six pieces plus the services of an equal number of pieces from nondivisional units. A British division had seventy-two 25-pounders, plus an average of sixteen heavier pieces from the medium regiment normally attached to each division.[5]

Though not as damaging as the shortage of firing battalions, another principal casualty of rapid expansion was the plan to provide each infantry division with an *Arko* of its own as well as observation units. (The latter were battalions and independent batteries capable of surveying positions, providing meteorological data, making artillery maps, and, most important of all, sound and flash ranging. Some were equipped with captive balloons for direct observation.) With these assets, the division would have been, as it had been at the beginning of World War I, the sole echelon concerned with the employment of field artillery, capable of commanding a number of attached units in addition to its battalions. However, as there were only enough *Arkos* and observation battalions to provide, on average, one to every corps, the Germans often had to form ad hoc corps artillery organizations.[6]

Table 8.1
Number of German *Arkos* and Observation Units

Date	Divisions	*Arkos*	Observation Units
September, 1939	102	16	48
May, 1940	145	45	45
June, 1941	179	59	63

It is to the credit of the German artillerymen that they usually resisted the temptation to abandon the flexibility inherent in their traditional artillery organizations (both the "one-stop-shopping" doctrine of 1914 and the more intricate task organization of the Bruchmüller era) for a French-style division of labor between division and corps artillery. Though there were occasions where an *Arko* and an observation unit formed the skeleton of an artillery groupment directly subordinated to a corps headquarters and used primarily for counterbattery and other general support tasks, the general tendency seems to have been to use the flexibility inherent in the "floating" nature of the *Arko* and the nondivisional artillery units to create groupments custom tailored to the task at hand.

This willingness to mix and match artillery units and headquarters extended to the artillery regiments of divisions. If the numerous diagrams found in the German archives captured at the end of the war are any indication, German artillerists thought nothing of stripping the battalions from one artillery regiment and attaching them to another. The remaining regimental headquarters would then be used for another task—the command of a groupment formed from nondivisional units or battalions borrowed from yet another regiment.

For important operations—such as the seizure of the Maginot Line fort at La Ferté in 1940, the crossing of the Soviet frontier in 1941, the siege of Sevastopol in 1942, or the defense of the key railroad junction at Orsha in 1944—both the number and the task organization of German artillery units could be quite impressive. At La Ferté, for example, 259 artillery pieces—three battalions of 210mm heavy howitzers, three battalions of 100mm guns and one of 150mm guns, six battalions of 150mm howitzers, nine battalions of 105mm howitzers, and a battery of 88mm antiaircraft guns—plus three batteries of *Nebelwerfer* (multiple-rocket launchers firing smoke-producing rockets) formed a task force under the direction of *Arko* 7. The maneuver unit supported by all this fire was a single company of assault pioneers. (Additional close-in fire support for the pioneers was provided by an infantry regiment.)[7]

Such massive assemblages of artillery could be gathered only at the expense of other parts of the front. Thus the majority of German divisions on the eastern front had, on most occasions, to make do with the few dozen howitzers permanently assigned to them. Combined with a perennial shortage of ammunition, the fact that howitzers were both in short supply and critical to the defense led the Germans to take a number of steps to economize on artillery. The most important way of doing this was also the most traditional: beefing up the "hip pocket" artillery of the infantry.

This was a relatively easy step to take for two reasons. The first was that the heavy losses suffered by the infantry, which resulted, in 1943, in the reduction of the number of infantry battalions in most divisions by a full third, automatically increased the ratio of mortars, infantry guns, antitank guns, and heavy machine guns to riflemen and light machine gunners. The second was that mortars, both the 81mm model with which the Germans had entered the war and the 120mm version copied from the Soviets, were easy to provide with ammunition and even easier to make.[8]

Another means of beefing up the combat power of the infantry was the creation of assault artillery (*Sturmartillerie*). These turretless but comparatively well-armored and well-armed tanks were simply the reinvention of the infantry tank—a means of providing direct fire support to attacking infantry. The fact that assault guns (*Sturmgeschütze*) were marketed by their chief proponent in the interwar period (the future Field Marshal Erich von Manstein) as the modern incarnation of horse artillery ensured that they would be employed with more skill than the clumsy pillboxes-on-treads of the late 1930s and early 1940s.[9]

This skill was particularly noticeable in the defense. The artillerymen who commanded assault gun units revived the old technique of the *Lauerstellung*. Rather than taking prominent or even masked firing positions, they would hide in an inconspicuous spot until the enemy had advanced far enough to be attacked on an exposed flank or from the rear.[10] The virtuoso practitioner of this technique was Wachtmeister (Staff Sergeant Hugo Primozic, a professional NCO who had learned his trade in the horse-drawn artillery of the *Reichswehr*.[11]

Their many virtues notwithstanding, neither infantry heavy weapons nor assault guns could entirely replace the concentrated fire of multiple light and heavy howitzer batteries. Indeed, the proof of the importance to the Germans of the concentrated fire of divisional field artillery regiments can be seen not only in the instances where it was used but in the one major instance where they attempted to do without it. During the first half of 1943, the German Army High Command conducted a front-line experiment with a type of division in which firepower was organized in a very different way. This experimental division, built from the wreckage of an infantry division (the 78th) that had suffered heavy losses in the position warfare of November and December 1942, was known as the 78th Assault Division (*78. Sturmdivision*).

The basic building block of the assault division was the assault regiment (*Sturmregiment*). Created from the remnants of three regiments of the 78th Infantry Division, the assault regiment was not, strictly speaking, an infantry unit. Rather, with its extraordinarily generous allocation of heavy antitank weapons and its field artillery battalions, it was an entirely new type of unit. The first battalion of each assault reigment was the assault battalion (*Sturmbataillon*). It was composed of four assault companies well equipped (with eighteen MG42 light machine guns and two 81mm mortars) for conventional infantry work. In addition, each assault company was provided with six 75mm antitank guns. These served both as antitank guns and as a form of direct fire, accompanying artillery attacking targets such as bunkers.[12]

The second battalion was a field artillery battalion of nine 105mm howitzers. This battalion, drawn from the artillery regiment of the old 78th Infantry Division, was not merely in direct support of the assault regiment. According to the design promulgated by the Army High Command, it was to be as much an organic part of the assault regiment as the assault battalion and the independent companies. Still more firepower was provided to the assault regiment in the form of a heavy infantry company reminiscent of those of contemporary mountain and light infantry battalions. This company was authorized four infantry guns (two 75mm and two 150mm), six medium (81mm) mortars, and eight MG- 42 heavy machine guns.

Although the bulk of the field artillery had been distributed among the three assault regiments, the assault division retained a relatively large artillery regiment. Commanded by the headquarters of the artillery regiment of the old 78th Infantry Division, the new artillery regiment consisted of a conventional battalion of heavy field howitzers (150mm), an assault gun battalion (*Sturmgeschütz Abteilung* 189) of about thirty assault guns, and an antiaircraft battalion (*Heeres Flak Abteilung* 293) with two batteries of 88mm guns and one battery of light (20–37mm) antiaircraft weapons. A heavy mortar battalion of thirty-six 120mm mortars (three companies of twelve mortars each) provided one more source of heavy firepower for the division.

The unwillingness of the leadership of the 78th Assault Division to dispense with concentrated field artillery fire can be seen in a map exercise conducted soon after the division was reorganized. The problem was a two-division attack with limited objectives in the hilly terrain southeast of Rshew, a town on the Volga 100 or so miles west of Moscow. The goal of the mock attack was to seize a piece of Soviet-held high ground that provided a bridgehead over a local river, a salient pushing into the German lines, and an observation post that allowed shelling of an important north–south railroad.

The plan of attack determined in the course of the map exercise called for a simultaneous, V-shaped, frontal attack by the two divisions. Although both divisions were to be reinforced by artillery battalions borrowed from other divisions and the corps artillery, the main effort was clearly with the 78th Assault Division. Of the fourteen available artillery battalions, it was allocated nine. The other division (the 216th Infantry Division) had to make do with five.

Within the 78th Assault Division, a division-level main effort was formed by reinforcing one of the assault regiments with two-thirds of the available 120mm mortars and assault guns. This local main effort was also allocated the lion's share of the field artillery. Of the nine battalions assigned to support the 78th Assault Division, seven—the assault regiment's 105mm howitzer battalion, the division's 150mm howitzer battalion, plus the five borrowed battalions—were placed behind the assault regiment forming the main effort. The other two battalions—105mm howitzer battalions of the other two assault regiments—remained in direct support of their parent assault regiments.

The fire plan for the attack dispensed with any fire prior to the assault troops leaving the German lines. "Surprise," wrote the commander of the assault forming the main effort, "is the essential precondition for success." Instead, a number of fire missions were prepared, each to be fired on receipt of a request (*Anforderung*) from the assault regiment's commander. There was, for example, a brief but intense (all available tubes) preparatory bombardment to be fired on the Soviet main line of resistance just before the assault troops broke into that position.

Communication with the artillery was by means of a field telephone line and radio link connecting the assault battalion of the assault regiment with its artillery battalion. This battalion, in turn, was connected to the other artillery battalions supporting the 78th Assault Division by means of a task-organized artillery command system. The key feature of this system was a single artillery headquarters—the regimental headquarters of the divisional artillery regiment of the 78th Assault Division—with operational control over all nine battalions firing in support of the 78th Assault Division. This headquarters was also reponsible for consulting with the assault regiments and drawing up the fire plan.[13]

Even in the somewhat artificial light shed by the map exercise, it was clear that making field artillery battalions parts of the maneuver regiments raised a number of problems. First, it put the assault regiment commanders in the business of positioning and resupplying batteries, tasks that conflicted with their primary duty of leading from the front. Second, putting artillery battalions under the command of the assault regiments unduly complicated the massing of fire. That is, to effect cooperation, the field artillery battalions had to be put back under the operational control of the regimental headquarters. Thus, the field artillery battalions were in the awkward position of belonging administratively to the infantry while getting many of their orders from the artillery.

These problems became even more evident when, later that winter, the 78th Assault Division was committed to combat. In an after-action report submitted in March, after the division had had an opportunity to carry out some actual attacks with limited objectives against Soviet positions, the commanding general recommended that the 105mm howitzer battalions be pulled out of the assault regiments and returned to the artillery regiment. He also recommended that the assault gun battalion be taken out of the artillery regiment and made directly answerable to the division commander.[14]

The artillery regiment that resulted when this recommendation was approved looked much like most other German artillery regiments at the time. Like the others, the artillery regiment of the 78th Assault Division had a headquarters, one heavy (150mm) battalion, and three light (105mm) battalions. The only difference was that the artillery regiment of the 78th Assault Division retained its antiaircraft battalion, a unit whose 88mm guns had proven themselves capable of supplementing the indirect fire of the field artillery battalions.[15]

Fresh memories of the 78th Assault Division's attempt to do without the massed fire of artillery units larger than battalions may have played a role in the German Army's next major experiment in division organization, the 18th Artillery Division. In contrast to the 78th Assault Division, which had been extraordinarily rich in direct fire weapons, the 18th Artillery Division was conceived of as a formation that acted exclusively through concentrated indirect fire. Its principal combat units were nine fully motorized artillery battalions, one of which had its howitzers mounted on armored, self-propelled, fully-tracked chassis.

The original concept was for the 18th Artillery Division to serve as a "focus of efforts weapon" (*Schwerpunktwaffe*) with which the Army High Command could powerfully reinforce an army corps or similiar organization in a particularly critical situation. So that it could move rapidly from one sector to another, the division was to be entirely motorized. (This was easily achieved by adding six additional artillery battalions to an armored division whose tank, *Panzergrenadier*, and combat engineer units had just been transferred to other formations.) So that the 18th Artillery Division could rapidly mass the fire of all available batteries on single targets, it was provided with an experimental fire control battery (*Feuerleitbatterie*).[16]

The fire control battery might best be described as an overgrown version of the French *poste central du groupe*. With communications links to as many as eighteen firing units (whether single batteries, battalions, or detachments of varying size) and an almost unlimited number of observers, its job was to translate the tactical decisions of observers into a coordinated set of firing commands. Like its French antecedent, the fire control battery had the advantage of greatly simplifying the work of battery commanders trying to cooperate with other batteries to produce the simultaneous impact of scores of shells. The great danger was that the battery commander would be deprived of his role as a tactical decision maker.[17]

This latter danger was greatly mitigated by the fact that the fire control battery was a supplement to, rather than a replacement for, traditional German fire control procedures. The batteries of the 18th Artillery Division, as well as any batteries under its operational control, retained their battery observation posts and forward observers, as well as procedures that made the battery commander, with his eyes on the battlefield, a tactical decision maker. These other observers were used for missions that were not of direct interest to the division as a whole: battery, battalion, and regimental concentrations; barrages (rarely); as well as registration and harassing fire by means of roving pieces (*Arbeitsgeschütze*). Only when traditional methods would not do the job—particularly when the fire of a large number of batteries needed to be concentrated quickly—did the fire control battery come into action.[18]

The innovation of the German fire control battery was not merely one of scale. The heart of the battery (or, more precisely, its mind) was an electronic computer linked to a series of teletype machines. The computer, which was "aware" of the location of every German firing unit, quickly converted the call for fire from the observer into a series of fire commands (azimuth, range, type of projectile and fuse, number of rounds, etc.) that, three to five seconds later, were automatically transmitted by teletype.[19]

In addition to making use of the forward observers and observation posts of the artillery batteries, battalions, and regiments, the fire control battery was in contact with a number of special observers riding in armored command vehicles (*Panzerbefehlswagen*). Escorted by assault guns (from the 18th Artillery Division's assault gun company) and often provided with man-pack radios so that they could use observation points too small to hide an armored vehicle, these observers belonged to neither battery nor battalion but to the division as a whole. They were, in contrast to the second lieutenants and NCOs who served as battery forward observers, experienced battery (and, in some cases, battalion) commanders. Most important, they had the authority to bring down the concentrated firepower of an artillery regiment or even the whole artillery division on whatever point they designated.[20]

In a sense, these armored observers were the descendants of the artillery liaison officers of 1918. Like their predecessors, the armored observers were not tied to any particular firing unit but had the means to gather the services of available artillery units. The armored observers represented a step up from the artillery liaison officers of World War I in that their use of radio and their links to the fire control battery allowed them contact with a larger number of potential firing batteries. Another advantage enjoyed by the armored observer as the practice of sending armored observers out in teams of two or three. This not only allowed continuous observation while on the move (one observer in an overwatch position while the others changed position) but also permitted the observation of a tactical event from two or three different vantage points.[21]

For counterbattery work, the 18th Artillery Division had an observation battalion. Identical to the observation battalions that were usually attached to army corps and directly subordinated to *Arkos*, this observation battalion had three tasks. The first was to establish its intelligence network of listening and observation posts and balloons. The second, particularly important if the fire control battery was to be of any use, was to carry out a thorough survey so that the entire division could be on the same grid. Last (but certainly not least) was to command the counterbattery effort. That is, rather than telling off a particular battalion or regiment for counterbattery work, the division put units under the operational control of the observation battalion.[22]

In situations where the 18th Artillery Division was operating with a formation that had access to an *Arko* or observation battalion of its own, one of these might be assigned the responsibility for the counterbattery effort. This freed the 18th Artillery Division to do what it was designed to do: rapidly concentrate its fire on single points where that fire would have a decisive impact on the outcome of a battle. The 18th Artillery Division, after all, was no better equipped for identifying and combating Soviet batteries than an *Arko* commanding a similar number of firing batteries. The combination of the fire control battery and the armored observation vehicles, however, gave it a unique means of cooperating with the hard-pressed infantry.

The very conditions that brought the German Army to the point of forming the 18th Artillery Division made it difficult for that division either to prepare itself properly for its assigned task or to go into action as a complete unit. The formation of the division in November of 1943 coincided with a major Soviet offensive. As had already happened with countless other formations in the process of organizing or retraining, the half-trained, undermanned, and incompletely equipped 18th Artillery Division found itself trying to plug a gaping hole in the German disposition. Because no infantry was available, the observation battalion, antiaircraft battalion, and practically every unit other than firing batteries were used as close-combat troops. And even though eight firing batteries (of an authorized total of twenty-four) had yet to arrive on the eastern front, nine batteries were taken away for service with other divisions. The result was a formation that consisted of little more than the artillery of a full-strength infantry division firing in support of a handful of amateur infantrymen trying to stand in the way of the main effort of a multiarmy Soviet offensive.

Saved from an inevitable disaster by the timely intervention of German armored troops, the 18th Artillery Division managed to rebuild itself to the point where it could go into action, two months later, in a manner befitting its original concept. Subordinated to an army corps and placed behind infantry divisions, it was able, on a few occasions, to command (but not mass) the fire of sixteen or seventeen artillery battalions (nine of which were organic and seven or eight of which were from the infantry divisions).[23] The chief innovation of this period was the reorganization of the light and mixed heavy battalions. The three mixed heavy battalions were replaced by three "pure" battalions—two of light field howitzers and one of 100mm guns. In addition, the five battalions equipped with either light or heavy howitzers each replaced their three four-piece batteries with two six-piece batteries.[24]

This latter change had the advantage of reducing the ratio of "overhead" (battery command and service personnel) to gun crews and thus cutting the number of men needed by an artillery battalion by a third without diminishing the firepower of the battalion. It also made it possible for the fire control battery to be linked directly to a larger percentage of the 18th Artillery Division's batteries. The disadvantages attendant upon larger batteries—the difficulty of finding firing positions, the additional time needed to displace, the larger target offered, and the decrease in the length of front that a battalion could cover—were less important for the units of the 18th Artillery Division than they were for the artillery of infantry or armored divisions. The batteries of the 18th Artillery Division, after all, were reinforcing artillery, intended to act as independent units only in exceptional cases.[25]

Before the 18th Artillery Division was able to perfect its technique, the situation that had brought it into being had changed. In 1942 or 1943, a German formation that could place the massed fire of fifteen or so artillery battalions on any point of a front of about ten kilometers was a match for the main effort of any Soviet offensive. By 1944, however, the scale of Soviet breakthrough attempts had increased to the point where the main effort of each attack might be spread over a front of twenty kilometers. To counter such attacks, the Germans would need a far larger number of artillery pieces. The fact that most artillery pieces could not reach all points along the full length of such a front, moreover, rendered impractical an organization whose purpose was to concentrate the fire of all its pieces on one point. Thus, as early as February 1944, the 18th Artillery Division was forced to spread its regiments along a front so long that division concentrations were no longer possible.[26]

Having suffered heavily in the "cauldron" battles of the spring of 1944, the 18th Artillery Division was disbanded in July of that year. Its component parts were used to build elements of the next German experiment with massed artillery fire, a modular structure in which a variable number of army artillery brigades (*Heeresartilleriebrigade*) and artillery corps (*Artilleriekorps*) would be assembled under the command of a floating headquarters. The brigades were composed of four battalions; the corps, of six battalions. The weapons with which these units were equipped varied widely, and included large numbers of antiaircraft guns and pieces of foreign manufacture. The floating headquarters consisted of existing *Arkos* for corps operations, *Harkos* (*Höhere Artillerie Kommandeure*, higher artillery commanders) for army work, and *Generale der Artillerie* to command the ad hoc artillery organizations of army groups.[27]

The units equipped with tube artillery were joined in these groupings by organizations equipped with *Nebelwerfer* (smoke projectors). These were rocket launchers of various sizes that had originally been designed to lay smoke screens but, by 1944, had proved themselves to be an excellent means of delivering high explosives. Though far less accurate than tube artillery, the *Nebelwwerfer* had the advantage of being able to fire a large number of rockets in a short period of time. When it came to the concentration of much fire on a single point, this capability made units equipped with *Nebelwerfer* a reasonable substitute for much larger tube artillery units. A *Nebelwerfer* brigade in 1944, for example, had 124 launchers, each with six to eight launch tubes. By way of contrast, the 18th Artillery Division was authorized only 108 pieces of field artillery.[28]

As a result of the experience of three years of fighting against the Soviets, the German Army that fought in France and Belgium in 1944 and 1945 was eager to try the technique of massed artillery fire against the largely English-speaking armies of the Soviet Union's Western allies. Their big opportunity for doing this came in December 1944, when Hitler launched his last great offensive, the attack through the Ardennes that has come to be known as the Battle of the Bulge. For this offensive, the Germans managed to scrape together 1,001 light pieces (75mm guns, 88mm antiaircraft guns, and 105mm howitzers), 639 heavy pieces (guns over 100mm, howitzers over 120mm), and 957 *Nebelwerfer*.[29]

The great strength of the American artillery, in the Ardennes during December 1944 and elsewhere, lay not so much in its tubes as in all of the other elements that make up field artillery. The weapons in the Americans' arsenal were remarkably similar to those of the Germans. Like the Germans, their basic light field piece was a 105mm howitzer. Similarly, their heavy divisional piece was a 155mm howitzer not unlike the German 150mm piece. Although lacking a weapon comparable to the 100mm long-range gun, the Americans had a 155mm gun to compete with the German 150mm gun and an 8-inch howitzer to match the German 210mm howitzer.

These superficial similarities notwithstanding, the American approach to field artillery was as different from that of the Germans as the German approach from that of the French. There was good reason for this. The American Army, which had entered World War I with little more than had been needed to chase Pancho Villa, had, in 1917 and 1918, been ushered into the twentieth century with the help of a French midwife. French military missions were present at the creation of the American Expeditionary Force. French instructors taught at American schools. French manuals were translated verbatim and issued not as reference material but as doctrine. American units were attached to French organizations for on the job training.[30]

What was true for the American Expeditionary Force as a whole was especially true for the artillery. Unlike the infantry and cavalry, which had indigenous traditions to mix with those imported from France, the American artillery found itself under the tutelage of its French counterpart at the very moment when the stock of professional knowledge seemed the most incomplete. Combined with the fact that American artillery units were supplied almost exclusively with French matériel and the natural attraction that the French doctrine of the predominance of artillery had for any gunner, this conjunction of supply and demand resulted in a degree of imitation that can only be described as slavish.

French influence on American field artillery continued throughout the 1920s and 1930s. Though the Ordnance Corps, in obedience to the findings of the board (Westervelt Board) that had met after World War I to determine the ideal "family" of artillery pieces for the U.S. Army, was hard at work developing 75mm and 105mm howitzers, the American division artillery bore a strong resemblance to that of contemporary French infantry divisions. Like its French counterparts, the American infantry division of the interwar period consisted of two regiments, one of three 75mm gun battalions and one of two 155mm howitzer battalions. In both cases, the pieces were slightly modified weapons of French design. Heavier artillery, consisting largely of 155mm howitzers and 155mm G.P.F. guns, was also of French origin.[31]

Soon after it was introduced in France, the *poste central du groupe* found its way to the United States. Starting in 1935, officers at the U.S. Army Field Artillery School at Fort Sill, Oklahoma, began working with what they called the battalion fire direction center. By October 1941, both the method and a number of time-saving analog computers—slide rules and circular plotting boards ("whiz wheels")—had been fully integrated into the American field artillery's official way of doing business. At the same time, the innovators at Fort Sill were working on a method of doing for three, four, or five battalions what the fire direction center did for three or four batteries.[32]

While these techniques were being perfected, the fall of France tested the faith of the American gunners in their French mentors. Following, as it did, on the heels of one of the waves of Germanophilia that seem to hit the U.S. Army every twenty years or so, the German defeat of France destroyed the willingness of American field artillerymen to go into World War II with either the weapons or the techniques of its predecessor. Indeed, the responses to a questionnaire circulated among U.S. Army field artillery officers on the eve of America's entry into World War II indicates a wide variety of opinions on the ideal composition of the artillery of an infantry division. While the organization most often recommended consisted of three battalions of the new American-designed 105mm howitzers and two of 155mm howitzers, there were proposals that ranged from the use of the 105mm howitzer as the only divisional piece to the employment of various combinations of 75mm guns, 75mm pack howitzers, 105mm howitzers, and 155mm howitzers.[33]

The solution finally arrived at (in early 1942 for divisional artillery and mid-1943 for corps artillery) bore a strong resemblance to contemporary German organization. The artillery of an infantry division was to consist of four twelve-piece battalions, three of 105mm howitzers ·and one of 155mm howitzers. Corps artillery was formed by assembling independent battalions under floating group (i.e., regimental) and brigade headquarters. Indeed, at the superficial level, the chief difference between U.S. and German field artillery during World War II was the fact that, save for a few batteries of pack howitzers carried by mules, all U.S. field artillery was either towed by motor vehicles or self-propelled.[34]

Like their German counterparts, the American artillerymen displayed a marked fondness for massing the fire of battalions and multiples of battalions on single targets. The fire control techniques and devices developed at Fort Sill in the prewar years, combined with numerous radios, allowed them to do this quickly and efficiently. Rich supplies of ammunition allowed them to do it often. The favorite American version of this basic technique was the "time on target" mission, in which the time at which the various batteries fired was staggered, in order that all rounds might arrive at the same time. The introduction in 1944 of the variable-time fuse, which permitted more reliable airbursts than older time fuses, made this technique particularly dangerous for German troops caught in the open.[35]

The only area in which American artillerists seem to have failed to catch up with the Germans was the massing of the fire of many divisions.[36] The culprit here seems to have been the relatively inflexible nature of American command arrangements. Whereas the Germans were perfectly happy to put divisional artillery under the direct operational control of another artillery headquarters (whether artillery division headquarters, *Arko*, independent regimental headquarters, observation battalion, or 18th Artillery Division), the Americans seem to have resisted such infringements on the autonomy of division commanders. As with the French, there remained a wall between division and corps artillery that prevented the kind of unitary leadership that had been central to German artillery practice since the days of Bruchmüller.[37]

In the last year of the war on the eastern front, the greatest enemy of the German ability to exercise unitary leadership was the growing Soviet ability to exploit the cracks in the German defensive crust with deep thrusts by tank units. As had been the case in France in 1940, these thrusts made artillery units more concerned with local antitank defense than fire missions, disrupted the links (wire communications, ammunition resupply, liaison) essential to the sustained action of masses of artillery, and made it difficult for the German batteries and battalions to withdraw as intact units. In the Ardennes fighting of 1944 and 1945, the German ability to mass artillery was disrupted by the initial success of the German breakthrough. Lacking sufficient transport for all but a tiny minority of the pieces involved in the operation, the German artillery was generally unable to follow in the wake of the victorious tanks. As a result, the American ground forces, aided, once the weather cleared, by ground attack aviation, were able to defeat the Germans.[38]

The irony of both situations was that the Germans ended World War II in the same position as the army they had defeated near the beginning of the conflict. Richly provided with artillery and fully capable of pouring tremendous volumes of fire on enemies within range of their guns and howitzers, the Germans were simultaneously unable to move and extremely vulnerable to the mobility of others. As in 1940, neither self-sacrifice on the part of the troops nor first-class shooting was any substitute for the ability to react quickly to either danger or opportunity.

NOTES

1. For a detailed picture of the degree to which German infantry on the eastern front was reduced to a shadow of its former self, see Timothy A. Wray, *Standing Fast: German Defense Doctrine on the Russian Front During World War II, Prewar to March 1943* (Fort Leavenworth, KS: U.S. Army Combat Studies Institute, 1986).

2. For the testimony of senior German generals on this matter, see Basil H. Liddell-Hart, *The German Generals Talk* (New York: Quill, 1979), pp. 210–20.

3. von Hobe, "Erfahrungen aus dem Kämpfen der Infanterie-Division Gross-Deutschland in der Zeit vom 28.6–25.12.1942," dated May 1943, U.S. National Archives, Captured German Records, Series T-78, Roll 620.

4. Tables of organization contained in the folder A.O.K. 6, Ia, Anlagen Band 2, "Kriegsgliederungen vom 1.7.43 bis 8.10.43," U.S. National Archives, Captured German Records, Series T-315, Roll 1475.

5. Shelford Bidwell and Dominick Graham, *Fire-Power: British Army Weapons and Theories of War, 1904–1945* (Boston: George Allen and Unwin, 1985), p. 239.

6. Joachim Feist, "Formationsgeschichte der Artillerie in zwei Jahrhunderten," *Artillerie Rundschau*, no. 3 (1967): 96–97.

7. Rudolf Berdach and Erich Dethleffsen, *Der Artillerie gewidmet* (Vienna: Berdach, 1975), pp. 14–16 and appendix III.B.1; and Roger Bruge, *Faites sauter la Ligne Maginot* (Paris: Fayard, 1973), pp. 211–69. The latter work contains the definitive account of the fall of the fort at La Ferté.

8. For more on German use of mortars during World War II, see "Guderian's Newsletter—Mortars," *Tactical Notebook*, Mar. 1992.

9. Erich von Manstein, *Aus einem Soldatenleben* (Bonn: Atheneum Verlag, 1958), pp. 243–50.

10. von Hobe, "Erfahrungen aus dem Kämpfen der Infanterie-Division Gross-Deutschland."

11. Bryan Perrett, *Knights of the Black Cross: Hitler's Panzerwaffe and Its Leaders* (New York: St. Martin's Press, 1986), p. 111.

12. Information about the organization of the 78th Assault Division is derived from tables of organization microfilmed at the U.S. National Archives, Captured German Records, Series T-315, Reel 1099. For a detailed description of the 78th Assault Division and its battles, see the series beginning with the June 1992 issue of *Tactical Notebook*.

13. The overall artillery headquarters for the operation was provided by Artillery Regiment 178, the artillery regiment of the 78th Assault Division. Under it, three groupments were formed. One consisted of the three 105mm battalions of the assault regiment plus the heavy (150mm howitzer) battalion of Artillery Regiment 178. The second consisted of three battalions (two with 105mm howitzers and one with French 105mm guns) under the command of the artillery regiment of the 216th Infantry Division (Artillery Regiment 216). The third consisted of two battalions of heavy artillery—a "pure" battalion of 210mm howitzers and a mixed battalion of 150mm howitzers and 100mm guns. "Anlage 6 zu 78. Sturmdivision Ia Op. Nr. 30/43 gen Kdo. vom 30.1.43," U.S. National Archives, Captured German Records, Series T-315, Roll 1100.

14. "78. Sturm-Division Ia/Nr. 63/43 g. Kdos., 16.3.1943," U.S. National Archives, Captured German Records, Series T-78, Roll 620.

15. Ibid.

16. Wolfgang Paul, *Geschichte der 18. Panzer-Division 1940–1943 mit Geschichte der 18. Artillerie-Division 1943–1944* (Reutlingen: Preußischer Militär-Verlag, 1989), pp. 288–91.

17. Artillerie-Division Ia/Art Nr. 114/43 geh. "Merkblatt für das Schießen mit Feuerleit-Batterie," dated 3.12.1943, U.S. National Archives, Captured German Records, Series T-315, Roll 704.

18. Artillerie-Division Ia/Art Nr. 65/43 geh. "Richtlinien für die Organisation der Beobachtungsstellen und deren Nachrichtenverbingdung," dated 11.11.1943, U.S. National Archives, Captured German Records, Series T-315, Roll 704.

19. Wilhelm Berlin, Hans Joachim Froben, and Konrad Roehr, "Reconaissance Artillery," U.S. National Archives, Foreign Military Studies, Ms P-023, p. 88.

20. For more modest tasks, they were also able to make direct liaison with individual artillery battalions. 18. Artillerie-Division Ia/Art Nr. 20/44 geh. "Artillerie-Befehl Nr. 2," dated 8.2.44; 18. Artillerie-Division Ia/Art Nr. 260/44 geh. "Artillerie-Befehl Nr. 4," dated 19.2.44; 18. Artillerie-Division Ia/Art Nr. 229/44 geh. "Einsatz des gep. V. B.," Verwendung von Sturmgeschützen für V. B.," dated 13.2.44; and 18. Artillerie-Division Ia/Art Nr. 40/43 geh. "Richtlinien für den Einsatz von gepanzerten V. B. in Zusammenarbeit mit Sturmgeschützen," dated 28.10.43. U.S. National Archives, Captured German Records, Series T-315, Roll 704.

21. Karl Thoholte, "A German Reflects upon Artillery," *Field Artillery Journal*, Dec. 1945, pp. 709–15.

22. le. Beobachtungs-Abteilung (mot) 4, "Bemerkungen zu dem Vermessungseinsatz innerhalb einer Art.-Division," dated 12.11.43; and 18. Artillerie-Division, Ia Nr. 113/43 geh., "Grundsätzliche Bemerkungen auf Grund der Planspiele, der Feuerleitungsübung und der Gefechtsschießen," dated 2.12.43, U.S. National Archives, Captured German Records, Series T-315, Roll 704.

23. 18. Artillerie-Division Ia Nr. 203/44 geh. "Dem Generalkommando XXXXVI. Pz. Korps," dated 9.2.44, U.S. National Archives, Captured German Records, Series T-315, Roll 704.

24. Tables of organization found in U.S. National Archives, Captured German Records, Series T-315, Roll 704.

25. Wilhelm Berlin and Heuther, "Die Spitzenvertretung der Artillerie in den Obersten Führung des Heeres, 1938–1945," U.S. National Archives, Foreign Military Studies, Manuscript P-041, p. 102.

26. 18. Artillerie-Division Ia Nr. 203/44 geh., 9.2.44.

27. Berlin and Heuther, "Spitzenvertretung," p. 105.

28. Hermann Jung, *Die Ardennen-Offensive, 1944/45* (Göttingen: Musterschmidt, 1971), p. 349.

29. Ibid.

30. In the course of one of these attachments, a French gunner expressed the relationship between the armies of the United States and the French Republic: "We had the impression of having received a draft of replacements, whom we had to assimilate as quickly as possible." The commander of this American unit went even further when he said to his hosts: "You know how to make war because you have fought for three and a half years. We, who have just arrived in the firing line, are ignorent of how to handle ourselves. Give us the instruction which we need. To be better and more rapidly trained, we have adopted your weapons and your regulations. We have confidence in you. We put ourselves entirely in your hands." Pierre Arnoult, *Guerre d'artilleur*, (Paris: Les Livres

de Deux Guerres, 1939), p. 53. For an example of verbatim translation of regulations, see U.S. War Department, General Staff, War Plans Division, *Artillery Firing* (Washington, DC: U.S. Department Printing Office, 1918). For the memoirs of a senior member of one of the many French military missions to the United States, see Paul Azan, *The Warfare of Today* (Boston: Houghton Mifflin, 1918). The lesson plans of the largely French instructional staff of the American Expeditionary Force's staff officers' school at Langres, France, are on file at the U.S. National Archives in Washington, D.C.

31. U. Birnie, Jr., "Memorandum for the Chief of Staff, Subject: Organization of Corps and Army and Division," dated June 20, 1937. Records of the Chiefs of Arms, Office of the Chief of Field Artillery, Correspondence, 1917–1942, U.S. National Archives, RG 177, Box 15, Folder 320.2, AA-49/C.

32. Frank E. Comparato, *Age of the Great Guns* (Harrisburg, PA: Stackpole, 1965), pp. 240–43.

33. "Analysis of Questionnaire of Field Artillery Matters," Records of the Chiefs of Arms, Office of the Chief of Field Artillery, Correspondence, 1917–1942, U.S. National Archives, RG 177, Box 17, Folder 320.2, AA-65/CA-5.

34. Shelby Stanton, *Order of Battle, U.S. Army, World War II* (Novato, CA: Presidio Press, 1984), pp. 28–29.

35. For anecdotes, see Ralph B. Baldwin, *The Deadly Fuze: Secret Weapon of World War II* (San Rafael, CA: Presidio Press, 1980).

36. Thoholte, "A German Reflects upon Artillery," p. 714.

37. One might argue that the German habit of putting all of the artillery for a particular operation in the hands of a single commander goes back to the pre-1914 practice of making the division the only echelon of command concerned with the tactical employment of artillery. The organization and scale were different, but the ideal was the same.

38. Thoholte, "A German Reflects upon Artillery," p. 714. The author of this article, General Karl Thoholte, served as the commanding general of the 18th Artillery Division and as the *General der Artillerie* in command of the artillery of the three German armies that attacked in the Ardennes in 1944.

9

Postwar Developments

To say that the two atomic bombs that ended World War II in the Pacific wrought a strategic revolution would be somewhat of an understatement. For the first time since the eighteenth century, when professionally led field armies displaced fortresses as the chief bulwark of European states, the fundamental measure of military might had changed. The military calculus no longer consisted, as it had for two hundred years, of counting rifles, sabers, and guns. Instead, a nation's influence in the councils of the mighty was weighed in megatons.

But just as the displacement of the fortress by the field army did not render the fortress entirely useless, so the primacy of atomic weapons failed to consign, as many predicted, conventional armies to the dustbin of history. What atomic weapons did do, however, was change the way these armies were used. This, in turn, eventually had a profound impact on the way artillery was designed, organized, and employed.

The first martial sacrifice to be laid on the altar of nuclear weapons was conventional warfare between atomic powers. Not only did conventional armies provide convenient targets for atomic weapons, but even the most ruthless leaders (Joseph Stalin and Mao Tse-tung) were unwilling to take the risk that conventional war might escalate into nuclear war. For those dissatisfied with the map of the world, this left two options— limited conventional war in which the nuclear powers kept their armies a safe distance apart, and guerrilla war. In most cases, the way taken by aggressive states was a mixture of the two.

The first war of this sort to invite a response from a modern, Western army took place in Indochina. The Western army involved (that of the French Union) fought as in earlier colonial wars. While many artillery pieces—a handful of field guns attached to the garrison of a fort or a mobile column—were present, field artillery in the traditional European sense was not. The one exception was the decisive battle of the conflict, the siege of Dien Bien Phu.

This latter battle is memorable not merely because it sealed the fate of Indochina but also because the insurgents won largely because they had better artillery. The Viet Minh had 200 field pieces (mostly 105mm howitzers) and rocket launchers arrayed on a narrow horseshoe of high ground surrounding the French position. The French had twenty-four 105mm howitzers and four 155mm howitzers obligated to fire *à tous azimuths*. And while the French guns inflicted horrible casualties on the Viet Minh infantry and sappers, whether either they or the French ground attack aircraft were able to knock out a single Viet Minh field piece is still unknown.[1]

The second nonnuclear war of the Atomic Age took place in Korea. Once more, the artillery park of the Western powers was but a shadow of what it had been at the end of World War II. This time, however, the enemy was even less able to put howitzers in the front lines The resulting dynamic would have a profound effect on both the outcome of the war and the way that the U.S. armed forces of the three decades that followed the Korean War would view artillery.

Like World War I in France and Belgium, the Korean War can be summarized as a campaign of rapid maneuver that bogged down into a stalemate. In the first phase (from June 1950 to June 1951) the few batteries that were available on either side were incapable of anything resembling the massed fire that had been commonplace in 1944 or 1945. While this was often, especially in the case of the Americans, of very high quality, it paled in comparison to the quantity of artillery available to British, American, Soviet, and even German commanders of the latter half of World War II. In the second phase (from June 1951 to July 1953) the troops that fought under the United Nations flag dug in and waited for peace talks to end the war that Kim Il Sung had begun. In that portion of the war, the United Nations troops, like their fathers and grandfathers in World War I, relied heavily on artillery to do the bulk of the killing in both defense and attacks with limited objectives.

During the first, mobile phase of the Korean War, the lack of artillery was a serious problem for the United Nations forces. Officered largely by veterans of World War II, American and Commonwealth units in particular were in the awkward position of having learned to fight a style of warfare whose fundamental assumption was that three or four battalions of field artillery would be available to support each battalion of infantry at the moment of truth. When, however, the moment of truth came, the truth was that the proportion was closer to one artillery battalion for every three or four infantry battalions.

When used with ingenuity and skill, and a certain willingness to concentrate at the right time and place, this proportion was sometimes enough for discrete operations. In early February 1951, for example, two batteries of 105mm howitzers firing in direct support of the American 21st Infantry Regiment allowed an understrength rifle company to retake a hill that it had recently lost to a Chinese regiment. The centerpiece of the artillery plan was a one-battery rolling barrage, directly observed by the artillery battalion commander, and moved forward by commands from the riflemen crawling behind it. The other battery fired on enemy positions on a neighboring hill, preventing the Chinese there from enfilading the attacking Americans.[2]

In most cases, however, there was simply not enough artillery to do all that was expected of it. The British 29th Brigade, fighting on the Imjin River in late April 1951, found that its one field regiment of twenty-four 25-pounders, supplemented by a single battery of 4.2-inch mortars, was not up to the job of cooperating with four infantry battalions attacked by Chinese infantry in division strength. The problem was not one of coordination. The proven British system of putting battery and troop commanders up front with the supported units was working well. The problem was, rather, one of scale.

The seven-and-a-half-mile front held by the British brigade was too large to be held continuously. As a result, the men of the three forward infantry battalions were divided among a number of hilltop positions, with company positions clustered together to form battalion positions and gaps of as much as two miles between battalions. In the later years of World War II, a British force would have solved this problem by "stonking" the low ground between the battalion positions. Without the number of guns needed for such tactics, however, the British were reduced to helping the infantry defend their strong points.

Suffering terribly from the intermittent fire of single British batteries, the Chinese were nonetheless able to infiltrate between the hard-pressed rifle companies. In a repetition of the events of March 21, 1918, this enabled the Chinese "storm troopers" to threaten the firing positions of the British 25-pounders. Again, as in March 1918, the consequent silencing of the guns deprived the British defense of its glue. Within hours, the brigade was forced to withdraw. One of its battalions, running out of infantry ammunition and deprived of its main means of killing Chinese, was annihilated.[3]

Such disasters were not repeated once the United States managed to reassemble a portion of the artillery park that it had left in various corners of the world during the mad rush to demobilize in 1945. As early as May 1951, a Chinese attack similar to the one that did so much damage to the 29th Brigade came to grief along the "No Name Line" erected by the Americans just north of Seoul. Some of the credit for this victory must be laid at the feet of the exhaustion of the attackers. The bulk of the damage done to the Chinese, however, was inflicted by the American artillery.

On one occasion, in a fire mission worthy of 1944 or 1945, fourteen battalions of light and heavy American field artillery fired a "time on target" concentration that sent 2,500 shells against a single target in less than two minutes. And while massed fire on this scale, produced by more than ten times the number of field pieces available to the 29th Brigade on the Imjin, was not always available to each and every infantryman, similar concentrations became a hallmark of the defense of the "No Name Line."[4]

The need for massed fire in Korea revived American interest in multiple-rocket launchers. This time, however, there was neither the multiplicity of designs nor any question about who was to operate the weapons. A single model—a truck-mounted launcher that fired 4.5-inch rockets—equipped provisional rocket batteries manned by field artillerymen. As might be expected from the experience of World War II, this weapon did a good job of killing enemy troops caught in the open.[5]

As the ebb and flow of the first year of the Korean War gave way to position warfare, the emphasis shifted from the massed fire of many battalions responding to a crisis to far fewer guns firing the same sort of missions fired by the artillery behind the trenches in the day-to-day fighting of World War I. As had been the case thirty-odd years earlier, the constant use of field artillery to support friendly patrols, repel enemy patrols, interdict enemy movement, and silence enemy guns proved a far greater drain on stocks of ammunition than the more spectacular, but less frequent, massing of a score or more batteries. The solution sought in the winter of 1951–1952 was the same as that sought in the winter of 1914–1915—strict rationing of shells on the basis of a set number of rounds per gun per day.[6]

In another repetition of World War I trench warfare, the American infantrymen who served in the static phase of the Korean War got used to the idea that artillery would always be available. This was reinforced by the "democratization" of communications brought about by the radio.

Whereas most World War I armies restricted the right to call on the services of the local battery to infantry battalion commanders or their superiors, the wide distribution of radios gave every patrol leader the ability to request the timely delivery of a few shells.

In the eyes of those with little knowledge of other ways of employing artillery, the experience of position warfare in Korea often led to the view that artillery was a sort of utility. That is, many Americans began to believe that artillery fire was a serivce that, like gas heat, piped-in water, or electricity, could be summoned at will by the "customer." The corollary to this view was that, like access to the products of a public utility in civilian life, access to artillery fire was a right that could be exercised regardless of the larger tactical situation.

Two factors contributed to the American tendency to view artillery as a utility. One was the way the system worked. A short radio or field telephone conversation by a forward observer connected an infantry patrol or outpost to a large and elaborate grid of batteries, fire direction centers, fire support coordination centers, and the like. Like customers turning on electric switches or water faucets, the infantrymen did not see the furious activity that was set in motion by the forward observer's call. All they saw was the resulting product.

The second was the political climate of the static phase of the Korean War. Once the movement stopped, the American political leadership gave up trying to win the war and began a series of negotiations that eventually resulted in the continued partition of the Korean Peninsula. Operations were thus reduced to the holding or the improvement of the line. Not only did this result in most United Nations infantrymen doing their jobs within easy range of lots of friendly artillery, it also facilitated the deliberate emplacement of batteries, surveying of positions and reference points, stockpiling of ammunition, and establishment of secure communications essential for converting discrete artillery units into a single artillery system.

The idea that American field artillery was a utility persisted through the late 1950s and beyond. The chief advocates were the field artillerymen, and the main audience was the infantry. As early as the late 1940s, American artillerymen began to notice both a malaise in their own arm and a large case of selective amnesia on the part of the other arms. While the popular press extolled the glories of atomic warfare, rockets, and, above all, the air force, the infantry and tank commanders seemed more and more influenced by peacetime exercises (in which artillery fire existed primarily on paper) and less by the still recent events of World War II. Their response was to preach multiple-battalion massed fire and lobby for the establishment of higher-level artillery headquarters capable of organizing such fire.

In the massed fire business, however, higher artillery headquarters lost the job to a new agency, the fire support coordination center (FSCC). Originally used in the Pacific as an ad hoc means of coordinating the actions of Marine ground attack aircraft with the work of land-based artillery (both Army and Marine) and fire from naval vessels, the FSCC became a permanent part of Marine organization for combat immediately after World War II. A few years later, the Army adopted the practice.

Staffed by representatives from the various units providing firepower—air squadrons, groups, and wings; artillery batteries, battalions, and regiments; naval vessels; and (eventually) mortar platoons—FSCC was a standing committee that answered to the commander of the unit or formation being supported. When time was available, it drafted the kind of fire support plans that were once the exclusive province of the artillery. In most cases, however, the FSCC was in a reactive mode, assigning targets to various fire support agencies for "servicing." In other words, the FSCC was a clearinghouse that matched producers with consumers.

When led by a strong officer (often called the fire support coordinator), this matching process had an autocratic quality. Such a leader could, and often did, play the role of Bruchmüller in his glory days, swiftly allocating resources in accordance with an overarching plan.[7] If, however, the leadership was not there, the FSCC would resemble more a parliamentary committee than a military organization, with all sorts of horse-trading going on to see who would attack which target. Given that the "horse traders," cooped up in a tent or armored command vehicle, rarely had firsthand knowledge of either the battlefield or the condition of the fire support agencies, the probability was high that fire support planning would bear little relationship to the situation on the ground.[8]

At its best, the FSCC provided rapid "deconfliction" between the various units providing fire support—assigning the best weapon to the target while ensuring that friendly shells did not shoot down friendly planes. It was particularly good at organizing suppression of enemy air defense missions—artillery fire that suppressed enemy antiaircraft weapons moments before friendly aircraft arrived to deliver their ordnance.

Even at its best, however, the FSCC, like the notion of firepower as a utility that it helped to see the light of day, was closely linked to static warfare. Born of the "run up the beach and hunker down" amphibious operations of World War II and refined in the static phase of the Korean War, the FSCC functioned best when the pace of operations was slow. To function at all, it required a first-class communication net of a kind that is rarely available to fast-moving armies. To function well, moreover, the FSCC required targets that had the good grace to stay still while a "weaponeer" matched them with an artillery fire mission or flight of aircraft.

Despite its growing strength, the view that conventional artillery was part of a larger fire support power grid was not, at least in the 1950s, universal. Its strongest competitor was close support—the idea that light field artillery was best used as independent batteries and battalions of relatively light weapons cooperating directly with maneuver units. This "institutional undertow" may have received some impetus from the memory of island fighting in the Pacific and the mobile phase of the Korean War. The biggest boost of the close support school, however, came from the two most important new weapons of the time: tactical nuclear explosives and helicopters.

Tactical nuclear weapons, whether fired from 280mm artillery pieces, delivered by unguided rockets, or dropped from aircraft, made the concentration of conventional forces a dangerous proposition. While this was certainly true for infantry and tanks, it was doubly true for artillery. Not only would five or six field artillery battalions along a conventional division front of a few thousand meters be vulnerable to destruction by one or two tactical nuclear weapons, they would also have little reason to get so close to each other. After all, anything that massed howitzers could do could be done far better by a single tube firing what would soon be called the "silver bullet."

For both the Army and the Marine Corps, the immediate response to the prospect of a nuclear battlefield was to resurrect battalion and regimental combat teams. The composition and nomenclature of these organizations varied somewhat. The concept, however, was the same. Just as had been the case with Percin's teachings prior to World War I or the original organization the German 78th Assault Division of 1943, the idea was that field artillery, freed from the need to mass anything more than a battalion's worth of artillery on a single target, should be tied more closely to the supported maneuver unit.

The Army formed its combat teams by attaching one or more independent six-to-twelve-tube direct support artillery units to a battle group of four (later five) rifle companies. Five of these battle groups, five direct support artillery units, and a general support artillery unit designed to shoot nuclear rounds made a Pentomic division. If the division was a "straight leg" infantry division, the direct support artillery units would be small battalions composed of one battery of 155mm howitzers and another of

105mm howitzers. The general support artillery unit of the infantry division was likewise a small battalion with one eight-inch howitzer battery and one "Honest John" battery armed with nuclear-tipped rockets. The airborne version of the Pentomic division had even less artillery. Its direct support artillery consisted of five 105mm howitzer batteries and five 4.2-inch mortar batteries; its general support unit was a single "Honest John" rocket battery.[9]

The Marine Corps was somewhat more conservative in its organizational philosophy but radical in its choice of equipment. It institutionalized the World War II practice of forming landing teams. A howitzer battalion, along with other support elements, was added to an infantry regiment to form a regimental landing team. On a smaller scale, a single battery (plus other "cats and dogs") was added to an infantry battalion to form a battalion landing team.[10] The independence of both types of landing teams was considerably enhanced by the fact that Marine infantry units of the 1950s were well supplied with 81mm and 4.2-inch mortars.

The weapon of choice for the field artillery of Army battle groups was a somewhat lighter version of the 105mm howitzer that had formed the mainstay of U.S. Army division artillery in World War II. The Marine Corps, on the other hand, preferred even lighter weapons. Somewhat nostalgic for the 75mm pack howitzers that had equipped the bulk of Marine artillery battalions in World War II and impressed by the great "bang for the buck" offered by the 4.2-inch mortar, Marines married the two to produce the "howtar." This weapon combined the recoil mechanism, wheeled carriage, and stable sights of a howitzer with the more lethal shell and high rate of fire of a mortar. Its range fell between that of the 4.2-inch mortar (5,500 meters) and the 105mm howitzer (10,500 meters).[11]

Marine interest in the "howtar" was spurred by the need to make Marine landing teams as light as possible. In traditional amphibious operations, such lightness had been an important but not paramount virtue. Surface landings, Marines of the 1950s believed, were too vulnerable to atomic weapons. The future of amphibious operations, therefore, belonged to the helicopter. As a result, lightness became even more important. Howtars, which could be moved with less than half the lift needed to move the same number of 105mm howitzers, seemed to provide the answer.

Despite the interest in lighter pieces for close support of battle groups, not all artillery developments in the 1950s were made in the service of mobility. Launchers were needed to fire tactical nuclear weapons, and though the Army's Field Artillery Branch displayed great enthusiasm for rockets, there was a good deal of work done on weapons that, in previous eras, would have fallen into the category of superheavy artillery. Leading the pack was the 280mm "Atomic Annie" howitzer. Further down the pecking order came the self-propelled version of the World War II-vintage eight-inch howitzer and, on the same mount, a 175mm long-range gun. These latter two weapons could also be used to fire conventional artillery rounds, a capability that would soon prove useful.

The war that both the U.S. Army and Marine Corps prepared for in the 1950s never came. Instead, the U.S. armed forces found themselves involved in what subsequent generations of historians will probably refer to as the Second Indochina War. Like the First Indochina War, the Second Indochina War was simultaneously a guerrilla war and a limited conventional war. This, combined with the fact that many of the same actors and all of the terrain from the first conflict were present for the second, resulted in many similarities. On a tactical level, however, the big difference was one of firepower. For while the French were often less well supplied with artillery than the Viet Minh, the U.S. forces in Vietnam almost always had the firepower edge.

At the beginning of the war, American troops brought with them a combination of the weapons that had been chosen for tactical nuclear warfare (the helicopter, the 4.2-inch mortar, the howtar, and the lightweight 105mm howitzer, as well as self-propelled 155mm howitzers, 175mm guns, and 8-inch howitzers) as well as the weapons of World War II (105mm and 155mm howitzers). The tactics that evolved to make use of these weapons, however, bore little resemblance to those of either World War II or hypothetical nuclear warfare.

Though there were exceptions, particularly during the siege of Khe Sanh and numerous artillery raids, these weapons were employed in batter-sized fire bases that were spread over the countryside. Operating from these fire bases, batteries fired a large number of rounds over days, weeks, months, and even years. Only occasionally, however, were they in a position to strike at targets large enough to warrant the fire of more than one battery. Evidence for this comes from the evolution of battalion organization. While there were many American artillery battalions that improvised additional batteries, there were few instances where batteries were augmented by additional pieces. On the contrary, some artillery battalions found four-gun batteries to be as effective as standard six-gun firing units.[12]

The key virtues for American artillery in Vietnam were coverage and responsiveness. With the chief use of artillery being the firing of a few rounds to rescue a small infantry patrol in contact with an even smaller number of enemy infantrymen, there was little danger that there would not be enough rounds. Rather, trouble happened when the handful of rounds that were needed failed to materialize at the right time and place. This, however, did not happen very often. Indeed, thanks to the radio and the what might be called customer-service orientation of U.S. field artillery units, both coverage and responsiveness became so good that many American infantry companies went into battle without their 81mm mortars.[13]

In some parts of Vietnam, infantry commanders found that the power and reliability of the supporting artillery, naval gunfire (in coastal regions), and ground attack aircraft was such that they could greatly reduce the size of infantry patrols. Instead of using battalion sweeps and platoon patrols, these commanders sent out four-, five-, or six-man teams equipped with little more than radios and personal defense weapons. Though not always successful, these "Stingray" teams managed, over the course of the four years of heaviest American involvement, to inflict far more damage on the enemy at a cost of far fewer casualties than conventional infantry battalions.[14]

The logic of this "infantry finds, artillery kills" arrangement was pushed to its limits by the 11th Marine Regiment (a field artillery organization equipped with weapons that ranged from 4.2-inch mortars to 175mm guns) during its last year in Vietnam (1970–1971). As fewer and fewer infantry patrols were sent out into the bush, the job of interfering with enemy "housekeeping" was assumed by long-range artillery fire. Some of this was observed by posts located on selected hilltops. Much, however, was unobserved fire directed at targets—bases, arms and rice caches, rocket and mortar positions, assembly points, and trails—that had been located by either the intelligence community or informal means.

The accuracy of fire observed from permanent observation posts was greatly enhanced by the use of the integrated observation device (IOD), a 400-pound apparatus that resulted from the mating of a pair of ship's binoculars with a night observation device and a laser range finder. With a daytime range of 10,000 meters (reduced at night to about 4,000 meters), the IOD allowed Marine observers to locate accurately most points within range of their 105mm and 155mm artillery pieces. This, in turn, permitted the observers to fire for effect without the inconvenience of firing ranging shots.

In a situation where there was no infantry or other arm to fix the enemy in position while the artillery got its bearings, the ability to deliver battery volleys against unsuspecting troops in the open greatly increased the damage inflicted by the "artillery alone" policy. Proof of this was provided by the vehemence with which the North Vietnamese attacked Marine observation posts in the area. Once it was clear that these attacks would not succeed—the observation posts were, of course, the best-located points in the whole system—the North Vietnamese bowed to the inevitable, moved their infrastructure elsewhere, and waited for the Americans to go home.[15]

That lavish American use of artillery and other forms of long-range firepower in Vietnam saved American lives is indisputable. The American willingness to drop a battery's worth of shells on suspected enemy locations, as well as the habit of firing harrassing and interdiction missions along routes that the enemy *might* have been using, was not without cost. On the one hand, the seemingly random shelling, with inevitable loss of civilian life, limb, and property, made more credible the communist assertion that the United States had come to Vietnam to build an empire. On the other hand, the fact that the shelling was rarely coordinated with the action of other arms in such a way that the enemy was dealt a decisive blow, made the enemy soldier somewhat contemptuous of the overall American effort. For while the average enemy soldier in Vietnam, like his counterpart in previous wars, would have preferred that the Americans fire far fewer shells, he learned to adjust well enough so that the Americans tired of firing shells before the Viet Cong and North Vietnamese tired of living with them.[16]

In an era when the guerrilla and the physicist seemed to conspire to push "normal" warfare into the dustbin of history, the old-fashioned soldier could always take comfort in the conventional nature of the perennial Arab–Israeli conflict. Short, sharp campaigns decided by short, sharp battles unencumbered by fallout, chemical contamination, or (until the *Intefadah* of the late 1980s) difficulty in distinguishing fighters from noncombatants provided reassurance that armies in the style of 1944 and 1945 still had a role to play in the Atomic Age. Somewhat less comforting to both Americans and Soviet soldiers was that the one army whose approach to conventional warfare proved most successful in the Middle East declined to copy their methods. In the case of artillery, as well as tanks, infantry, and aviation, the Israeli Army was happy to make use of both American and Soviet weapons. When it came to tactics, however, they decided to follow the blitzkrieg style (what is now called maneuver warfare) perfected by the Germans.

Unlike older armies, whose adoption of maneuver warfare was hampered (and often prevented) by the burden of centuries of peacetime soldiering capped by the dead hand of trench warfare, the Israelis practiced blitzkrieg from the very beginning. Influenced by the teachings of Orde Wingate, Liddell-Hart, and (quite ironically) Erwin Rommel, the Israeli forces that fought during the major campaigns of the Arab–Israeli wars (1948, 1956, 1967, 1973, and 1982) displayed a remarkable capacity for tactical flexibility, improvisation on the spot, and, most important, the maintenance of a high tempo of operations.[17] At first, artillery played a tiny role in the Israeli approach to the art of war. Over the years, as equipment became available and conceptions matured, the Israelis made increasing use of field artillery.

In 1948, the field artillery at the disposal of the newborn state of Israel consisted of 650 men divided among eight batteries. These were armed with a variety of obsolete and improvised weapons, including 65mm mountain howitzers of pre-World War I vintage, 75mm quick-firers of various origins, and the homemade Davidka siege mortar.[18] These batteries were used independently, often in direct support of infantry brigades. Given their limited numbers, they were able to do little more than augment the fire of the principal indirect-fire weapon of the Israeli army of 1948, the infantry mortar. Close to 900 of these (mostly British two- and three-inch models) were in the hands of the 30,000-odd first-line combatants on the Israeli side, giving the Israelis of 1948 a proportion of mortars to rifles far greater than that of the British division and slightly greater than that of a German or American division of World War II.[19]

Thanks largely to the inadvertent generosity of Arab armies, which often left their 25-pounders on the battlefield, the number of field artillery pieces in Israeli service had, by 1956, grown to 150.[20] Now organized in British-style eight-gun batteries that were attached to maneuver units as circumstances dictated, the field pieces had to share the role of close support with 120mm mortars. Evidence of the Israeli willingness to sacrifice weight of fire in order to increase responsiveness could be found in their frequent practice of attaching single four-gun troops to task forces of battalion size or smaller.[21]

The techniques for using the limited firepower provided by the Israeli batteries of the 1950s and 1960s were reminiscent of those of the German mobile tradition of both world wars. Artillery troops were placed close to the front of the long columns of tanks and armored personnel carriers. Troop and battery commanders rode with division, brigade, and battalion commanders, ordering fire on the move. And while there was frequent consultation between the leaders of maneuver units and their supporting artillery commanders, great emphasis was placed on the need for artillerists to use their initiative to seek out targets. Even in situations (such as the fighting in Jerusalem) where the prospect of collateral damage was great, the Israelis depended on the good judgment of artillery officers rather than any formal agency to ensure that fire landed on enemy troops rather than friendly forces or innocent bystanders.[22]

As the Israeli Army as a whole was transformed from a collection of foot mobile units that fought primarily in inhabited areas to a gasoline-powered force capable of operating in the desert, great efforts were made to make the Israeli artillery as mobile as the tank forces and the mechanized infantry. The easy half of this project was to mount 120mm mortars, which were beginning to be built in Israel, on half-tracks of American manufacture. A more difficult, and therefore time-consuming, project was the provision of self-propelled guns and howitzers.

The first self-propelled field pieces in the Israeli service were 105mm howitzers mounted on light tank chassis (AMX-13) obtained from France in 1954.[23] While only a single eight-gun battery of these was available during the 1956 war, they proved their worth to the Israeli authorities. As a result, the years between 1956 and 1967 were marked by Israeli attempts to improvise additional self-propelled artillery by mounting a variety of American and French 105mm and 155mm pieces, as well as locally produced 155mm howitzers and 160mm mortars, on the chassis of Sherman tanks.[24]

By 1967, the Israeli artillery had received a number of modern field pieces—mostly 105mm and 155mm howitzers—that doubled its 1956 inventory. The Arab states, however, were also improving their artillery parks, replacing their World War II-vintage equipment (often 25-pounders of British manufacture) with Soviet weapons (particularly 122mm and 130mm guns) capable of throwing heavier shells to a greater range. The net result was that the Israelis, unable to best the Arabs in artillery duels, used other means—deep penetrations by tanks or strikes by ground attack aircraft—to put the Arab guns and howitzers hors de combat.

This was true even of the battle that saw the greatest concentration of Israeli artillery in the first twenty years of that state's existence: Ariel Sharon's attack with limited objectives at Um Katef in the Sinai on the night of June 5, 1967. Although the target of the attack was an Egyptian strong point known to contain at least 160 field pieces, none of Sharon's 100 or so guns and howitzers (six battalions of eighteen pieces each) got involved in an artillery duel. The job of neutralizing the Egyptian guns so that Sharon's division could deploy was done by ground attack aircraft. The task of finishing off the Egyptian batteries was given to commandos landed by helicopter.[25]

The use of these unconventional means of dealing with the Egyptian artillery allowed the Israeli guns to concentrate on supporting the attacking

infantry and tanks. At first, the Israeli artillery limited itself to overwatch-
ing the silent advance of the leading waves of Israeli infantry. Once that
wave was discovered and the Egyptians began to fire, the Israelis let loose
with a "jumping barrage." That is, each tube in the Israeli "grand battery"
fired at a single target. After a few minutes, all tubes switched to a second
target, gave it the same treatment, and then went on to a third. At irregular
intervals, the Israeli batteries would return to an "old target" in the hopes
that the defenders would have left their shelter and taken up exposed firing
positions. Ten minutes of this jumping barrage was enough to convince
the Egyptians to keep to their shelters, whether they were being fired on
or not. As a result, Israelis were able to get into the Egyptian position and
root out the defenders with comparatively light casualties.[26]

In the years after 1967, the Israeli Army's continued emphasis on close
support, combined with the fact that mortars were being produced in
Israel, led to a growing consensus in favor of 120mm and even 160mm
mortars as the indirect fire weapons of choice. Initially, this trend toward
mortars threatened to push guns and howitzers even further to the margin
of the Israeli art of war. As time went on, the liberation of Israeli cannon
artillery from the close support role made possible its expansion during
the two decades that followed the lightning victories of the Six Day War.

Israeli demand for artillery that could shoot at long range against targets
that were not in direct contact with friendly tanks or infantry began in the
early 1960s. Beaten twice in mobile warfare, the Arab leaders of the time
began to look for ways of keeping up the struggle against Israel without
risking the honor of their armies or the reputation of their generals. Part
of the solution to this problem was provided by terrorism. Another tactic
was long-range artillery and multiple-rocket launcher bombardment of
Israeli frontier settlements. Yet another part of this strategy of attrition was
the attempt to deprive Israel of much of its water by diverting the River
Jordan.[27]

The Israeli response to all three parts of the Arab campaign involved
artillery. The proximity of Arab to Israeli that made possible the shelling
of Israeli border towns also facilitated the work of the Israeli artillery.
As a result, Israeli guns could retaliate for bombs thrown by Palestinian
commandos, respond to Syrian (and, beginning in 1968, Egyptian)
harassing fire, bombard Egyptian oil refineries and the cities of Suez and
Ismailia, and shell the workers trying to reroute the Jordan.[28]

For the first time since the bombardment of Paris in 1918, states were
attempting to use artillery as a strategic weapon that would influence
politics without the intermediary steps of the battle and the campaign.
While rarely decisive—the one exception being the prevention of the

hijacking of the Jordan River—these bombardments and artillery duels played a large role in the daily political maneuverings of the governments that paid for the ammunition. It is thus not surprising that between 1967 and 1973, the Israeli artillery almost doubled in size. When the Arabs invaded again in 1973, the Israelis could put 570 guns of 100mm or more in the field.[29]

The long-range weapons that made this expansion possible were provided by the United States. Thanks to the growing rapprochement between Israel and the United States (which became, by the late 1970s, something resembling an alliance), the Israeli artillery was able to acquire the long-range artillery (primarily self-propelled 175mm guns) needed for this sort of war. In the 1973 October War, the employment of these long-range weapons dropped from the strategic to the operational level as they were pushed forward to bombard targets of direct significance to the Israeli campaign: antiaircraft missile sites, the airport at Damascus, the bridges across the Suez Canal, and the one good road linking Cairo to the city of Ismailia.[30]

At the same time that their big guns were shelling at long range, the Israelis found a new use for their more modest artillery pieces. The October War was the first in which precision guided antitank missiles had been employed by both sides. The Egyptians, in particular, showed a talent for using Soviet-made Saggers to knock out large numbers of Israeli tanks. The Israeli response to this new threat was to make sure that no tank went into battle without the close cooperation of mechanized infantry and close support artillery or mortars. For while the Saggers were both light and accurate, they were very vulnerable to machine gun fire and shell fragments. Their guidance systems were so delicate, moreover, that even a near miss was enough to make the gunner "jump" and thus lose control of his tank-killing "model airplane."

Largely as a result of their experience in the October War, the Israelis formed independent brigades of thirty-six self-propelled 155mm howitzers. These units, composed of three twelve-gun battalions, seem to have been designed for short, intense concentrations of fire against targets of interest to divisions and higher echelons. To mass the fire of these guns more effectively, the Israeli electronics industry was asked to develop a modern fire control computer. And, to provide a mobile observation post, an Israeli aircraft firm designed and built remote-control vehicles with TV cameras in their noses. The result was a unit that, when attached to a task-organized armored or mechanized division, bore a strong resemblance to the division artillery of a French armored division of the same time period.[31]

In keeping with the theme of a great deal of fire falling in a small area in a very short time, the Israeli artillery has displayed a sustained fondness for multiple-rocket launchers. Starting after the 1967 Six Day War with 240mm Katyushas captured from Arab armies, the Israelis soon developed similar weapons of their own. These included improved rockets for their truck-mounted launchers of Soviet manufacture as well as a 160mm system of local design and manufacture. This latter system, known as the LAR-160, though mounted on old tank chassis, is a thoroughly modern weapon whose range (30,000 meters) and ease of use approaches that of the multiple launch rocket system.[32]

The artillery of western European armies of the postwar period followed the same general path of development as the Israeli artillery of the same period. This was not accidental. On the one hand, the Israelis closely monitored European weapons designs and operational concepts. On the other, the Europeans, having no conventional wars of their own, closely followed the Arab–Israeli wars for information that would help them design their own conventional forces. For most of the 1970s and 1980s, the problem of NATO was remarkably similar to that of Israel. Both were faced with the need to defeat huge numbers of enemy tanks in short but intense wars that might take place with little or no warning.

In the case of NATO, the tank mania reached its height in the mid-1970s, when the Soviet conventional buildup that began with the fall of Nikita Khrushchev in 1964 started to bear fruit. At first, the NATO response concentrated on the problem of Soviet tanks. All arms—infantry, aviation, armor, and artillery—were put to work to find direct means of putting those tanks out of action. For infantry and aviation, this meant various kinds of antitank guided missiles. For tanks and artillery, tank mania threatened to turn every tube into a species of antitank gun.

At a time when the U.S. Army was giving up its 105mm howitzers for a new familiy of 155mm howitzers, the traditional means of turning a field piece into an antitank gun (elevation near zero and open sights) was out of the question. Instead, two rather different approaches were tried. One was to turn 155mm howitzers into launchers for antitank guided missiles. The other was to fill shells with a number of "bomblets" that were designed to penetrate the relatively thin armor on the top of Soviet tanks.

Despite the great enthusiasm with which they were introduced, neither of these approaches fit well with traditional field artillery organization or equipment. The cannon-launched antitank guided missile that made it out of development and into production was a laser-guided device called Copperhead. Copperhead's first problem was that of "ruggedizing" the missile so that its complex guidance system would survive the stress of being fired from a howitzer. The second problem was that firing Copperhead required the services not merely of an entire firing battery but also of a forward observer equipped with a laser designator.

The first problem was eventually overcome. The second problem remains. For while there may be situations where it is worth taking a battery out of battle in order to destroy a small number of tanks, a system such as Copperhead has few advantages (such as a higher angle of fall and a less visible launch signature) over direct-fire, precision-guided munitions such as the TOW missile. It has, moreover, even fewer advantages compared to the dozen or so direct-fire guided missiles that might be purchased and manned for the same amount of treasure and talent needed to field a battery of 155mm howitzers.

Bomblets also promised to tie up a large number of batteries. Because of the limited volume of a 155mm shell, only a few bomblets (about sixteen of the smaller type) could be carried in each round. This meant that a large number of rounds would have to be fired to achieve the kind of saturation needed to ensure that a live bomblet landed on the roof of every tank in the target area. The need to fire a large number of rounds, in turn, would result in the requirement for either a long, drawn-out bombardment (which would give the tanks time to escape and expose the firing battery to counterbattery fire) or the massed fire of many batteries (which might be hard to organize).

The solution to both bomblet problems was found in rocketry. Unguided rockets, fired in ripples like the Soviet Katyusha, German *Nebelwerfer*, or American Calliope of World War II, could carry a far greater number of bomblets than an equivalent number of howitzer shells. Once the competent authorities realized this, the U.S. Army set about obtaining a new multiple-rocket launcher designed expressly to drop bomblets on tank formations. Indeed, once realized, the economies to be gained by this approach were so promising that even when it was discovered that most bomblets were not as effective against tanks as had initially been hoped, the American multiple-rocket launcher continued to be developed as a means of attacking Warsaw Pact artillery, especially the self-propelled howitzers that started to enter the Soviet bloc inventory in the late 1970s. The result was the multiple launch rocket system (MLRS), a weapon that can send hundreds of bomblets out to a range of over 30,000 meters in less than a minute.[33] Other NATO armies of the 1970s and 1980s displayed a similar sustained interest in multiple-rocket launchers. Most of this interest was manifested in the decision of Germany, Italy, Britain, and France to buy into the MLRS program. Germany and Spain, however, fielded lighter multiple-rocket launchers of their own—weapons that filled the gap between 155mm howitzers and long-range weapons such as MLRS.

The trend toward multiple-rocket launchers was part of a larger trend in the 1980s that might be called neoclassicism—an approach to conventional warfare that was based largely on the Prussian–German–Israeli tradition of maneuver warfare as it might apply to a NATO–Warsaw Pact confrontation.[34] Although the Soviet Union continued to produce tanks, Western armies freed themselves found their previous fixation on the single weapon and took the more sensible approach of looking for ways of destroying Soviet tank formations. Part of the reason for this was institutional maturity—soldiers wresting military analysis from the often myopic views of engineers. Another part was the growing Soviet artillery arsenal, a weapons park that included, for the first time, large numbers of self-propelled howitzers.[35]

The chief tenet of neoclassicism was combined arms—the idea that different weapons acting in concert to create dilemmas were more powerful than weapons working on their own. Insofar as artillery was concerned, neoclassicism brought a renewed appreciation for the advantages of both close support of maneuver units and massed fire in battalion strength or greater. At the same time, it brought an increased appreciation for the role of decisive maneuver in modern combat. This, in turn, put the accent on mobility.

The standard artillery piece of the neoclassical period—comparable in popularity to the 75mm quick-firer of the first two decades of this century—was the self-propelled 155mm howitzer. As was the case with the light quick-firer, not all nations had as many self-propelled 155mm howitzers as they would have liked. The reasons, however, were often more financial than doctrinal. For most armies of this period agreed that modern field artillery consisted of a weapon similar to the U.S. M109 organized in battalions of at least eighteen pieces. No consensus, however, lasts forever. The strategic environment that gave birth to neoclassicism— NATO and the Warsaw Pact facing each other across the inter-German border—is no more.

NOTES

1. Robert H. Scales, Jr., *Firepower in Limited War* (Washington, DC: National Defense University Press, 1990), pp. 54–61.

2. Carl Bernard, "Action on Hill 296 by Company L, 21st Infantry, 'Sleeping Bag Hill,'" unpublished ms. on file at ISAT, Inc., Alexandria, VA, pp. 2–3; interview with Colonel Bernard, Aug. 14, 1992.

3. Max Hastings, *The Korean War* (New York: Simon and Schuster, 1987), pp. 208–27.

4. Scales, *Firepower in Limited War*, pp. 16–17. Assuming that the fourteen battalions each had eighteen tubes, 252 tubes fired on this mission. The British field regiment at Imjin had an authorized strength of twenty-four tubes. The ratio was thus 10.5:1.

5. The American multiple-rocket launcher was less successful in fighting for its own survival in the postwar drawdown. As soon as the war was over, the rocket batteries were disbanded. Bruce I. Gudmundsson, *On Time and Under Budget: The Multiple Launch Rocket System* (Cambridge, MA: John F. Kennedy School of Government, 1987), p. 2.

6. W. G. Hemmes, *The U.S. Army in the Korean War: Truce Tent and Fighting Front* (Washington, DC: U.S. Government Printing Office, 1966), p. 352, as quoted in J.B.A. Bailey, *Field Artillery and Firepower* (Oxford: Military Press, 1989), p. 237.

7. This was the case with the FSCC that controlled the guns, howitzers, and aircraft that did the bulk of the killing at Khe Sanh. For an excellent description of this, see Scales, *Firepower in Limited War*, pp. 120–32.

8. This opinion is based on my personal experience with a Marine Corps Reserve infantry battalion FSCC during the mid-1980s.

9. U.S. Department of Defense, Office of Public Affairs, "News Release no. 395-59," in file folders HRC 322.Divisions and HRC 321.Divisions, Pentomic, Office of the Chief of Military History, Washington, DC.

10. F. P. Henderson, "Amphibious Artillery of the Future," *Marine Corps Gazette*, Dec. 1955, pp. 29–36.

11. The "mortar-howitzer" was proposed by 1st Lt. C. J. Spring, Jr., USMC, in an article of the same name in *Marine Corps Gazette*, Sept. 1955.

12. David Ewing Ott, *Vietnam Studies: Field Artillery, 1954–1973* (Washington, DC: Department of the Army, 1975), p. 172; artillery raids are discussed on pp. 184–85.

13. Shelby Stanton, *Order of Battle, Vietnam* (Washington, DC: U.S. News Books, 1981), p. 53.

14. Francis J. West, Jr., "Stingray '70," *U.S. Naval Institute Proceedings*, Nov. 1969, pp. 27–37.

15. Graham A. Cosmas and Terrence P. Murray, *U.S. Marines in Vietnam: Vietnamization and Deployment, 1970–1971* (Washington, DC: U.S. Government Printing Office, 1986), pp. 300–03.

16. For more on this and related issues, see Scales, *Firepower in Limited War*, passim.

17. For more on the intellectual history of the Israeli ground forces, see Brian Bond, *Liddell-Hart: A Study of His Military Thought* (London: Cassell, 1977), ch. 9.

18. Louis, Williams, *The Israel Defense Forces: A People's Army* (Tel Aviv: Ministry of Defense Publishing House, 1989), pp. 235–37. The most complete description of this early arsenal claims that the following weapons were on hand at the end of 1948: fifty Krupp 65mm mountain howitzers (other sources claim that these were French 65mm mountain howitzers), fifty Krupp 75mm (other sources claim that these were French 75mm quick-firers), thirty-two Mexican 75mm pieces, twenty-four French 120mm howitzers, thirty-six Davidkas, and twelve German 50mm guns (taken, I presume, from wrecked Mark III tanks and mounted) on homemade carriages. Leo Heiman, "Firepower in Sinai," *Ordnance*, Nov.–Dec. 1968, p. 274.

19. Trevor N. Depuy, *Elusive Victory: The Arab-Israeli Wars, 1947–1974* (New York: Harper & Row, 1978), pp. 44–45, 90, 93, 100–01.

20. Ibid., p. 212.

21. For example, the patrol led by Major Mordechai Gur into the Heitan Defile in the Sinai on Oct. 30, 1956, consisted of a battalion's worth of motorized infantry supported by four 120mm mortars mounted on half-tracks. Ibid., pp. 172–74. During the same conflict, the 27th Armored Brigade was divided into two battalion combat teams, each provided with a single troop of four self-propelled 105mm howitzers. Moshe Dayan, *Diary of the Sinai Campaign* (New York: Harper & Row, 1966), app. 4.

22. Heinman, "Firepower in Sinai," p. 275.

23. Eric Hammel, *Six Days in June: How Israel Won the 1967 Arab–Israeli War* (New York: Charles Scribner's Sons, 1992), pp. 65, 89. See sources erroneously refer to these self-propelled howitzers as "self-propelled 105mm guns."

24. For the best single description of these weapons, as well as the Israeli artillery park as a whole, see Terry Gander, *Modern Military Powers: Israel* (New York: Military Press, 1984), pp. 83–94.

25. Dupuy, *Elusive Victory*, pp. 258–60; D. D. Campbell, "The Gunners in the Arab–Israeli Six-Day War of 1967," *Journal of the Royal Artillery*, Sept. 1968, pp. 132–37; Edward Luttwak and Daniel Horowitz, *The Israeli Army, 1948–1973* (Lanham, MD: University Press of America, 1983), p. 290.

26. Heiman, "Firepower in Sinai," pp. 274–75.

27. Dupuy, *Elusive Victory*, p. 224.

28. The most spectacular of these strategic artillery bombardments took place during the war of attrition along the Suez Canal that started in 1968. Chaim Herzog, *The Arab–Israeli Wars: War and Peace in the Middle East* (New York: Random House, 1982), pp. 178–79; and Ze'ev Schiff, *A History of the Israeli Army, 1874 to the Present* (New York: Macmillan, 1986), pp. 218–22.

29. Dupuy, *Elusive Victory*, p. 608.

30. Ibid., pp. 533, 594–95; and Edgar O'Ballance, *No Victor, No Vanquished: The Yom Kippur War* (San Rafael, CA: Presidio Press, 1978), pp. 246, 296.

31. Henri Hure, *The Field Artillery in the French Armed Forces: An Example of French–American Military Cooperation* (Fort Sill: OK: U.S. Army Field Artillery School, ca. 1984).

32. Gander, *Modern Military Powers: Israel*, pp. 83–84. For a detailed look at the LAR-160, see Tamir Eshel, "MLRS in the IDF, Mobile Rocket Launchers from Israel," *Defence Update International*, no. 54 (1985): 58–64.

33. For a detailed treatment of the development of the MLRS, see Gudmundsson, *On Time and Under Budget*, (Cambridge, MA: John F. Kennedy School of Government, 1987), passim.

34. Although there is no "manifesto" for this movement, the 1982 edition of the U.S. Army's FM 100-5 "Operations" remains one of the central documents of what I have chosen to call "neoclassicism."

35. David Eshel, "Soviet Self Propelled Artillery," *Defense Update International*, no. 49 (1984).

10

Conclusion: The Future of Artillery

The story of field artillery in the present century is largely the tale of the great divorce, of the removal of the guns and their leaders from the close combat of the infantry and the tendency for a single combined arms battle to divide into two separate struggles. Almost as soon as this happens, however, a new class of weapon—whether it be the mortar, the infantry gun, the tank, the assault gun, or, most recently, the automatic grenade launcher—finds itself in the role recently abandoned by the "proper" field artillery.

Current developments in conventional field artillery promise to exacerbate the great divorce. Base-bleed shells and rocket-assisted projectiles give the current generation of 155mm howitzers the ability to reach ranges once the exclusive province of long-range guns. Satellite communications, larger command posts, computerized command and control systems, "deep battle" doctrine, and elaborate staff procedures also serve to separate the gunners from the battlefield.

There is, however, one development that promises to reverse this trend. This is the invention of the fiber optic guided missile. Invented at the U.S. Army's Redstone Arsenal, various models of this weapon are currently under development in Japan, the United States, France, and Germany. Their ranges vary from ten to thirty kilometers, and their payloads usually consist of a hollow-charge armor-piercing warhead. The chief virtue of this weapon, however, is neither range nor payload. Missiles that can outdo it in both categories have been available for nearly half a century. What makes the fiber optic guided missile revolutionary is its unique guidance system.

Taking advantage of the ability of fiber optic cable to transmit large volumes of data, the fiber optic guided missile is able to send television pictures of unprecedented clarity from a camera in the nose of the missile to a monitor in front of its gunner. Armed with this information, the gunner, for the first time since the general introduction of indirect fire nearly a century ago, is able to see *exactly* where his round is going. Though located further from the target than even the heavy artillerymen of both world wars, a fiber optic guided missile gunner has a view of the battlefield that the commander of a field gun battery in 1870 would envy.

The potential of this weapon to bring an end to the "great divorce" is enormous. A gunner with the ability to get a general picture of a battlefield while his missile is flying over it and then cause it to swoop down on a target while he gets a closer and closer look at the intended victim will be free of the problems that have plagued interarm cooperation from the beginning. When uniforms and equipment markings can be seen clearly up until the very moment of impact, losses from friendly fire should be greatly reduced. When accuracy is no longer a matter of intricate cooperation and methodical preparation is but inherent in the design of the weapon, infantrymen will no longer have to choose between having a great deal of fire support and being close enough to be able to exploit its effects.

In a sense, the fiber optic guided missile will turn the clock back to 1870. What is now done by surveyors, tables, charts, computers, weather stations, devices for measuring muzzle velocity, and the well-worn pencil of the artillery officer will be done by the wrist of a young man raised on video games. The technique of artillery will have disappeared. All that will be left is tactics.

Bibliography

Wherever possible, I have given the most recent English edition of a published work. In those cases where I have referred to both an English translation and a foreign-language original, both versions are listed.

Anonymous. "Remarks on the Organization of the German Artillery." *Journal of the Royal Artillery*, Jan.–Feb. 1923.

Anonymous. "Taktische Strömunguen und Bewaffnungsfragen in der französischen Artillerie." *Vierteljahreshefte für Truppenführung und Heereskunde* 10, no. 3 (1913).

Azan, Paul. *The Warfare of Today*. Boston: Houghton Mifflin, 1918.

Bacevich, A. J. *The Pentomic Era*. Washington, DC: National Defense University Press, 1989.

Bailey, J. B. A. *Field Artillery and Firepower*. Oxford: Military Press, 1989.

Balck, Wilhelm. *Tactics*. Translated by Walter Krueger. Fort Leavenworth, KS: U.S. Cavalry Association, 1914.

——— . *Development of Tactics—World War*. Translated by Harry Bell. Fort Leavenworth, KS: General Service Schools Press, 1922.

——— . *Entwickelung der Taktik im Weltkriege*. Berlin: R. Eisenschmidt, 1922. Second German edition of preceding item.

Baldwin, Ralph B. *The Deadly Fuze: Secret Weapon of World War II*. San Rafael, CA: Presidio Press, 1980.

Barnett, Correlli, Shelford Bidwell, Brian Bond, John Harding, John Terraine. *Old Battles and New Defenses: Can We Learn from Military History?* London: Brassey's Defense Publishers, 1986.

Batchelor, John, and Ian Hogg. *Artillery*. New York: Charles Scribner's Sons, 1972.

Benary, Albert, ed. *Das Ehrenbuch der deutschen Feldartillerie*. Berlin: Verlag Tradition Wilhelm Kolk, 1933.

Berdach, Rudolf, and Erich Dethleffsen. *Der Artillerie gewidmet*. Vienna: Berdach, 1975.

Berendt, Richard von. *Das 1. Garde Fußartillerie Regiment im Weltkrieg*. Berlin: Druck und Verlag von Gerhard Stalling, 1928.

Berlin, Wilhelm, Hans Joachim Froben, and Konrad Roehr. "Reconnaissance Artillery." U.S. National Archives, Foreign Military Studies, ms. P-023.

Berlin, Wilhelm, and Huether. "Die Spitzenvertretung der Artillerie in der Obersten Führung des Heeres, 1938–1945. Ihre Aufgaben, Mittel, und Wirkungsmöglichkeiten." U.S. National Archives, Foreign Military Studies, ms. P-041. (Paper copies of manuscripts and translations in the Foreign Military Studies series can be found at both the U.S. National Archives in Washington, DC, and the U.S. Army Military History Institute at Carlisle Barracks, Carlisle, PA. Microfiche copies can be ordered from the U.S. National Archives.)

Bernhardi, Friedrich von. *On War Today*. London: Hugh Rees, 1913.

———. *Germany and the Next War* (London: E. Arnold, 1914.

Bidwell, R. G. S. "The Development of British Field Artillery Tactics 1940–1942: The Desert War." *Journal of the Royal Artillery*, Mar. 1968.

———. "The Development of British Field Artillery Tactics: Old Principles–New Methods 1940–1943." *Journal of the Royal Artillery*, Sept. 1968.

Bidwell, Shelford. *Gunners at War*. London: Arms and Armor Press, 1970.

Bidwell, Shelford, and Dominick Graham. *Fire-Power: British Army Weapons and Theories of War 1904–1945*. Boston: George Allen and Unwin, 1985.

Bierman. "Die Entwickelung der deutschen Minenwerferwaffe." In Paul Heinrici, ed., *Das Ehrenbuch der deutschen Pioniere*. Berlin: Verlag Tradition Wilhelm Kolk, 1932. (Many German authors before World War II published books and articles without giving their first names.)

von Böckmann. "Betrachtungen über unsere Artillerietaktik." *Vierteljahreshefte für Truppenführung und Heereskunde* 8, no. 2 (1911).

Bond, Brian. *Liddell-Hart: A Study of His Military Thought*. London: Cassell, 1977.

Bruge, Roger. *Faites sauter la Ligne Maginot*. Paris: Fayard, 1973.

Bruchmüller, Georg. *Die deutsche Artillerie in den Durchbruchschlachten des Weltkrieges*. Berlin: E. S. Mittler und Sohn, 1922.

———. *Die Artillerie beim Angriff im Stellungskrieg*. Charlottenburg: Verlag "Offene Worte," 1926.

———. "Die Artillerieführung bei den großen deutschen Angriffen imn Jahre 1918." *Wissen und Wehr* (1931): no. 4.

Burne, A. H. "The French Guns at Bertrix, 1914." *Journal of the Royal Artillery* 63, no. 3 (Oct. 1936).

Comparato, Frank E. *Age of the Great Guns*. Harrisburg, PA: Stackpole, 1965.

Corum, James Sterling. "The Reichswehr and the Concept of Mobile War in the Era of Hans von Seeckt." Ph.D. diss. Queen's University, Kingston, Ontario, 1990.

Cron, Hermann. *Die Organisation des deutschen Heeres im Weltkrieg*. Berlin: Ernst Siegfried Mittler und Sohn, 1923.

Davenport, Guiles. *Zaharoff*. Boston: Lothrop, Lee, and Shepard, 1934.

Deiß, F. W. *Die Hessen im Weltkrieg, 1914–1918*. Charlottenburg: Dr. Wilhelm Glaß & Co., 1939.

Doughty, Robert A. *Seeds of Disaster: The Development of French Army Doctrine, 1919–1939*. Hamden, CT: Archon, 1985.

Dupuy, Trevor N. *Elusive Victory: The Arab—Israeli Wars, 1947–1974*. New York: Harper & Row, 1978.

Farsac. "Organisation de l'artillerie dans le corps d'armée." *Revue d'artillerie*, Oct. 1920.

Farwell, Byron. *The Great Anglo-Boer War.* New York: W. W. Norton, 1990.

Feist, Joachim. "Formationsgeschichte der Artillerie in zwei Jahrhunderten." *Artillerie Rundschau*, no. 3 (1967).

Ferrard, Stephane. *Les Matériels de l'armée de terre française, 1940.* Paris: Charles-Lavauzelle, 1984.

Fischer, K. "Neuzeitliche Artillerie—eine Schriftumsübersicht." *Wehrtechnische Monatshefte*, Feb. 1938, pp. 78–80.

Fuller, J. F. C. *Armored Warfare.* Harrisburg, PA: Military Service Publishing Co., 1943.

Germany, Oberkommando des Heeres. *Merkblatt für den Dienst im Stabe eines Artillerie-Kommandeurs.* Berlin: Ernst Siegfried Mittler und Sohn, 1938.

Germany, various agencies. *Der Welkrieg 1914–1918.* Berlin: E. S. Mittler und Sohn. (This is the German official history of World War I, the last volume of which is currently being completed.)

Glaise-Horstenau, Edmund, ed. *Österreich-Ungarns letzter Krieg.* Vienna: Verlag der Militärwissenschaftlichen Mitteilungen, 1936.

Gold, Ludwig. *Die Tragödie von Verdun.* Berlin: Gerhard Stalling, 1926.

Golovine, Nicholas N. *The Russian Army in the World War.* New Haven: Yale University Press, 1931.

von Graevenitz. "Ein italienische Angriff auf das italienische Feldartillerie-Material." *Militär-Wochenblatt*, no. 157/158 (1905).

Great Britain, War Office, General Staff. *Field Service Regulations of the German Army.* London: Harrison and Sons, 1908.

Guderian, Heinz. *Die Panzertruppen und ihr Zusammenwirken mit den anderen Waffen.* Berlin: E. S. Mittler und Sohn, 1943.

Gudmundsson, Bruce. *Storm Troop Tactics: Innovation in the German Army 1914–1918.* New York: Praeger, 1989.

Haber, L. F. The *Poisonous Cloud: Chemical Warfare in the First World War.* Oxford: Clarendon Press, 1986.

Hamilton, John A. I., and L. C. F. Turner. *Crisis in the Desert: May–July 1942.* Cape Town: Oxford University Press, 1952.

Hamilton, Nigel. *Monty: The Making of a General, 1887–1942.* New York: McGraw-Hill, 1981.

Hammel, Eric. *Six Days in June: How Israel Won the 1967 Arab–Israeli War.* New York: Charles Scribner's Sons, 1992.

Hastings, Max. *The Korean War.* New York: Simon and Schuster, 1987.

Hanslian, Rudolf. *Der chemische Krieg.* Berlin: E. S. Mittler und Sohn, 1937.

Henderson, F. P. "Amphibious Artillery of the Future." *Marine Corps Gazette*, Dec. 1955.

Hérr, Frédéric Georges. *L'Artillerie, ce qu'elle a été, ce qu'elle est, ce qu'elle doit être.* Paris: Berger Levrault, 1924.

Herzog, Chaim. *The Arab–Israeli Wars: War and Peace in the Middle East.* New York: Random House, 1982.

Hiegel, Henri. *La Drôle de guerre en Moselle, 1939–1940.* Sarreguemines: Editions Pierron, 1983.

Hinze, Rolf. *Die hannoversche Artillerie.* Privately published by the author, 1977.

Hoffbauer, C. von. *Die deutsche Artillerie in den Schlachten und Treffen des deutschfranzösischen Krieges 1870–71.* 3 vols. Berlin: n.p., 1873–78.

Hoffmann, Max. *The War of Lost Opportunities.* London: Keegan Paul, 1924.

Hoffmann, Max. *The War of Lost Opportunities*. London: Keegan Paul, 1924.

Holden-Reid, Brian. *J. F. C. Fuller, Military Thinker*. New York: St. Martin's Press, 1987.

Hure, Henri. *The Field Artillery in the French Armed Forces: An Example of French–American Military Cooperation*. Fort Sill, OK: U.S. Army Field Artillery School, ca. 1984.

Joffre, Joseph J. C. *Mémoires du Maréchal Joffre (1910–1917)*. Paris: Librairie Plon, 1932.

Jung, Hermann. *Die Ardennen-Offensive, 1944/45*. Göttingen: Musterschmidt, 1971.

Kleeman, Ulrich. *Streiflichter zur Kriegsführung in Nordafrika*. U.S. National Archives, Foreign Military Studies, ms. D104.

Köhn, Herrmann. *Erstes Garde Feldartillerie Regiment und seine reitende Abteilung*. Berlin: Druck und Verlag von Gerhard Stalling, 1928.

Korolkov, G. K. "The Battle of Lodz: November 2–December 19, 1914." Translated by Charles Berman. Washington, DC: U.S. Army War College, 1939. Unpublished ms.

Prince Krafft zu Höhenlohe-Ingelfingen. *Letters on Artillery*. Quantico, VA: U.S. Marine Corps, 1989.

Kuhl, Hermann von. "The Execution and Failure of the Offensive." Translated by Henry Hossfeld. Unpublished translation of *Entstehung, Durchführung und Zusammenbruch der Offensive von 1918*. Berlin: Deutsche Verlagsgesellschaft für Politik und Geschichte, 1927.

———. *Der Weltkrieg*. Berlin: C. A. Weller, 1933.

Liddell-Hart, Basil Henry. *The Remaking of Modern Armies*. London: John Murray, 1927.

———, ed. *The Rommel Papers*. New York: Harcourt, Brace, 1953.

Lombarès, Michel de. "Le '75,'" *Revue historique des armées* (1975): 96–102.

———, ed. *Historie de l'artillerie française*. Paris: Lavauzelle, 1984.

Lossberg, Fritz von. *Meine Tätigkeit im Weltkriege 1914–1918*. Berlin: E. S. Mittler und Sohn, 1939.

Lucas, Pascal Marie Henri. *L'Évolution des idées tactiques en France et en Allemagne 1914–1918*. Paris: Berger-Levrault, 1923.

Ludendorff, Erich. *Ludendorff's Own Story*. New York: Harper and Brothers, 1939.

Maercker, Ludwig. *Vom Kaiserheer zur Reichswehr*. Leipzig: R. F. Koehler, 1921.

Manchester, William. *The Arms of Krupp, 1587–1968*. Boston: Little, Brown, 1968.

Manstein, Erich von. *Aus einem Soldatenleben*. Bonn: Atheneum Verlag, 1958.

Matuschka, Edgar Graf von. "Organisationsgeshichte des Heeres, 1890–1918." In *Handbuch zur deutschen Militärgeschichte 1648–1939*. Frankfurt am Main: Bernhard und Graefe Verlag für Wehrwessen, 1968.

Meier-Welcker, Hans. *Seeckt*. Frankfurt am Main: Bernard und Graefe, 1967.

Mellenthin, F. W. von. *Panzer Battles: A Study of the Employment of Armor in the Second World War*. Norman, OK: University of Oklahoma Press, 1956.

Middlebrook, Martin. *The Kaiser's Battle, 21 March, 1918: The First Day of the German Offensive*. London: Allen Lane, 1978.

Nordenfelt, Thorsten. "Quick Firing Guns in the Field," *Journal of the Royal United Service Institution* 32, no. 143 (1888): 1–24.

O'Ballance, Edgar. *No Victor, No Vanquished: The Yom Kippur War*. San Rafael, CA: Presidio Press, 1978.

Paine, George H. "Accurate Shooting in Trench Warfare," *Field Artillery Journal* 7, no. 4 (Oct.–Dec. 1917).

Paul, Wolfgang. *Geschichte der 18. Panzer-Division 1940–1943 mit Geschichte der 18. Artillerie-Division 1943–1944* (Reutlingen: Preußischer Militär-Verlag, 1989.

Perrett, Bryan. *Knights of the Black Cross: Hitler's Panzerwaffe and Its Leaders.* New York: St. Martin's Press, 1986.

Polster. "Minen- und Bombenwerfer Frankreichs." *Kriegstechnische Zeitschrift,* 1917, pp. 153–56.

Poydenot, O. "Fire Manoeuvre or the Application of Fire and Its Control in the French Artillery." *Journal of the Royal Artillery,* April 1938. Translated by T. G. G. Heywood.

Prussia, General Staff, Historical Section. *The War in South Africa.* Translated by W. H. H. Waters. London: John Murray, 1907.

Regling, Heinz Volkmar. *Amiens 1940: Der deutsche Durchbruch südlich von Amiens 5. bis 8. Juni, 1940.* Freiburg im Breisgau: Verlag Rombach, 1968.

Rossi-Landi, Guy. *La Drôle de guerre: La Vie politique en France 2 septembre–10 mai 1940.* Paris: Armand Colin, 1971.

Rupprecht, Crown Prince of Bavaria. *In treue Fest: Mein Kriegstagebuch.* Munich: Deutscher National Verlag, 1929.

Scales, Robert H., Jr. *Firepower in Limited War.* Washington, DC: National Defense University Press, 1990.

Schiff, Ze'ev. *A History of the Israeli Army, 1874 to the Present.* New York: Macmillan, 1986.

Schmidt-Richberg, Wiegand. "Die Regierungszeit Wilhelms II." In *Handbuch zur deutschen Militärgeschichte 1648–1939.* Frankfurt am Main: Bernard und Grafe Verlag für Wehrwessen, 1968.

Schott, J. "Material der Artillerie." *Von Löbell's Jahresberichte über das Heer- und Kriegswesen* 27 (1900): 370–71.

———. "Die gegenwärtige Ausrüstung der Feldartillerie mit Kanonen." *Militär-Wochenblatt,* no. 144 (1905): 3326–3332.

Schulte, Bernd F. *Die deutsche Armee, 1900–1914: Zwischen Beharren und Verändern.* Düsseldorf: Droste Verlag, 1977.

Scheel. *Das Reserve Feldartillerie Regiment Nr. 70.* Berlin: Druck und Verlag von Gerhard Stalling, 1923.

Scott, E. D. "Howitzer Fire." *Field Artillery Journal* 6, no. 4 (Oct.–Dec. 1916): 525–26.

Seekt, Hans von. *Aus Meinem Leben.* Leipzig: von Hase und Koehler, 1938.

Showalter, Dennis E. *Railroads and Rifles: Soldiers, Technology, and the Unification of Germany.* Hamden, CT: Archon Books, 1975.

Spring, C. J., Jr. "Mortar-Howitzer?" *Marine Corps Gazette,* Sept. 1955.

Stanton, Shelby. *Order of Battle, U.S. Army: World War II.* Novato, CA: Presidio Press, 1984.

Stein, Hans Rudolf von. "Die Minenwerfer Formationen 1914–1918." *Zeitschrift für Heeres und Uniformkunde,* 1959, 1960.

Stolfi, Russel H. S. *A Bias for Action: The German 7th Panzer Division in France and Russia, 1940–1941.* Quantico, VA: Marine Corps Association, 1991.

Sulzbach, Herbert. *With the German Guns.* London: Leo Cooper, 1973.

Trythall, Anthony John. *"Boney" Fuller: Soldier, Strategist, and Writer, 1878–1966.* Baltimore: Nautical and Aviation, 1989.

U. T. "Taktik der Feldartillerie." *Von Löbell's Jahresberichte über das Heer- und Kriegswesen* 27 (1900).

U. T. "Taktik der Feldartillerie." *Von Löbell's Jahresberichte über das Heer- und Kriegswesen* 27 (1900).

——— . "Taktik der Artillerie des Feldheeres." *Von Löbell's Jahresberichte über das Heer- und Kriegswesen* 37 (1910).

——— . "Taktik der Artillerie des Feldheeres." *Von Löbell's Jahresberichte über das Heer- und Kriegswesen* 39 (1912).

Vasselle, Pierre. *La Bataille au sud d'Amiens, 20 mai–8 juin 1940*. Abbéville: Imprimerie F. Paillart, ca. 1963.

Vogt, Adolf. *Oberst Max Bauer: Generalstabsoffizier im Zwielicht 1869–1929*. Osnabrück: Biblio-Verlag, 1974.

Waline, Pierre. *Les Crapouillots, 1914–1918: Naissance, vie, et mort d'une arme*. Paris: Charles-Lavauzelle, 1965.

Watson, M. G. "Redrawing the Circle." *Journal of the Royal Artillery*, Sept. 1986.

Werneburg, Rudolf. *Königl. preußisches Reserve-Feldartillerie-Regiment Nr. 7*. Oldenburg: Gerhard Stalling, 1926.

Wisser, John P. *The Second Boer War, 1899–1900*. Kansas City, MO: Hudson-Kimberly, 1901.

Wray, Timothy A. *Standing Fast: German Defense Doctrine on the Russian Front During World War II, Prewar to March 1943*. Fort Leavenworth, KS: U.S. Army Combat Studies Institute, 1986.

Zaloga, Steven, and Victor Madej. *The Polish Campaign, 1939*. New York: Hippocrene, 1985.

In addition to the above-listed books, articles, pamphlets and manuscripts, I made extensive use of French, German, and American materials on file at the U.S. National Archives in Washington, DC, and the archives of the Service Historique de l'Armée de Terre at Vincennes, France. Documents from the latter are identified by the initials SHAT, followed by the carton number. I also made frequent reference to fact sheets and articles published by *Tactical Notebook*, a service of the Institute for Tactical Education in Quantico, VA. Acknowledgment of the use of specific materials published by this organization can be found in the notes.

Index

Radio communications, 146
Rafales, 21
Raids, 71, 99
Regimental landing teams, 150
Regimental organization, 25
Reims, battle of (July 15, 1918), 91–106
Remotely piloted vehicles, 157
Réserve Générale d'Artillerie, 108
Rheinische Metallwaren und
  Maschinenfabrik (Rheinmetall), 74
Riga, battle of (September 1917), 82
River crossings, 82
Rolling barrage, 70, 88, 93, 100
Rommel, Erwin, 120, 154
Roving pieces (*Arbeitsgeschütze*), 133
Russian Army, Siberian riflemen of, 56
Russo-Japanese War (1904–1905), 17,
  34
Russo-Turkish War (1878), 33

Saar Offensive (September 1939), 114
Sagger (Soviet antitank guided missile),
  157
Salient, 58
Sarre Offensive (September 1939), 114
Scales, Robert H., Jr., ix
Schell, Adolph von, 4
Schmidt von Knobelsdorf, 58
Schwerpunkt (main effort), 23
Schwerpunkt und Aufrollen (penetration
  and exploitation), 77
Schwerpunktwaffe (focus of efforts
  weapon), 132
Scott, E. D., 30
Sedan, battle of (1870), 2
Serbia, 32
Sevastopol, 128
Sharon, Ariel, 155
Shrapnel, 5, 18
Siege gun, German 150mm "ring
  cannons," 48
Siege mortar: German 280mm, 36;
  German 305mm, 36; German
  420mm, 36
Siegfried Line, 114
Signal flares, 55, 71
Signal rockets, 71, 98
Slide rules, 138

Smokeless powder, 4
Soissons, France, 48
Somme, battle of (July 1916), 81, 88
Sound Ranging, 72, 98
Splintering effect, 111
Stalin, Joseph, 143
Standing barrage, 46, 71, 88
Stingray teams, 152
Strategic artillery fire, 156
Sturmartillerie (assault guns), 129
Sturmgeschütze (assault gun), 129
Suez, Egypt, 156

Tactical nuclear weapons, 149
Tank mania, 158
Tank warfare, 116
Tarnow, Poland, 53
Taylor, Frederick W., 109
Telephones, 19, 71, 73, 98
Terminal ballistics, 89
Thrust line, 120
Thürheim, Baron von, 4
Time-on-target, 146
Trench artillery, 69, 74
Trench mortar: British 81mm Stokes,
  79; French 58T, 75; French 75mm
  Jouhandeau-Deslandres, 80; French
  81mm Stokes, 81; German 170mm,
  76; German 250mm, 76; German
  76mm, 76, 79; improvised, 76
Tufkanone (Tank-und-Flieger Kanone),
  heavy, 117
Tufkanone (Tank-und-Flieger Kanone),
  75mm, 117

Um Katef, battle of (1956), 155
Unitary shell (Einheitsgeschoß), 35
U.S. Army, 21st Infantry Regiment, 145
U.S. Army Military History Institute, vii
U.S. Marine Corps, 11th Marine
  Regiment, 152

Vailly, battle of (October 30, 1914), 44
Verdun, 57. *See also* Fleury; Herbebois
Vietnam, 151
Vimy Ridge, 51
Vregny Plateau, battle of (January 12,
  1915), 48

About the Author

BRUCE I. GUDMUNDSSON, who is affiliated with the Institute for Tactical Education, is the author of *Stormtroop Tactics: Innovation in the German Army, 1914–1918* (Praeger, 1989). He has written a number of articles on military history and tactics for journals such as the *Military History Quarterly* and the *Marine Corps Gazette*. He is currently working, with John A. English, on a revision of English's classic study *On Infantry*.